W9-BLF-531

AMERICA'S

HEROES

AMERICA'S HEROES

The Changing Models of Success in American Magazines

Theodore P. Greene

NEW YORK • OXFORD UNIVERSITY PRESS • 1970

Library of Congress Catalogue Card Number: 70–117214

Printed in the United States of America

Preface

THIS BOOK BEGAN, too many years ago, from my desire to discover what had happened to individualism in America. Individualism interested me not as an actual pattern of behavior, not as a formal structure of ideas, but as a pervasive attitude toward life. Somehow, at the heart of most of the debates over public policy, most of the moralistic judgments, most of the human difficulties which I had observed by 1948 lay an ultimate appeal to something Americans seemed to think of as individualism.

I began, then, with an assumption that the whole cluster of values, expectations, and prohibitions associated with individualism had become an irrelevant, irrational barrier to the development of a more humane, more pragmatic society and of more varied forms for individuality in America. At the time this assumption seemed to be widely shared, at least among intellectuals. This study now reaches completion, however, after remarkable swings in American perceptions of their experience and their possibilities. The 1950's bewailed "conformity" and chastised youth for their loss of enterprise and daring. The 1960's have quailed before the radical, at times antinomian, individualism of a generation which could often see no good in institutions and which sought a variety of experiences for the individual self that Ralph Waldo Emerson had never quite envisioned. Seldom has the historical climate shifted thus effectively to curb the initial bias of an historical inquiry. The result, I trust, displays more balance than would otherwise have been achieved. It is as faithful an account as I can render of some important attitudes which were present at crucial moments in the popular culture of America.

My debts in this extended enterprise have been many and varied. Richard Hofstadter has been from the beginning immensely helpful, leaving me free to develop my ideas but invariably attentive, encouraging, and suggestive when given a chance. Several members of the Sociology Department at Columbia University gave me early help in devising procedures for sampling and ordering magazine materials: Paul F. Lazarsfeld, Leo Lowenthal, and the late C. Wright Mills. Walter Metzger, Eric McKitrick, Carl Hovde, and Daniel Bell read an earlier version of this study and offered a number of judicious suggestions. Among my colleagues at Amherst College, Edwin Rozwenc, John William Ward, John Halsted, and George Juergens gave the manuscript the benefits of their particular interests and perspectives. I am particularly grateful to Professor Ward for showing me his own work-in-progress on the history of American individualism and for his continuous encouragement. Many students in my seminar on The Progressive Generation have read chapters in manuscript and stimulated further ideas in seminar discussion and papers. The Trustees of Amherst College granted me a year's leave and a Trustee Fellowship during which the writing was largely completed. Sheldon Meyer has been a tactful and helpful editor with a balky and procrastinating author. Finally my wife Mary, my daughters Dorothy and Jennifer, and my son Stephen sustained me through periods when the author might well have been finished though the book was not.

T.P.G.

Amherst, Massachusetts
January 1970

Contents

Part Three

THE IDOLS OF JUSTICE

1904–1913

Part Four

THE IDOLS OF ORGANIZATION

1914–1918

List of Tables

AMERICA'S

HEROES

Prologue

The Search for Changing Models of Success in America

The biography of illustrious men furnishes the most instructive history of the times in which they lived, as it is from their sentiments and examples that each age derives its complexion.
Monthly Anthology, *1803*

ARE AMERICAN VALUES, basic American attitudes toward life, undergoing profound changes in our day? Has the American "character," in fact, already experienced a polar shift between the past and the present? Few generations in a constantly changing America have been as aware of change—even fewer have seemed as uneasy about change—as our own. Seldom has historical perspective upon our anxieties seemed as necessary, and yet seldom if ever have historians found it as difficult to provide perspective upon many of the kinds of questions which trouble the age. If historians are to be faithful to the task of suggesting where we are by showing more fully where we have been, they must continue to raise some relatively unexplored questions about the American past. If historians are to raise questions about the changes in basic, pervasive American attitudes, they must turn to relatively unexamined historical materials as their guides. This book is an effort to embark upon those tasks.

I

The most dramatic descriptions of a radical shift in American attitudes have come from sociologists. A host of educated readers in the 1950's responded to lengthy sociological studies which pictured modern Americans as drastically different from their forebears. The authors of *The Lonely Crowd* explained the change as one from an inner-directed character to an other-directed character. In their view the American of the past was a work-centered, frankly competitive, moralistic individual who took his directions from both the principles and the competitive drive for achievement inculcated in his childhood. The American of the present, however, was seen as the product of a populous, affluent, and bureaucratic society. Trained in childhood to respond to the expectations of his peers, this other-directed modern man emerged as more concerned with consumption than with production, oriented more to the personnel than to the job, devoted more to morale than to morality, and tending to consider response from others an end in life as well as a means.[1]

This conception of a polar contrast between the present and the past was further reinforced by the widespread popularity accorded William H. Whyte's *The Organization Man.* As Whyte described the shift, generations of individualists imbued with the Protestant Ethic had been succeeded by a present generation dominated by a Social Ethic which insisted upon the individual's subordination to the group and the organization.[2] The Riesman and Whyte books in turn drew upon a whole body of sociological literature which dramatized in various ways the split between modern Americans and their ancestors. Both books referred to the distinctions between an old middle class of independent entrepreneurs and the new middle class of bureaucratic functionaries which were elaborated in C. Wright Mills's *White Collar.*[3] Both books cited as evidence of their polar shift a pioneering article by Leo Lowenthal which argued that America's popular heroes had switched from the Idols of Production to the Idols of Consumption.*

What all these writings had in common was a sharp polarity between the past and the present accompanied at times by an apparent nostalgia for many aspects of the past. Their descriptions of the present were informed, perceptive, complex, and based upon a variety of observations and studies. Their contrasting images of the past, however, often seemed simplistic, romanticized, and unsupported by any close analysis of historical materials. The result was a distorted perspective which dramatized the problems of the present by minimizing the tensions of the past.[4]

The initial scholarly response to these writings attempted to restore perspective by stressing continuity and denying any radical break with past American values. Historians joined other sociologists in asserting that Americans had always been noted for many of the characteristics of the other-directed man. Critics cited the comments of foreign observers like Tocqueville and Martineau in the 1830's to demonstrate the continuous tendencies in American society toward conformity and the suppression of individuality. The polar values of individualism versus conformity were not, they argued, a difference between the past and the present. Rather these represented the continuing tension between the historic American values of personal achievement

* Leo Lowenthal, "Biographies in Popular Magazines," reprinted in William Peterson, ed., *American Social Patterns* (Garden City, N.Y., 1956), 63–118. This article, first called to my attention by Richard Hofstadter, provided the original impetus to my own study. Professor Lowenthal also kindly reviewed some of my original plans. As my own examination of magazine biographies progressed, however, I found myself differing with Lowenthal's very favorable assessment of the Idols of Production around 1900 and questioning some of his despairing conclusions about the Idols of Consumption in the magazines of the 1940's. Lowenthal's very stimulating and often perceptive article seems finally too simple an application of European theories about mass society to American materials which seem only in part to support the analysis.

and of social equality. Americans had always lived within this tension, their views of the successful life had always reflected it, though from time to time one pole might be emphasized more than the other.[5]

What this debate revealed, above all, was how little we really knew about past changes in the basic American conceptions of a successful life. While Riesman and Whyte obscured previous changes by their dramatic device of contrasting the present to a past of inner direction and individualism, the critics also obscured historical changes by emphasizing the continuity of past and present. The historian's task still remained: to chart the past's own continually changing dynamics; to insist upon the integrity and multiplicity of our various pasts; to recognize the past's right to problems as serious, ideas as dysfunctional, values as questionable as those of the present; and thereby to gain more authentic perspectives upon the present.

II

How can the historian hope to chart with any accuracy significant changes in past American values? What materials may provide him with a relatively reliable index to these changes? Upon what concept can he focus to reveal most clearly crucial shifts of emphasis in American attitudes? What methods can he employ to identify changes with some precision and to reduce subjective selection or distortion of his materials? Those who venture into the history of popular culture have been forced to discover evidence and procedures appropriate for their quest.

Never has the general magazine in America been thoroughly examined as an index to changes in the nation's life and values. Too derivative and pedestrian for the literary scholar, too diffuse and secondary for the historian, magazines have generally fallen into a limbo between academic disciplines. Even the few serious histories of American magazines do not lend themselves to any coherent effort to compare the attitudes of one period with those of another.[6]

Yet Americans were long known as a nation of magazine-readers, and the general magazine came to depend for success upon its ability at any particular moment to meet the interests, the attitudes, the changing mood of a general audience. Until the advent of radio, movies, and television after 1920, the magazine was in fact the only regular medium of communication which reached beyond the local community. More far-ranging and reflective than the newspaper, more immediately responsive to change than the school book, more continuous than the best-selling book, the general magazine offers to the historian one of the more promising indexes to change in national values.

Such an index must, however, be used with some care. The general magazine of 1800 was in many ways a different institution from its successor in 1900. The economics of magazine publishing passed from a stage of virtual patronage to one of independent entrepreneurship and finally to that of large corporate organizations catering to mass audiences for the benefit of other large corporate advertisers. The editors of magazines changed from independent professional men to independent businessmen and finally to managers employed to keep the constituent parts of vast publishing empires running profitably. These changes in the fundamental structure of the general magazines might seem to invalidate comparative study of their contents as a reliable index to changing attitudes.

A more sophisticated view will recognize, however, that it is these very shifts which insure the usefulness of magazines as a guide to the timing of social change. The general magazine has proved to be far more rapidly responsive to changing social and economic conditions in America than other institutions which reflect and reflect upon the nation's values. The church, the school, the publishing of books, even the style and the conventions of politics demonstrate inherent resistances to change which cause them to lag behind developing conditions. Where these institutions cannot afford to change too rapidly, the general magazine cannot afford *not* to be responsive to its immediate environment. For this reason the nature of the general magazines in most periods of our national history gives significant clues to the dominant features of contemporary society.

This book, therefore, assumes that a more complex, more precise sense of changing values in our past can be gained from a sustained analysis of general magazines. Each part of this book opens with a chapter on major developments within the world of magazines during a particular period. At each stage the structure of magazine publishing reflected significant aspects of the nation's contemporary economic and social structure. At each stage, too, the magazines themselves reflected many of the dominant attitudes and tensions of the time, the changes in popular interests and popular moods, the recognition of changing circumstances and present challenges to older values. These chapters, then, set the context within which at each period a particular constellation of American values emerged. They help to explain the timing and to understand the dynamics of change in American conceptions of the successful life which are described in the remaining chapters.

The primary intellectual difficulty in the study of general magazines, one on which many writers have foundered, is the very diffuseness of their contents. Without some clear conception on which to focus, without some conscious limitation to particular magazine materials, the historian cannot reconstruct any coherent comparative order in the changing values of the past. This study focuses on the model of success, the dominant image of a successful life, which emerges in the magazines of a particular period. It seeks for that model of success primarily in the biographical articles included in the general magazines. It assumes that each generation and, at times of rapid social change, even each decade have looked at the world with a different sense of values, of needs, and of possibilities for life. Each period has had its own dominant hero-image into which it may recast the idols of the past. Each era has admired some particular character type, some form of career, some standard of success more than others.

The biographical articles in the most popular general magazines are in themselves among the most transient and least worthy forms of literature. For that very reason, however, they may be the most accurate available guide to any contemporary consensus about the successful life. Intended only to gain the immediate interest and approval of their readers, these magazine biographies can lay some claim to represent those figures in which the men of their time were most interested and those standards of success which were most approved. In every general magazine, editors have been forced to decide which individuals their audience might judge worthy of biographical treatment. In every magazine biography, writers have brought to bear their contemporary sense of what was possible and what was desirable in life. Popular fiction might reveal more of the heroic aspirations of an age, but biography demands that a tension be maintained between aspiration and reality.

This search for the changing models of success in America focuses, therefore, upon the biographical articles in general magazines. At four distinct stages in the nation's development it attempts to reconstruct from these biographies what Americans in each period felt to be the characteristics of a successful life. It notes which occupations provided the most magazine heroes in a particular period. It judges which standards of success were dominant, which standards remained recessive, in each period. It determines how the magazines described their heroes in body, mind, and character; what personal habits their heroes were noted for; how their heroes were supposed to conduct relations with other people; and what seemed to be the approved road to success.

In order to curb the author's subjectivity, to reveal more precisely significant changes in the models of success, and to draw attention to the presence of subordinate elements in the hero-image of a period, tables of statistics have been introduced where these seemed appropriate. Readers should be warned, however, that results reported in numbers are not necessarily as definitive as the use of numbers implies. Too many arbitrary decisions were made at times in compiling statistics for these statistics to have "scientific" reliability. Since it seems important that the intellectual historian investigating the materials of popular culture should learn to use statistics judiciously, it seems equally important that his statistics should not be assumed to bear more weight than they can reasonably carry. In these matters quantification may serve better as a suggestion of complexity than as a spurious means to simplicity. More often than not, the compiling of these statistics led to a discovery of tension, an awareness of necessary qualification within an apparently simple stereotype of some period's heroic image. From a search conducted in this manner we may begin to chart with some confidence the nature and the timing of significant changes in American conceptions of the successful life.

III

No one will deny that individualism, in one sense or another, has been a central value throughout American experience.[7] Few will question the immense influence which the image of the self-made man has exercised in American social myth. These perceptions have led to a persistent view of *the* American model of success as properly and almost exclusively that of the Individualist—the autonomous man who finds self-fulfillment through the unaided and unremitting exercise of his energies and abilities (usually in business) with a necessarily consequent rise in his economic and social status. This is, in fact, what Americans are generally assumed to mean by "success."

Countless apostles of the success cult have testified to their faith in this vision of life through a voluminous flow of inspirational tracts, how-to-do-it manuals, exemplary biographies, autobiographies, and reams of popular fiction. Many other writers, also accepting this as *the* characteristic American vision, have deplored it as the primary blighting influence on our life, our literature, and our grasp of social reality. Historians who have turned their attention to the documents of this success literature have stressed the continuity of emphasis upon the self-made man.[8] Even social analysts like Riesman, Whyte, and Lowenthal derived much of their dramatic impact by setting off a contemporary picture of Americans against *the* traditional model of individualism.

Yet there are reasons to suspect that this traditional model of the successful life has not been the only one and has not always been the dominant one in our historical experience. The insistence of New England Puritans upon individual conversion, personal accountability to God, and diligence in one's earthly calling may have provided cultural roots for a later conception of the self-made man. But faithful Puritans always regarded Arminianism, the notion that any man could earn salvation through his own good works, as a heresy and always balanced their individualism with a strong concern for the social covenant and the community. The Enlightenment, in turn, may have provided cultural ideas to liberate the individual from tradition, from the paternal state, the mercantilist economy, the inherited social hierarchy, and the established church. It may have grounded a social order upon the "natural rights" of the individual. But the essential vision of the founding fathers was a public philosophy, not a private one. The great contemporary hero of the new nation was Washington far more than Franklin. And even Franklin's famed *Autobiography* was no more a treatise on the way to wealth or the road to self-fulfillment than an account of the appropriate strategies for social effectiveness and public improvement. To reduce the earlier American conceptions of a successful life to preliminary editions of Horatio Alger is to demean the integrity of the past and to deprive ourselves of a liberating perspective. It is also to obscure that remarkable constellation of ideas, institutions, and historical developments which, at one particular period in our history, did make individualism the central idea in American culture.

Looking back from his old age, Ralph Waldo Emerson remembered that the period beginning around 1820 had at its center the belief "that the nation existed for the individual." "This idea," he concluded, "roughly written in revolutions and national movements, in the mind of the philosopher had far more precision: the individual is the world." * As historical observer, Emerson identified with some precision that era when an absorbing faith in the self-sufficient, natural, free-willed, intuitively moral individual emerged to capture American imaginations. As philosopher, Emerson himself most fully revealed that moral perspective from which the world could be seen as the individual.

The decades after 1820 formed the historical moment when individualism found its name, found its embodiment in contemporary heroes, found its celebration by writers and poets, found too the beginning of its vulgarization in the literature of "success." The word itself came to public attention when the translator of Tocqueville's *Democracy in America* had to invent an English equivalent for the French "individualisme." In Tocqueville's eyes the American effort to base a social order upon the individual person was a precarious enterprise since it seemed to sever vital social relations while leaving individuals exposed to the tyranny of the majority. But by 1842 the *Democratic Review* was proclaiming proudly, "The age of individualism is already upon us." [9] Americans hailed Andrew Jackson as the

* Edward Waldo Emerson, ed., *The Complete Works of Ralph Waldo Emerson* (Boston, 1903), Vol. X, 325–26, as quoted in the second chapter of a forthcoming book by John William Ward on the history of the idea of individualism in America. I am greatly indebted to this manuscript for enhancing my perception of this period as I am to its author for his encouragement of this present study at crucial moments.

new man of the New World, self-reliant, strong-willed, and naturally moral.[10] In Abraham Lincoln they came to see the highest embodiment of the ideal, a self-made man of the most humane instincts who suffered for his people and lived to set men free.

Meanwhile Emerson was urging young men to see "that if the single man plants himself indomitably on his instincts, and there abide, the huge world will come round to him." [11] And Walt Whitman was celebrating himself in the "Song of Myself" since "what I assume you shall assume / For every atom belonging to me as good belongs to you." The most eloquent and elevated prophets of American individualism were assuming a mystical, transcendent moral order in which the more that individuals became true individuals the more they would become linked to and serve one another. On a more mundane level a similar assumption in the economic thought of the era postulated an Unseen Hand which transformed individual enterprise and acquisitiveness automatically into social benefits. In its political rhetoric the period wavered between images of the simple, self-sufficient, republican yeoman and of the ambitious, enterprising liberal capitalist.[12] What united these divergent conceptions was the common ideal of the free individual, free from all the constraining traditions of the past and superior even to the social institutions of his present.[13]

Within this context of ideas and of what contemporaries loved to call their "free institutions," the great, traditional model of the self-made man, the Individualist, came to fruition. It was so powerful an ideal, it seemed so uniquely American that its hold on American imaginations would endure for generations after the conditions which had created it passed away. It would continue to appear to many as *the* American model of the successful life. Yet this ideal, an ideal which seemed to hold the individual above all social institutions, was itself the product of a particular social and cultural context. We may rightly question whether Americans had not in fact cherished a rather different model of success before 1820. And we may properly look for that point in history when changing conditions led Americans to recognize the inadequacy and the irrelevance of this particular idol.

Previous historical studies of American conceptions of the successful life have concentrated their attention upon the nineteenth-century exponents of this traditional model. Whitney Griswold has exposed some of the ironies inherent in their idolatry of the successful individual. Irvin Wyllie has revealed many of the genuine moral and social attributes with which the success writers clothed their image of the self-made man. John Cawelti has explored some of the changes which this central tradition underwent even during its period of dominance, and he has described perceptively many of the tensions and contradictions evident in the success literature of the nineteenth century.[14] One could still write an interesting book, using the general magazines and the magazine biographies from 1820 to 1890 as a guide, to chart more precisely the developments, the changes, the tensions within this nineteenth-century model of individualism. A summary sampling of the magazines at intervals throughout this period suggests that older conceptions of the successful life maintained an influence well into the nineteenth century and that magazine biographies presented a rather more complex and less sentimental picture than the success materials which have thus far been examined.

The individualistic model of success which emerged to dominate most of the nineteenth century has, in fact, been so thoroughly studied that its features have obscured an earlier ideal and its actual decline has not been closely charted. The focus of this book, therefore, lies first upon the magazines and magazine biographies of the new nation before 1820. By sketching the contemporary lineaments of these heroes of the young republic it seeks to demonstrate that the traditional model of individualism is not the only one upon which Americans can lay historic claims. The study then leaps over those years from 1820 to 1890 in order to focus again upon the period when changing conditions brought individualism under great strain. In three successive stages during the quarter century from 1894 to 1919 it demonstrates how popular magazines responded to that strain by first intensifying, then supplementing, and finally transforming the individualistic model of success.

The hope of the book is that a more complete perspective upon our past may free us both to draw upon that past and to escape from its sometimes compulsive hold for more humane, more relevant visions of a successful life in our own day.

Part One

THE IDOLS OF ORDER

1787-1820

In which our hero emerges
as a Patriot, a Gentleman, and a Scholar
in magazines of gentlemen, by gentlemen,
and for gentlemen

Chapter 1

Magazines for the Few

The Anthology has never been a favorite with the publick at large, nor were they ambitious of popularity. . . . Amongst the subscribers to the Anthology they may proudly boast of the first names in the country, of those most distinguished by political knowledge, general information, extensive learning, the integrity of their publick conduct, and the virtues of their private life.

Monthly Anthology, *1808*

DURING the first generation of American life under the new Constitution, magazines were produced by the few for the few. Circumstances may have forced this condition upon them, but editors sometimes spoke of the limitation as a virtue. Many factors combined to give the leading magazines the tone of a gentleman's club. Their limited number of subscribers assumed the role rather of patrons than of customers. Their editors and publishers were more likely to be writers or professional men than business entrepreneurs. Their contributors resembled a loose, voluntary group of acquaintances and kindred spirits rather than paid employees. Their continual and often frustrated struggle for survival insured that hope of substantial profits would not long remain a dominant motive in continuing publication. All these characteristics would distinguish them sharply from the aggressively expansionist and prosperous periodicals of mass circulation which emerged in America one hundred years later. Any comparison of the magazine heroes of the early republic with those of a century later must first take account of the differences in the magazines of the two eras.

There is no reason to suspect that any of the early magazines were started with the positive intention of not making a profit. Certainly the fiercely competitive behavior of Benjamin Franklin and Andrew Bradford in launching almost simultaneously the first American magazines sprang from the financial hopes of these two rival printers in 1741.* Such hopes were encouraged by "The Success and Approbation which the MAGAZINES, published in Great Britain, have met with for many years past, among all Ranks and Degrees of People." [1]

Bradford's magazine expired after three numbers, Franklin's after six. Yet the example of magazine prosperity in Britain continued to be as inspiring as it was illusory to Americans for many decades after 1741. Other reasons too seemed to enhance the pecuniary prospects for American publishers. The costs of production promised to be low. Anywhere from one-third to all of the contents could be secured without charge from existing publications simply by judicious use of scissors. Before 1820 even original contributions were customarily submitted without any payment for publication. Printing costs were relatively high in America,† but this could induce printers to look upon maga-

* Charges and countercharges ran through early issues of both magazines. Franklin accused Bradford and his editor of stealing Franklin's idea for a magazine. In turn Franklin was charged with using his control of the Post Office to discriminate against the distribution of Bradford's publications.

† Despite the now-current myth that in these early days a newspaper or magazine could be started by anyone who could set type himself or hire a journeyman printer, scholars point out that printing costs on this side of the Atlantic ran high. It was difficult and costly to secure type, paper, ink, presses, and labor in America. See Daniel J. Boorstin, *The Americans, The Colonial Experience* (New York, 1958), Part 12 and Mott, *History of American Magazines,* I, 20.

zines as a promising way to utilize costly facilities in a country where the market for books was limited. Under these circumstances a magazine could hope for survival with a relatively small number of subscribers, enough to pay the printer's bills. Expansion of the subscription list beyond this point would be almost entirely profit. Charles Brockden Brown approached his first magazine venture with considerable optimism in 1799:

> Four hundred subscribers will repay the annual expense of sixteen hundred dollars. As soon as this number is obtained, the printers will begin and trust to the punctual payment of these for reimbursement. All above four hundred will be a clear profit for me; one thousand subscribers will provide $4,500 and deducting the annual expence will leave $2,700.[2]

Favorable calculations of this sort may have helped to launch the great majority of magazines which chose to disregard the repeated failures of their predecessors. From 1741 through 1785 Lyon Richardson lists twenty-four magazines started in the area of the United States.[3] Yet the average life for these periodicals was about a year, so that in this forty-five-year stretch there were many times when no magazine was in existence. With the return of prosperity after the post-Revolutionary depression, the rate of birth for magazines increased about ninefold.[4] The death rate, however, also remained high, and few of this new brood survived a year or two of precarious life. What were the factors which killed off so rapidly and so regularly these periodicals of the new nation? To understand those factors is also to understand why the more enduring magazines in this early period tended to resemble gentlemen's clubs rather than business enterprises.

Various problems of distribution and pricing served to keep circulations limited to particular areas and particular classes. Population was widely scattered outside the cities; roads were poor; and transportation facilities were restricted. Much depended, then, upon how much indulgence the regular postal service was willing to grant to the distribution of periodicals. Up to 1825 at least, the Post Office proved more of a barrier than a stimulus to magazine publication. Under the Ordinance of 1782 postriders were permitted to carry any periodicals they wished and to make arrangements for payment privately with subscribers.[5] This somewhat chaotic but workable practice was altered by the Postal Act of 1792 which strongly discriminated against magazines. Postriders were now permitted to carry newspapers in addition to the regular mail as before, but Congress specifically voted against extending the privilege to magazines. Some (but apparently not all) postmasters interpreted this as requiring full letter rates for any magazines.[6] A new Postal Act of 1794 did establish a special status for magazines, but the new status was scarcely more favorable. The new regulations stated that magazines "may be transported in the mails when the mode of conveyance and the size of the mails will permit of it." This gave local postmasters a full right to exclude magazines whenever they deemed them a burden. Even when accepted, moreover, they were carried at a rate of eight cents a copy for any distance over a hundred miles, with reductions for shorter distances. Annual carrying charges for a monthly magazine could thus amount to ninety-six cents, and this sum had to be paid by the subscriber.[7]

These high postal charges were themselves added to the already high prices for the magazines. From 1787 to 1820 annual subscription rates ranged from $2.50 to $6.00. At a time when a rural carpenter might receive less than a dollar a day, magazines were, according to Mott, "an unattainable luxury for workingmen." [8] Only those well-to-do citizens who might place a high value on magazine reading were tempted under these conditions to become subscribers. Circulations consequently remained low, and magazines seldom achieved any real financial success. Few magazines of the period ever printed any circulation figures. In Philadelphia, Matthew Carey's *American Museum* claimed to have achieved 1,250 subscribers before 1792, and *The Columbian Magazine* may have approached this figure. Both these exceptionally successful magazines, however, were forced to fold in face of the discriminatory Postal Act of that year. The first two decades of the nineteenth century saw the *Port Folio* reach an outstanding figure of 2,000, but more nearly typical was the *Monthly Anthology's* circulation of 440 in 1805. Charles Brockden Brown's first magazine, for which he had calculated a necessary minimum of 400 subscribers, expired after two years.[9]

Even the circulation figures failed to give a true measure of a periodical's financial strength. The fundamental mistake in Brockden Brown's optimistic estimates lay not in his figures but in his assumption that all subscribers would actually pay their bills. Over and over again these early editors were forced to print the same complaint and the same plea:

> Please to *Read* it! Somehow or other, many persons who subscribe to newspapers and magazines never bother themselves to make payment. When the Printer gives by way of advertisement a *general dun,* they either think that they are not called upon or whether they pay or not it will be of little consequence as the debt is small, or they content themselves with thinking that *sometime or other* they will call or send him the money due, or otherwise they will send him some articles of produce to discharge their accounts. . . . He now requests *All* who are indebted to him (Post-Riders are also desired to remember that *they* are included in the word *All*) to come and settle with him.[10]

The delinquent subscriber remained the chief disappointment to editors' hopes and the most frequently cited cause for magazine failure. The ratio of delinquency also seemed to multiply with distance, a fact which combined with the state of transportation and the postal regulations to keep magazines largely localized. Despite the pretensions of an occasional editor's prospectus, therefore, no magazine up to 1820 could make any valid claim to national influence.

These circumstances not only produced the high death rate for magazines; they also meant that to survive a periodical must fulfill certain requirements. It must rely upon a faithful core of four to eight hundred readers. These must be relatively prosperous; they must be close enough to the place of publication to avoid high postal charges; and they must be close enough to the publishers both in location and in social acquaintance to feel responsibility for payment. More importantly, perhaps, these circumstances meant that to continue publication a magazine's sponsors must have some motivation beyond the desire for monetary gain. As magazines passed the second or third year of existence and as profits remained elusive, they tended to find consolation in their literary and social functions. The proprietors of *The Columbian Magazine* found themselves in such a situation:

> They have uniformly declared that the emoluments which might well have been expected from their undertaking formed but a secondary object; and in truth, as the account stands, after something more than two years of labour and expence, unless they have succeeded in affording a rational entertainment to their readers, they must suffer the mortification of a defeat in every hope.[11]

The career of the *Monthly Anthology* was held by one of its creators to reinforce a similar lesson: "It serves to furnish an instance in addition to so many others, to warn those persons who engage in literary labour with any view to direct profit that they will be certainly disappointed; and if the pleasure of the employment and the satisfaction of doing the state some good will not suffice, they had better never engage in the pursuit." [12]

Understandably, then, the men responsible for these early magazines were persons who found some personal satisfaction along with some social usefulness in the task and who generally had some other occupation to help sustain them. Mott concludes that "Editorial salaries were . . . either (1) non-existent; or (2) what was usually the same thing, contingent on the financial success of the periodical; or (3) in the case of magazines edited by members of the firms that published them, included in the payments for other duties; or (4) comparatively small honoraria paid to professional editors."[13] Joseph Dennie of the *Port Folio* was one of the very few editors able to devote his time almost exclusively to his editorial function. The more common pattern found clergymen, professors, or lawyers filling editorial posts on a part-time basis or continuously for brief stretches away from their more regular occupations. Some magazines had multiple editors of this sort who described themselves as "a society of gentlemen." Printers, engravers, and booksellers, as in the case of *The Columbian Magazine,* might combine their talents for editorial service. The result was that editing a magazine retained some connotations of the gentlemanly dilettante, a conception which also had its effect on the contents of these periodicals.

Above all it was the contributors who generally gave the tone of a gentleman's club to these early enterprises. In some cases they quite literally fulfilled this description. The *Port Folio* depended for much of its original material upon the members of the Tuesday Club in Philadelphia, a group of young lawyers and doctors, mostly college graduates, Federalist in politics, ambitious of literary fame, and fond of good food, good wit, and good society.[14] Other magazines stemmed from the Friendly Club of New York, the Delphian Club of Baltimore, or the Literary Club of Walpole, New Hampshire. Without some such reliable source of copy, editors found original writings difficult to secure, though some managed to build up a circle of contributors through personal friendships and even in some cases payment of an "honorarium." Charles Brockden Brown, who made the most strenuous efforts of any American to support himself by his writing, lamented the fact that there were no full-time professional writers in the new nation. For contributors as well as editors the magazines called upon the talents of other professions: clergymen, lawyers, educators, doctors, politicians, but especially upon the lawyers. The *Port Folio* paid special tribute to the role of the legal profession in supporting magazines:

> Lawyers are unquestionably the best patrons which literature can hope to find in this country. . . . Quick to invent ingenious and useful papers and powerful to disseminate them; eager to encourage and generous to reward merit, they frequently unite in one the author, the publisher, and the patron.[15]

In their creators, their contributors, and their audience the magazines of the early republic were intimately linked with the outlook and the concerns of lawyers, that occupational group which would strike Alexis de Tocqueville as a trace of "aristocracy" amid a generally democratic America.

Magazines of this sort naturally tended to reflect the interests and standards of the upper class, of what the *Monthly Anthology* described as "the first names in the country, of those most distinguished by political knowledge, general information, extensive learning, the integrity of their publick conduct, and the virtues of their private life."[16] They stressed literary nationalism, social usefulness, sound morality, gentlemanly taste, and serious information. They spoke of their "ambition to diffuse useful knowledge, and inspire a taste for literature among their fellow citizens." They found satisfaction in "the pleasing consciousness of having done the state some service."[17]

To choose a sample from among these magazines on the basis of circulation would be both impossible and inappropriate. None of them could be classified under the term of "mass media" purporting obviously to reveal the standards and assumptions most attractive to a wide national public. None of them, moreover, remained in existence throughout the generation from 1787 to 1820. It would seem wiser, then, to select a few magazines which together spanned most of this period, which by their relatively long life demonstrated some hold upon their limited audiences, and which seem fairly to represent the general character of magazines described here. *The Columbian Magazine,* the *Monthly Anthology,* and the *Analectic Magazine* fulfill these criteria. Biographical articles in these three periodicals may fairly be assumed to demonstrate the characteristics of the successful life which served as models for American upper classes in this early generation.

The Columbian Magazine or *Monthly Miscellany* began publication in September, 1786, at Philadelphia.[18] Its various sponsors and editors over a six-year career corresponded well to the pattern of interests and occupations already described. The five original founders included three prominent printers and booksellers, an engraver, and Matthew Carey, who had become known as an editor, publisher, and author. Proprietorship shifted around among various members of the group for three years and then came to lodge with "a Society of Gentlemen" who have thus far remained unidentified. The editorship, which paid a modest salary, was variously held by Matthew Carey, by Francis Hopkinson—poet, judge, signer of the Declaration of Independence—and by Alexander James Dallas—lawyer, later Secretary of the Treasury and Secretary of War, father of a Vice President. At one point Jeremy Belknap—clergyman, historian, writer—was sounded out for the editorial post but replied that a Boston church was offering him a higher salary. The editorial as well as the proprietary functions were taken over by the unknown "Society of Gentlemen" in 1790 when the magazine's name was changed to *The Universal Asylum, and Columbian Magazine.* After a relatively long and flourishing life for that era, the enterprise came to an end with the Postal Act of 1792, which in effect closed off postal distribution for magazines.

A Preface to the first volume announced *The Columbian*'s purpose to serve posterity as "a future criterion of the opinions and characters of the age." By observing the lofty sentiments and earnest purposes revealed in its contents, "however superior the wisdom of succeeding generations shall prove, posterity may at least be taught to venerate the purity and virtue of their fathers; and, if they find nothing in this work to increase their stock of knowledge, neither will anything be found to vitiate their taste, or contaminate their manners."

For its contemporary readers, however, *The Columbian* did much to increase the general stock of knowledge. It printed frequent articles on agriculture, on the state of manufactures, on recent inventions, and many scientific papers. Readers were kept informed of the activities of the American Philosophical Society. Historical and geographical pieces ranged from Jefferson's *Notes on Virginia* and William Byrd's "Description of the Dismal Swamp" to original contributions by Jeremy Belknap, David Rittenhouse, and others. Posterity would actually find more to praise in its knowledgeable prose than in the virtuous and mannered fiction or the ephemeral and conventional verse. As a "criterion of the opinions and characters of the age," succeeding generations can profitably turn to the biographies which were a fairly regular staple, one appearing in every second or third issue. Matthew Carey inaugurated these early with his life of General Nathaniel Greene. Jeremy Belknap followed with a series, "The American Plutarch," on such historical figures as John Winthrop, John Smith, and Sir Ferdinando Gorges. Sketches of Washington, Franklin, Jefferson and lesser known figures were reprinted from other sources or taken from funeral orations and addresses of tribute. These biographies appeared in a context where serious men of affairs were striving to provide serious information about their world and to preserve elevated standards for their age. It will not be surprising that posterity in our case finds a high sense of social responsibility, a respect for intelligence, and a regard for private virtues in the heroes of these biographies.

Though the *Monthly Anthology* of Boston attained a longer life than *The Columbian,* this was not because it catered more fully to popular tastes. The *Anthology,* in fact, seems to have survived with a circulation from one-third to one-half that of *The Columbian.* Its advantage lay in sponsorship by a more coherent "Society of Gentlemen" who took more personal satisfaction from the publication and who disdained more willingly considerations of profit. The result was further to intensify the class-consciousness of the magazine's tone and contents.

The *Anthology* was started in 1803 by a Boston schoolmaster and Harvard graduate named Phineas Adams.[19] After six months he felt compelled to hand over responsibility to the Reverend William Emerson, who in turn "induced two or three gentlemen to join with him in the care of the work." This informal group was replaced in 1805 by the establishment of the Anthology Society whose operation has been described by one of its members:

> The club was regularly organized and governed by certain rules; the number of resident members varied from seven or eight to fifteen or sixteen. It was one of the rules that every member should write for the work: the contributions were in some cases voluntary, in others were assigned by vote. . . . A few of the members, I believe, never wrote anything.[20]

The Society met every week for dinner, "literary chat," the reading of contributions, and the assigning of responsibilities. Members included the leading literati of Boston: clergymen, physicians, Harvard presidents and professors, lawyers, and some businessmen. The names of John T. Kirkland, George Ticknor, Alexander H. Everett, and Winthrop Sargent graced its roll of resident members, while Daniel Webster, Josiah Quincy, James Kent, and Benjamin Silliman were numbered among the corresponding members. From the pleasures of fellowship and of intellectual discourse, from the pride of place and of social station, from a sense of duty and social obligation the magazine drew the support which enabled it to survive for eight years. The Anthology Society backed the *Monthly Anthology* in much the same spirit with which they created a more enduring institution, the Boston Athenaeum. Their feelings toward the magazine were later summarized:

> Whatever may have been the merit of the *Anthology,* its authors would have been sadly disappointed if they had looked for any other advantages to be derived from it than an occasional smile from the public, the amusement of their task, and the pleasure of their social meetings. The publication never gave enough to pay the moderate expense of their suppers, and through their whole career they wrote and paid for the pleasure of writing.[21]

After the demise of the *Anthology* in 1811, a number of its sponsors soon felt the need for some comparable periodical and founded that august, scholarly landmark of nineteenth-century Boston, the *North American Review.*

In content the *Anthology* concentrated less on scientific and historical matters, more on literary ones than had *The Columbian.* It did run a regular section called "The Botanist" as well as a medical section. But far more of the magazine was taken up by reprints of extracts from recent books and by reviews of current literature. Interest in classical literature and in the efforts of translators remained high. A department of "Original and Selected Poetry" included far more of the "selected" than of the original. Periodical essays, editorial comments, religious discourses, a section for State Papers, and biographies filled out the bulk of the issues. The *Anthology* struck a somewhat provincial note with its brief items under the headings of Marriages, Intelligence, and Necrology. Most of these were restricted to the Boston or New England area. In biographies too it did not limit itself to the great national figures of past or present. The heading "Biographia Americana or Anecdotes of Professional, Learned, or Distinguished Characters in America" indicated a wide range which included Patrick Henry and Alexander Hamilton along with the more prominent local figures like Fisher Ames and many lesser known ministers, statesmen, scholars, doctors, and merchants. Biographies in the *Anthology* would reveal directly the standards and assumptions which this tight group of Boston's leaders applied in judging the merits of their contemporaries.

Special circumstances also aided the *Analectic Magazine* of Philadelphia to survive from 1813 through 1820. Its origin came from the enterprise of Moses Thomas, a bookseller and publisher. He had purchased a minor periodical which had struggled along by printing almost exclusively selections from the English reviews. In an effort to give his acquisition new vigor Thomas hired Washington Irving as editor for the "handsome" salary of $1,500 a year. That this sum did not disrupt the dilettante attitude customary with editors is evident from Irving's comments to his brother on the new job: "It is an amusing occupation without any mental responsibility of consequence. I felt very much the want of some such task in my idle hours; there is nothing so irksome as having nothing to do." [22] Early in 1813 the new editor changed the title to the *Analectic Magazine* and began introducing more original contributions from his own pen and from his own circle of literary friends which included his brother-in-law, J. K. Paulding, and Gulian C. Verplanck. After two years Irving found that this "periodically recurring task" did not fit his "desultory" course of life and handed over the editorial chair to an energetic Philadelphia lawyer, Thomas Isaac Wharton.

The greatest success of Irving's tenure had been his own series of biographies on the American naval heroes in the War of 1812. The naval cast thus introduced into the magazine was continued under the new editor with further naval biographies, a history of the United States Navy, and a department called "The Naval Chronicle." The very name of the magazine was changed to the *Analectic Magazine and Naval Chronicle*. This particular trend may have done much to win for both Irving and Paulding later offers of cabinet posts as Secretary of the Navy. It certainly did much for the magazine by capitalizing on a wave of popular nationalism and by making it virtually a service journal for naval officers. In these ways the *Analectic* found a reliable group of contributors among Irving's friends (they continued to write for the magazine even under Wharton) and a necessary nucleus of subscribers in naval circles. These advantages gave it a life of eight years, but in 1820 it changed character and promptly succumbed.

A major part of the *Analectic* always remained the selections from British sources. Both Irving and Wharton, however, printed much that was timely and original beyond their naval pieces. Several of the later items in the *Sketch Book* first appeared in the magazine. Original reviews of American, British, and French books were published as was some "literary and scientific intelligence." Substantial articles on travel and science were supplemented by valuable survey articles on American civilization, such as a study of education in the United States and a discussion of the fine arts here. The generally conservative tone of the magazine, its tendency to divide society automatically into higher and lower classes came through clearly in a book review in 1813. The reviewer used the occasion to take vigorous exception to the doctrine of perfectibility. He felt that the growth of knowledge and of specialization might well bring improvements in the mechanical and domestic arts, "But as to any general enlargement of the understanding, or more prevailing vigor of judgment, we will own that the tendency seems to be all the other way; and we think strong sense, and extended views of human affairs, are more likely to be found, and to be listened to at this moment, than two or three hundred years hereafter." While this would be the fate of "the higher and more instructed classes of society," he found that "the lower orders . . . have still less good fortune to reckon on." The growth of manufactures would produce "a fixed and degraded caste out of which no person can hope to escape." [23] That the magazine was intended solely for "the higher and more instructed classes of society" and that the existing order of society was on the whole more satisfactory than any likely alternative were prevailing assumptions in the *Analectic*.

Biography, though less frequent than in the *Monthly Anthology*, played an important role in the *Anelectic*'s career. The series of naval biographies appeared most prominently and at greatest length. But the roll of contemporaries so honored also included statesmen, writers, physicians, and a college president. Though the *Analectic* tended to stress nationalism and the military virtues more heavily than had *The Columbian* or the *Monthly Anthology,* its background and its assumptions insured that its biographies would also reflect the serious and gentlemanly standards of the upper classes.

Magazines by gentlemen, for gentlemen, and containing biographies about gentlemen thus provide our "criterion of the opinions and characters of the age" from 1787 to 1820. The model of success which emerges from these magazine biographies cannot substantiate any claim to wide popular appeal. When a periodical proudly boasted that it had "never been a favorite with the publick at large," the historian must accept it as the limited class publication which it was. In one obvious way, then, these magazines of 1800 provide a poor basis for comparison with the later popular periodicals of 1900. Changes in the biographical heroes represent not simply a change in time. They also reflect a shift from the outlook of a restricted upper class to that of a broad middle class. The aristocratic Rufus King, if he could have survived for a century to see the standards of success purveyed to a mass audience by the later magazines, might have concluded that "The unnatural genius of equality" had finally sapped "the foundations of all that had been built in the knowledge and virtue of the past." [24]

Yet for the historian primarily interested in change, the gentlemanly cast of the early magazines offers a significant starting point for tracing the development in American versions of the successful life. It is important to note that at the beginning of our national life the upper class, at least in the magazines, was able to make its own definition of success. Here gentlemen could find in magazine biographies the rigorous code of conduct by which they themselves lived. The class bias of the magazines was itself a significant measure of the ability of these leaders to impose their standards upon the young republic. For a whole generation before the stirrings of Jacksonian democracy the upper class held a monopoly of the symbols of success in the magazines. When the new popular periodicals after 1890 came to celebrate a radically different model of success, the change was in part a measure of the decline in the power of older established families and professions to set standards for the nation. The shift from class magazines to mass magazines does not negate comparisons of their heroic images. It encourages them and lends them added meaning as a clue to underlying social changes in America.

Chapter 2

The Heroes of the Young Republic

Duty. Here is another Roman clue to Washington: duty seen as a cluster of obligations. Obligations, be it noted, rather than some more modern word such as 'compulsions'; for these are not individual but social *necessities, and Washington was, if not a particularly sociable man, nevertheless emphatically a social being.*

Marcus Cunliffe, George Washington, Man and Monument

LATER GENERATIONS of Americans have often found it difficult to accept the Founding Fathers on their own terms. George Washington in particular has seemed too remote, too aloof, too irreproachable to stir the warmest human sympathies of his posterity.* Even Thomas Jefferson, our greatest philosopher of democracy, has not really become a widely popular, democratic hero. He has served more as a symbol of conflicting social and political ideas than as a human figure for popular identification and emulation.[1] As for John and John Quincy Adams, James Madison, Alexander Hamilton, and the other great names, their role seems far greater in the history books than in the Sunday

* See Marcus Cunliffe, *George Washington, Man and Monument* (New York, 1960), Ch. 5, for a perceptive discussion of the code of conduct held by Washington's generation and of the difficulty modern Americans have in understanding and appreciating it. The quotation from Cunliffe cited above appears on page 164 of his book.

supplements and the popular imagination. Alone among his contemporaries Benjamin Franklin has won the affection as well as the respect of later ages. Yet the Franklin who has achieved this response bears only a partial resemblance to the "good Dr. Franklin," eminent man of science, public-spirited citizen of his city and his nation, distinguished man of letters and of learning, who was revered as a model of the scholarly and patriotic virtues during those early years of the new republic.[2]

Americans have long since lost touch with the code of conduct, the standards, and the style which governed life among the nation's leaders in the decades around 1800. Though platitudinous orators may still recall us to the virtues of our forebears, though an eminent analyst of present society may call for a revival of the "public philosophy" which he finds shared by the Founding Fathers,[3] the times have changed. It now takes considerable historical imagination to see life through eighteenth-century eyes. Even the resources of a Rockefeller cannot erect at a restored Williamsburg the model of a successful life which was cherished by Southern planters and Northern professional men alike at the beginning of our national experience. If we sometimes suspect the motives and feel a taint of hypocrisy in the polished manners and rhetoric of the founders, that is partly because we cannot easily grasp the standards which they applied to themselves. If they occasionally seem too much like marble figures of antiquity, that is because the living meaning and relevance which they saw in the heroes of classical times have lost their power in modern America.

The heroic models of classically educated gentlemen in the new American republic were drawn from the earlier republics of Greece and Rome. Biographers very consciously compared themselves with the classical writers. One entitled his series on American heroes "The American Plutarch."[4] Another asked, with rhetorical flourish, "Why did I not receive from nature the genius and eloquence of the celebrated orators of Greece and Rome?"[5] They drew repeated parallels between their contemporary subjects and the ancient prototypes. Washington was compared with Fabius and Cincinnatus. Cicero's comments on the proper use of leisure were cited as the guide for a distinguished clergyman.[6] The patriotism of Fisher Ames was said to have "all the ardour, which inflamed the best men of Greece or Rome, tempered and guided by the solid convictions of a christian."[7] Life was conceived in terms of neo-classic standards inherited from the eighteenth century, not yet in terms of the romantic individualism which would emerge in succeeding decades. The first American magazine model of success was the neo-classic hero.

This classical emphasis in the early biographies ran far more deeply than the use of conventional classic symbols. It included a view of life which stressed the classic tradition of duty, of order, and of social obligation. It influenced the way in which writers thought of the functions of biography. It helped to shape every aspect of the model of success which emerges from their biographies. The classical overtones given to these early heroes cannot have been simply an effort to write in the approved, elegant style. Obviously the leaders of this generation found in the republican virtues of Rome a code of conduct which met many of the felt needs of their class and of their new nation.

The Functions of Biography in the Early Republic

The design of biography is to celebrate useful talents, to record patriotick labours, and to exhibit characteristick traits of virtue.

Monthly Anthology, *1808*

Biography in these early magazines catered to no frivolous purposes. Editors did not proclaim an intention to enliven their pages with "human interest" accounts of the great or the notorious. Writers did not concern themselves with actresses or celebrated tavern keepers. Details of the private lives of prominent citizens were not revealed to a curious public. To be sure, among the brief death notices of clergymen, professors, governors, and merchants in the sober *Monthly Anthology* there appeared mention of some individuals whose claim to fame stemmed from the simpler human concerns of a generation often afflicted with poor health and early death. Here were recorded in a few sentences the achievements of Tobias Ham, who had lived to the age of 102 years leaving 122 living progeny, or of Thomas Withington, whose "long life, 104 years, was rendered remarkable by his very constant attachment to drinking." [8] But editors and writers left no doubt of the more serious importance which they attached to their full biographical articles. Repeatedly in preamble or text biography was defended as a particularly worthy form of literature for the young republic.

What one editor described as the universal sentiment "to know something of those who, by their virtues or talents shed lustre on their age and country" [9] seemed an especially acute need in a new and self-conscious nation. A prime function of biography for this generation was its unabashed nationalism. What it meant to be an American, how America ranked among the nations of the world, these insistent questions of identity, could be answered in part at least by knowledge of the lives of eminent Americans. A magazine reviewer hailed "the patriotism of adding to the literature of our country, a book of national biography." [10] The heading for Jeremy Belknap's series of biographies in *The Columbian Magazine* promised to readers: "The American Plutarch; Or a Biographical Account of the Heroic and Virtuous Men, who have, at any time, been instrumental to the foundation and prosperity of the United States." [11] Though one writer noted that in a republic there was a special need to know about every political candidate,[12] the magazines did not run timely articles on candidates before elections. The nationalism of their biographies did not cater to the direct and obvious questions of the moment. Their appeal was to the fundamental pride and anxiety of a new people.

While American editors in this period accentuated the normal nationalistic function of biographies, the American context also led them to stress emphatically the didactic, moralistic functions customary in their English models.[13] A predominantly Protestant and middle-class nation could not fail to justify its interest in biography by reference to the edification of virtuous examples. As *The Columbian Magazine* explained, "Nothing excites more powerfully to virtuous deeds, than the examples of those whom they have rendered conspicuous. Man generally desires what he finds applauded in others." [14] The *Monthly Anthology* announced that, "The design of pronouncing encomiums on the dead is to promote the practice of virtue among the living." [15] And the *Analectic Magazine* agreed that history, "only when it deviates into biography, in portraying the actions of some extraordinary man, does it afford those practical models of conduct, or exhibit the consequences of ill regulated ambition, the consideration of which teaches philosophy by examples, and is truly the 'school of life'." [16] Editors took seriously the aims which President Washington had stated for American magazines: "I consider such easy vehicles of knowledge, more happily calculated than any other, to preserve the liberty, stimulate the industry and meliorate the morals of an enlightened and free people." [17] Biography was accepted, then, as an admirable means for stimulating moral impulses as well as inspiring national pride among Americans.

From some comments in the magazines one can sense a further function which biographies may have served for editors and readers of this generation, a function which served to distinguish these early biographies from those proffered to mass audiences a century later. Biographers who wrote about "Professional, learned, or Distinguished Characters in America" [18] could assume that their readers were also professional, learned, and often distinguished in their own right. Many readers could consider themselves on a par with the biographical heroes, and many might have personal knowledge of the man about whom they read. Even the biographers themselves were often fairly eminent persons like Washington Irving or Jeremy Belknap. As a result these biographies had somewhat the tone of an upper class defending itself against the leveling tendencies of the age. This tone was most evident, of course, in the more ardently Federalist magazines like the *Port Folio* of Philadelphia or the *Monthly Anthology* of Boston. The latter ran highly laudatory articles upon such Federalist worthies as Fisher Ames and Alexander Hamilton. It deplored "the vexations of a world, where the mass of its inhabitants without rule or reason give the reins of their conduct into the hands of passion and prejudice." [19] In its comments during 1808 on the ruinous effects of "political bigotry," its fears of egalitarian attacks upon upper-class standards were revealed:

> It is then that the distinctions, which beautify and preserve society, are, because they *designate* genius, learning, honour, virtue, piety, long-tried fidelity, and well-attested valour, exploded as so many palpable violations of the rights of man. . . . These engineers of ruin direct the popular fury against the strength and pride, against that native honour and inalienable magnanimity, which characterise the higher orders of a community, and constitute its defence and ornament.[20]

Whether writers consciously or unconsciously viewed their biographies as a defence of an upper class, certainly they betrayed the conception of a society in which there were fairly definite higher and lower "orders" and in which an individual assumed a fairly fixed "station" in life. The most revealing example of a prevailing artistocratic tone came in the commentary on "an instance of heroic courage, and loyal self devotion, on the part of a common sailor" which was noted in passing during the biography of a naval commander. The author took this occasion to add condescendingly:

> We love to pause and honor great actions in humble life, because they speak well for human nature. Men of rank and station in society often do gallant deeds, in a manner from necessity. Their conspicuous situation obliges them to do so . . . but an act like this we have mentioned . . . done by an obscure, unambitious individual, a poor sailor, can spring from nothing but innate nobleness of soul.[21]

With this one exception to prove the general rule, however, biographers restricted themselves to "men of rank and station." Their heroes invariably came at the least from a "respectable" family. They were then "called" or "appointed" or "destined" to a "dignified station in society." The metaphor of "station," of course, was not simply an inheritance from societies of fixed status, though it retained some of that implication. The hero, whatever place in society he might achieve, was said to regard it "as a station assigned to him by Divine Providence."[22] While this use of the term allowed play for social mobility and individual exertions, in the hands of biographers it also added a certain sanctification to social position.

The function of biographies in these magazines of the young republic was thus threefold. In the face of foreign aspersions or self-doubts about the quality of a new people, the lives of eminent Americans could be offered as testimony to the caliber of American society. In the light of a tradition which viewed biography as an ideal means for teaching morality by example, a highly moral people could find examples from their own ranks for this respected form of education. And finally for anxious members of "the higher orders" of the community, tributes to their fellow citizens who exemplified "genius, learning, honour, virtue, piety" and the other threatened distinctions could appear as bulwarks against an encroaching egalitarianism. Federalists might view the threat to learning and virtue as stemming from Jeffersonian doctrines.[23] Yet educated Jeffersonians would be no less anxious to rebuff the charges of their opponents by emphasizing their own dependence upon an aristocracy of talents and virtue.

The Hero as Patriot, Gentleman, and Scholar

He knew the dependence of a republick on the energy of its intelligent citizens, and generously contributed to the claims of his country. . . . In fine he was that honest man, whose duty was the spring, the rule, and measure of his conduct.

Monthly Anthology, *1805*

A classical age has been described as one which looks at the world through the eyes of society and which looks for the fulfillment of accepted social standards. A romantic age, on the other hand, looks at the world through the eyes of the individual and looks for individual fulfillment and expression. Certainly the magazine heroes of the young republic were those of a classical age. Never since this first generation has the American model of success so thoroughly emphasized the claims of duty and social obligation or so strongly discounted the value of personal ambition. The serious social purposes of biographies in the early magazines were paralleled by the serious social functions of their heroes. In magazines produced by public-spirited gentlemen for the benefit of kindred spirits the biographical hero was a patriot, a gentleman, and a scholar.

I
The Standards of Success

The standards of success applied to these heroes left no doubt of the basic orientation. Not personal fame, not material gain, not individual expression nor creative power, but social contribution, or "publick usefulness" as they usually phrased it, was the invariable standard. "To preserve from oblivion," said the *Monthly Anthology*, "such characters as have been eminently useful to society, ought to be the business of a biographer." [24] The honored lives were "models of public usefulness." [25] "The great aim" of one hero "was to fill his station with dignity, and to be useful to his fellow beings," while the death of another at the age of twenty-two was lamentable because of

> . . . his desire of usefulness—his wish to be one of those by whom society is enlightened and made better. If he had lived to take that station for which he seemed to be destined, he would have been one of those, who give its character to society; who guide and direct public opinion and feeling; and whose influence on the moral and intellectual condition of others, is felt far beyond the sphere in which they are personally known.[26]

The needs of young American nationalism and the emphasis upon social usefulness erected patriotism into an indispensable requisite for the heroes of this generation. It virtually became a Standard of Success in itself. Assertions that a college professor "was early in the Revolution and continued a warm friend to it" or that a merchant "was an upright, uniform, and unshaken patriot" who "early espoused, and during the whole course of his life, firmly maintained the cause of his country" [27] formed a standard part of biographical sketches. As the Revolution receded into the past and a magazine noted that, "Year after year the grave hides from our view the patriots who shed their blood in support of American independence," [28] other evidences of patriotism had to be adduced. Peacetime too held its triumphs of nationalism. A professor of anatomy had brought honor to the republic by publishing the first American work on medicine to be reprinted in Europe. His biographer could not neglect the occasion for patriotic rejoicing:

> To us all this should be a matter of pride and exultation, since by thus reflecting the light of science from the new upon the old world, we can alone be able to redeem the heavy literary debt we have incurred, and vindicate the insulted genius of our country, from the contumelious reproaches we have so long endured.[29]

The War of 1812, however, released the most ardent and the most extended paeans to nationalism among all the magazine biographies of these three decades. The heroes for a series of articles in the *Analectic Magazine* were the American naval commanders who early in the war won engagements with British ships. Their particular merit lay less in their courage, their naval proficiency, or their gentlemanly conduct than in the spur which they had given to national pride. Irving's biography of Captain Isaac Hull devoted a mere four pages to the life of his hero and to the *Constitution*'s capture of the *Guerriere*. He then expanded for five pages upon the national significance of this event. Americans could "hail this event as the dawning of a glorious era for our country; as the parent of a well-founded confidence in ourselves, without which neither nations nor individuals can ever be distinguished." The greatest need of Americans was some such inspiration:

> They want something to rally round; some brilliant light to allure them from afar off. . . . They want something to attract and concentrate their affections; to call them off from brooding over those virulent and petty local feelings which have of late occupied their attention. They want, in short, some great universal bond of union, distinct from any convention whatever, and that bond, we firmly believe is only to be found in National Glory.

Fortunately, continued Irving, these victories "form a little precious hoard of national glory, round which our hearts will rally at all times." [30]

Concern for the nation, for the society, rather than for the individual career pervaded the biographies of this generation in a manner that would virtually disappear within the magazines of the McKinley era. In its final judgment of why a man should be deemed heroic the eye of this generation remained firmly fixed not on the individual and what he had attained for himself but on society and what the hero might have contributed to it. Only once did this focus waver toward the individual, and that was in 1819 at the very end of this period. One of the *Analectic*'s naval biographies in that year clearly sensed what would be a major difference between the early ideal of public usefulness and the future goal of personal fame. The biographer noted that "Those who determine to live and labour for the cause of humanity, may choose with indifference the mode and place of their service—the fellowship of virtuous and elevated actions will raise them all to one kindred rank in the world." But the ambition for personal fame usually involved a more difficult course: "the pursuit of manly and permanent fame is generally cheerless or repulsive." It called for industry, resolution, self-denial, and "patient anticipation" of its "distant, though certain possession." Here sounded for the first time in the magazines the familiar notes of future hymns to success. Here in brief outline was the first magazine description of the ambitious, industrious, persevering, inner-directed individual who would capture the imagination of most nineteenth-century Americans.

But in 1819 the possible tension between these diverse careers was neatly resolved. The biographer quickly noted that there were some avenues to personal fame which did not involve the long, arduous pursuit which might seem "repulsive" to gentlemen. In "the profession of arms" individual ambition for fame could find early gratification. And the reasons for this, it becomes very evident in his explanation, were simply that a military career easily met the standard of social contribution:

> There is an interest and grateful feeling towards the fate of those, who offer their lives to the service of their country: their success is identified with the honor of their nation; public attention follows its steps with enthusiasm, and marks its issue with applause.[31]

The "profession of arms" did indeed provide, at least in time of war, a particularly appropriate way for reconciling the criterion of "publick usefulness" with an urgent quest for individual distinction. Perhaps the prevalence and apparent popularity of naval biographies in the *Analectic* owed something to a growing tension between two standards of success.

II
Description of the Hero

How were these early patriots described? What did biographers think worthy of remark about their physical appearance, their mental powers, and their character? Here too clear differences emerge between the hero-image of this generation and that of a century later.

Most significant, possibly, was the proportion of descriptive statements in each of these three categories. Little was said about the physical appearance of an individual, while twice as much attention was paid to his intellect and twice as much more to his character. The actual content of descriptive statements emphasized even more strikingly the stress upon mentality and character since the occasional references to bodily features simply used them to point to the qualities of mind and spirit. Writers noted a countenance "strongly marked with the lines of thinking" or an eye which not only "kindled with intelligence" but also "spoke the language of an ardent and noble mind" (surely a burning eye which talked was worthy of remark).[32] The predominant concern was revealed by an author who observed, "Even in their busts and paintings, we endeavor to trace the lineaments of their minds."[33]

The particular qualities of mind most admired were those fitting to the gentleman and the scholar. Not the prudential foresight of the business tycoon but a strong, active, comprehensive mind "improved by education and embellished by taste" distinguished the hero.[34] It would ideally possess "a store of rich and varied knowledge" as well as "a command of language."[35]

The heroic character was likewise that of a gentleman, conscious of his duty, moderate in all things, and displaying "the best habits of piety." The heroic virtues were self-restraint not self-expression, moderation not ambition, dignity not forcefulness, responsibility to one's accepted duty not making one's mark upon the world in new ways. The *Monthly Anthology* aimed to be "a judicious biographer of the great, and a persecutor of the ambitious." The model was "that honest man, whose duty was the spring, the rule, and measure of his conduct." He knew that "a continued spirit of moderation alone characterizes the virtuous individual." He was one of "those few mortals, who live according to nature, by leading a life of order, and doing everything in its proper season."[36] In an age when nature meant the fixed regularities of a Newtonian universe, the appropriate personal virtues of order, reason, duty, and moderation seemed only "natural" to moralizing biographers. After Darwin had helped to change the image of nature to one of unceasing struggle and evolution, the biographers of the 1890's would elucidate a new "natural" morality of ambition, forcefulness, and individual success.

III
The Hero's Personal Habits

What were the personal habits of the heroes of the early republic? Unlike modern magazine biographers who dwell upon the home lives of movie stars, the eating habits of baseball players, and the athletic activities of presidents, writers in the generation after 1787 showed little interest in the private consumption practices of their subjects. Only the most general of comments, and those only in two areas, referred to personal habits of the hero.

One area for such comments lay in sparing references to the use of leisure time. Here again the net effect was to add further touches to the gentlemanly image of the hero. One merchant's "taste for the fine arts" was recorded, as was another's proclivity for "inquiries into practical science" and a third businessman's relish for "the conversation of well bred men." A physician, busy as he was, "still did not neglect elegant literature, or the liberal arts." All that was required of the hero in his leisure time was briefly summarized in one article which quoted and then translated from Cicero: "I neither surrendered myself to inactivity and indolence; nor, on the other hand, to pleasures unbecoming a man of letters." [37]

Yet there was another activity which seemed highly desirable if not absolutely requisite for the hero. This was, of course, Christian faith and practice. No man was selected or praised solely for an exemplary Christian life. Only about one-third of the articles mentioned the religious aspect of their hero's life. The statements were usually brief. But this proportion was considerably higher and these statements were less perfunctory than would be the case in magazines after 1890.

The treatment of Alexander Hamilton was perhaps a fair indication of the relation which Christianity held to the hero in the eyes of many. After eulogizing Hamilton as soldier, statesman, lawyer, and man, the author went on to conclude, "As a Christian we are happy to add, he has not left the world to doubt of his faith and hope." Before his death Hamilton had "put a seal on his character" by declaring "his firm belief in the merits and atonements of a Saviour." [38] Christian faith, not enough for heroic status by itself and not a requirement for all heroes, did serve to "put a seal" on other virtues and accomplishments. A political and commercial leader was thoroughly praised, and the biographer rested content with his effort "when it is added to this, that religion was the base and crown of his virtue." A conventional ending for biographies of the period, particularly for memorials of the recently deceased, was a notation of the subject's "modest hope that he had closed with the terms of salvation proposed in the gospel." [39]

The greatest difference between this early generation's comments on the religious life of its heroes and those of the 1890's lay in the distinction between faith and behavior. For these early biographers the important religious question about the hero was whether he had accepted and believed in the Christian assurances of salvation. Only one of those writers who referred at all to religion did so with the obvious behavioristic and secular orientation revealed in his remark about a businessman who "was exemplary for his attendance on publick worship, and saw, what every wise man sees, a close connexion between the observance of religious institutions and the prosperity of a people." [40] By 1894 the tenor of this comment would become the dominant theme in statements about heroes' religion. Church membership, church donations, and church attendance might be noted, but the question of beliefs and faith would be restricted to social, economic, and political matters.

IV
The Hero's Relation to Others

The hero's relation to others is not easy to document from the evidence of the early biographies. They were written in such general language that few specific actions and few specific persons other than the hero ever appeared. Yet after reading numbers of them one gains a clear impression here again of their difference from later biographies. The preeminent relationships admired, beyond the very general notion of service to society, were those of friendship and cooperation, of affection and respect among equals. The hero repeatedly appears who was an "ardent and sincere friend," who had "many warm friends," and who was "warm, sincere, and constant in his friendships." Alongside Hamilton, "so esteemed by the public, so beloved in the circles of private friendship and of domestic life," came the clergyman honored because he "attempted not to exercise dominion over the faith of a brother; but was ever ready to cooperate with him." Even in the role of teacher the hero "blended the authority of the parent with the freedom of the friend." [41] Here was the atmosphere of the gentleman's club where men described equals to equals and praised friends for their friendship. It was quite different from the competitive struggle for fame and dominance described in later national magazines. Friendship and cooperation were desirable assets in the society of the political caucus and the business partnership, the ministerial association and the officer's mess in America's small navy.

V
The Road to Success

How did biographers treat the carving of a career, that subject which would seem to have such endless fascination for succeeding generations? The truth is that these early articles paid virtually no attention to this topic. For the gentlemen of the early republic the question was how well a man filled the station "assigned to him by divine Providence." The interest lay more in personal qualities than in careers. After all, the story of "the pursuit of manly and permanent fame" was considered "generally cheerless or repulsive." Hence the Road to Success of Joseph Barrell (fitting name for a merchant) was dismissed in one sentence: "Mr. Barrell was bred a merchant; and by his industry and enterprize, and the fair and honorable manner in which he conducted his business, he became eminent in his profession, and accumulated an ample fortune." Even more brief was the road of Thomas Davis: "Destined for commerce, while a youth, important concerns devolved upon him, in whose management he discovered that intelligence, integrity, and assiduity which promised and secured success in enterprise." [42] Thereafter their moral virtues and their public-spirited activities were described at length. The glamour of rags to riches, of the triumph over youthful hardships, had no place in the story of men "bred a merchant" or "descended from a rich and respectable family." [43] The dramatic rise of Alexander Hamilton had no place in an article which completely ignored any mention of his origins. There were some things which gentlemen chose to pass over.

VI

The Heroic Occupations

Finally the question of the hero's occupation remains. What were the most acceptable occupations for the heroes of the early republic? In what fields were the patriotic gentlemen of dignified station, dutiful conduct, and comprehensive minds assumed to be found most frequently? A statistical summary of the hero's occupation in seventy-three biographical articles from 1787 to 1820 appears in Table I.[44]

Not apparent in the table is the significant difficulty of classifying men by occupation in those days before the age of specializa-

Table I

Heroic Occupations, 1787–1820

A statistical summary of the hero's occupations in a random sample of biographical articles from four magazines published at various times between 1787 and 1820.

Occupation		No. of Articles	Per Cent of Articles
Politicians	9		
Soldier-Statesmen	5		
Professor-Statesmen	2		
Lawyer-Statesmen	1		
Business-Statesmen	1		
Total Politicians	18	18	25
Military			
Army	10		
Navy	7		
Total	17	17	23
Clergymen	10		
as Professors	3		
as College Presidents	3		
Total Clergymen	16	16	22
Professor-Scholars		6	8
Lawyers		5	7
Physicians		4	5
Businessmer		3	4
Writers		2	3
Women		2	3
	Total	73	100

tion. Heroes like Washington, Hamilton, and Franklin, as well as lesser figures, were not restricted to one line of activity. The table represents many arbitrary classifications based on the occupational emphasis of the articles themselves, but there can be no doubt of the preeminent importance given to the politicians, the military, and the clergy.* Obviously the traditional basic institutions of society—the state, the military and the church—still provided the major fields for a life worthy of the hero. Though America harbored no titled aristocrats, Americans seemed to share an aristocratic English view of occupational prestige. The younger sons of the Peerage might look upon the possibilities for a career in this same order. If they did not enter the government, the military services, or the church, then the university or the law might logically occur to them. Only the more unconventional sons of an ancient family would look to medicine or the taint of trade. Among the gentlemanly circles of even a new middle-class republic, inherited notions of status could be influential.

But this occupational ranking in American magazines did not reflect simply the English heritage. It may also have demonstrated, as will the changed frequencies of later periods, some sense of the felt needs of the new nation. One might well characterize these early heroes and their occupations as the Idols of Order. These were the activities necessary to provide and protect a more perfect Union, establish justice, insure domestic tranquillity, and promote the general welfare. To bring order to a new government and defend it against foreign enemies, to elucidate the moral order and man's proper relation to God, to maintain respect for learning and the orderly processes of scholarship, to emphasize the merits of legality, to heal disorders of the body, and to conduct business in a "fair and honorable manner"—these vocations were needed by a raw, young nation amid "the vexations of a world where the mass of its inhabitants without rule or reason give the reins of their conduct into the hands of passion and prejudice." [45] Nothing would seem to be of greater "publick usefulness." Surely no member of the Anthology Society would object to describing his heroes as Idols of Order.

* The very high proportion of clergymen is probably not representative of all magazines in this period. Most of the clergy in our sample appeared in the pages of the *Monthly Anthology,* a magazine which numbered somewhat more ministers among its sponsors than did other periodicals.

Occasional passing comments in the articles give further insight into their reasons for considering these occupations appropriate for a hero of this period. Politics and arms were almost taken for granted as heroic pursuits. The life of a minister or a doctor sometimes seemed to call for explanation:

> The life of a clergyman cannot be diversified. The profession, though of a publick nature is necessarily limited: But the situation is favorable for the best mental improvements; the cultivation of the good affections and the exercise of the amiable virtues. In the example of the worthy minister we may notice the silent growth of Christian excellence and the unobtrusive display of dignity and usefulness.[46]

So too it was explained that although a physician "may not compete with those who lead the arms of their country to victory, or control the decisions of her councils by their eloquence or wisdom, surely he has some honest claims to notice, who so sedulously endeavoured to minister to the miseries of his species, and extend the limits of science, to spread the blessings of benevolence, and uphold the empire of truth and knowledge." [47]

Where the importance of an occupation was not self-evident to readers, the underlying assumption emerged in statements indicating how this was one of those "dignified pursuits" in which the virtues and activities of the heroic, gentlemanly life could be cultivated. Whether certain dominant occupations created prestige for the virtues characteristic of their members or whether certain prized personal qualities lent status to occupations in which they were developed was a question which no biographer attempted to answer. On the evidence alone no historian can hope to solve this particular riddle of causation.

Two final points about this table of early occupations will appear significant when it is compared with similar tables for later periods. The relatively high frequency of professor-scholars makes the magazines of this generation unique in the history of general magazines in the United States. If we should include also the professors and college presidents who have been listed with the politicians and clergymen, the total of those involved to considerable degree in the scholarly life would approach 20 per cent rather than the 8 per cent noted in Table I. Add to this the fact that many other articles referred to the "excellent elementary and classical education" of their heroes and that none in these early years disparaged the value of "book-learning" in the way which would become customary among later generations. Note the presence among the heroes of two college undergraduates who had died in the course of their studies. One particularly was described as "a very worthy young man, who probably fell a victim to intense study." He had "set an example of industry worthy of universal imitation, and, with due attention to health," this example was "especially recommended" to students at Yale.[48] Remember the attention paid to mental qualities in descriptive statements and the hero's devotion to liberal and scientific studies in his leisure time. The evidence is overwhelmingly demonstrative of the respect for learning in this period among these magazine biographies.

Along with this high regard for the trained and cultivated intellect went a very low frequency of mention for the creative arts. Only two creative writers appeared in the heroic ranks. They were as much an oddity there as women. Magazines which elsewhere called for distinctive artistic achievements as a true measure of America's cultural nationalism did not give much biographical notice to creative artists, foreign or domestic, who might have served as models. Here especially the biographies of the 1890's with their prime concern for the creative individual, their neglect or disparagement of scholarship would offer a striking contrast, a clear indication of changed values within American society.

The magazine hero of the early republic had clearly defined features which would distinguish him from the model types of later generations. His concern for public usefulness found its outlet in the traditionally valued institutions of society—the government, the military services, and the church. He could also, though less often, find his "dignified station" in scholarship, the law, or medicine. If he came of an established family and displayed both public spirit and cultivated tastes, he might find it possible to attain heroic status as a merchant. But business in itself did not rank as a sufficient testing ground for the hero.

The essential question about these Idols of Order, however, was not thought to be the positions which they held. Certainly it was not how they had struggled through hardships to success. What was asked of the hero was how honorably he had filled his "appointed" station in life. Had he served his nation and his fellow citizens well? Did he display an educated mind? Had he made duty "the spring, the rule, and measure of his conduct"? Was he more a friend than a master to his fellows? Was his leisure devoted to liberal pursuits? Was religion "the base and crown of his virtue"? The hero who possessed these qualifications could give prestige to the new nation, could serve as a moral example to others, and could preserve reason and virtue against that egalitarianism which threatened to destroy all distinctions and all standards.

The hero of the young republic, at least in these upper-class magazines, was a patriot, a gentleman, and often a scholar. For thirty years and more he remained the undisputed model of success in magazine biographies. Yet the succeeding decades of an extended democracy, a rising industrialism, and a romantic individualism would raise irresistible challenges to this neo-classic ideal. The careers of Andrew Jackson, Abraham Lincoln, John D. Rockefeller, and Horatio Alger's *Ned the Newsboy* would not be viewed entirely in these early terms of duty, decorum, and devoutness. By 1890 the intervening years of individualism would have left only faint traces of this initial American model of success, and individualism in turn would be facing its own period of challenge.

Part Two

THE IDOLS OF POWER

1894-1903

In which our hero has become

the Master of His Environment and gains

national stature in new magazines of the people,

by business entrepreneurs, for profit

Chapter 3

The Magazine Revolution of the Nineties

In my study of the problem I became convinced that both the price and the magazines were wrong for wide circulation, and I worked out the idea of reducing the price of my magazine to ten cents, and of accompanying this radical change by an equally radical change in the character of the magazine—making a magazine of the people and for the people.

Frank A. Munsey

TO MOVE from the magazines of the early republic to those of the decade 1894–1903 is to be ejected from a gentleman's club and thrust into the market place. Instead of dilettante editors who saw in magazines "an amusing occupation" for "idle hours" one encounters energetic entrepreneurs ambitiously carving out successful careers in the promising new field of popular magazines. In place of the amateur contributor who penned graceful essays to please fellow members of the Tuesday Club there is the "magazinist," a regularly salaried writer on the staff of an incorporated periodical or a free-lancer attempting to win sufficient reputation so that editors will bid against each other for his articles and stories. The subscriber, that patron of literature numbered in the hundreds who was often slow to pay his bill to hard-pressed publishers, has given way to a unit of circulation numbered in the hundreds of thousands. Whether he pays his dime at the newsstand or his annual dollar to the circulation manager, it is in either case a matter of somewhat less urgency to the magazine's budget. His very presence on the circulation list has made it possible to raise the rates to advertisers who provide an increasing part of the magazine's revenue. The advertiser himself, flourishing a registered trademark and a brand name before a national market of consumers, is an entirely new figure on the scene. He will come to be its dominant figure during World War I, the man for whose benefit magazines will be constructed along the lines of an editorial formula carefully devised to tap a particular market appropriate to his products. But this will be a later phase of the revolution.[1] In 1894 editors are more concerned with finding a market for their magazines than for their advertisers. Their efforts to expand circulation in the decade after 1894 are successful enough to constitute a revolution in the magazine world. This revolution in turn gives a new and wider function to magazine biographies and to the image of forceful heroes which in these years they carry to a national audience.

The magazine revolution had been long in preparation over the course of time since 1820, but its full impact did not come much before the end of the nineteenth century. The total number of magazines in existence had risen to 575 by 1860. After the Civil War they multiplied at an amazing rate, virtually doubling in number every ten years until the total reached some 5,100 by 1895.[2] In that year the *Nation* observed that magazines were being born "in numbers to make Malthus stare and gasp."[3] The problem of infant mortality, the very limited survival period of the early magazines, was surmounted by a number of hardy periodicals which managed to endure for many decades. *Godey's Lady's Book, The Saturday Evening Post, Harper's Monthly,* and *The Atlantic Monthly* were examples of pre-Civil War magazines still being published in 1894. The distribution problem was largely solved by the improved transportation facilities which railroads provided and by increasingly indulgent treatment of magazines in the Post Office. Congress gave full second-class mailing privileges to magazines in the Postal Act of 1879. Still further assistance came in 1885 when second-class rates were reduced to one cent a pound. The system of rural free delivery after 1897 granted publishers easier access to country areas.

The circulation of individual magazines reached proportions that would have astounded Charles Brockden Brown. Feminine interest in *Godey's* secured for it a circulation over 100,000 as early as 1865. By 1890 Mott calculates that thirty-nine different periodicals were each circulating at least that number of copies while the leaders, *Ladies' Home Journal, Comfort,* and *Youth's Companion,* were approaching the half-million mark. The dimensions of the magazine world had greatly expanded since 1820. The numbers, the producers, the readers, and the variety of magazines had all multiplied many times by 1890. Yet there are some reasons for concluding that the most significant change in the relation of magazines to American society did not come before the publishing events of 1893.

Certainly that was the revolutionary year for the general magazine. As distinct from special-interest publications aimed at particular vocational or avocational interests, the general magazine has always attempted to represent the variety of interests which editors assumed were shared by the alert citizens of the time. Accepting the perceptiveness of editors in this matter, historians naturally prefer the general magazines as the best periodical measures of the concerns, the tastes, and the standards of an era. Whether these magazines simply reflect or actually shape the thinking of their readers is a riddle impossible and unnecessary to solve. In a search for the magazine heroes of any age the general magazines obviously appear to be the most significant hunting grounds.

With the exception of religious journals and a few publications centered upon the theatre, the magazines before 1820 were mostly general in nature. This type of periodical continued and increased in prosperity thereafter, but the greatest changes and the dramatic expansions of circulation before 1893 came in the special-interest field. *Godey's Lady's Book* and the *Ladies' Home Journal,* like the almost equally flourishing *Peterson's* and *Delineator,* were magazines for women. *Youth's Companion* was for children. The widest circulations were piled up by what were called "mail-order journals" such as *Comfort,* with its reputed 1,300,000 subscribers in 1894. *Comfort* and its many sister papers existed solely as a means for mail-order advertisers to reach vast numbers of potential customers among rural and lower-income families. The mail-order journals embedded their numerous advertisements in rather thin quantities of cheap fiction and household hints. They sold for an annual price of twenty-five or fifty cents, but they were less interested in collecting the subscription price than in collecting names of subscribers which could be sold to the mail-order advertisers. That this was the real situation became clear in 1907 when Congress refused second-class mailing privileges to periodicals whose subscribers did not pay in advance. Under this provision most of the mail-order journals promptly went out of business.[4] Since their "subscribers" showed insufficient interest in the mail-order journals to pay in advance even the small prices charged, the historian seems justified in dismissing them as any significant influence on popular culture, despite their impressive circulations.

While new audiences were being tapped by publications for women, for children, and for mail-order customers, the general magazines had remained fairly well limited to prosperous, educated members of the upper classes. The only structural changes in this field were the new means for reaching this kind of audience on a national scale, the presence of long-term professional editors, and the financially strong sponsorship provided by an intimate connection with publishing houses. The giants of the general magazine world in 1893 were *Harper's Monthly, Scrib-*

ner's, and the *Century*. These three were leaders not only in quality and prestige but also in circulation and advertising within their field. Circulations of the big three ranged between 150,000 and 200,000, while their only rival for prestige, *The Atlantic Monthly*, lagged far behind at about 12,000. Despite their more numerous subscribers, their copious and excellent illustrations, their greater proportion of fiction, a reader from the early republic might still have found in the three top general magazines of 1893 considerable similarity to the tone of his own gentlemanly periodicals.

A first link to older traditions was the continued high price of the big three. *Harper's* and the *Century* each sold for thirty-five cents an issue. *Scribner's*, beginning after the other two were solidly established, had ventured to compete at twenty-five cents, but even this rate limited its competition to the same affluent upper-middle-class market. A second link to the early magazines lay in the character of the editors. Though editorship had become a full-time, well-paid occupation, the editorial staffs of these leading magazines came from professional and literary backgrounds. They continued to think of their vocation as an art and a public service more than a business. Henry Mills Alden of *Harper's* had been a clergyman and author before his long career in the editorial chair. Richard Watson Gilder, defender of all "that which is dignified and conservative in the magazine world," [5] had been reared as a minister's son and won recognition as a poet before his long tenure with the *Century*. The editorial post at *Scribner's* was held by Edward L. Burlingame, son of a famous diplomat, a man educated in both American and European universities who had had long experience in publishing circles. These were men of letters, recognizable successors to Washington Irving, William Emerson, and Jeremy Belknap of an earlier day.

There was something still of the gentleman's club about these illustrious magazines. The *Century*, in fact, took its name from the Century Club of New York.[6] Editors and prominent contributors belonged to fashionable New York clubs. But the atmosphere surrounding these quality periodicals, the basic institution upon which they depended, was more precisely that of the reputable, established publishing house. From the great family publishing firms they took their origin, their business ethics, their tone, and their literary standards. *Harper's Monthly Magazine* began in 1850, according to Fletcher Harper, as "a tender to our business, though it has grown into something quite beyond that." [7] The *Century* began in 1870 as *Scribner's Monthly* with the prestige and backing of the elder Charles Scribner. When its editors wished to publish some books separately from the Scribner firm, the connection was dissolved and the name was changed in 1881. In its place Scribner established the last of this triumvirate, *Scribner's Magazine,* six years later.

From the Civil War to the 1890's magazines became distinct economic assets to publishing houses. Profitable in themselves, they provided a means to arouse interest in books through prior serialization as well as a way to attract prominent authors with the promise of publication and remuneration through two media. While the connection enhanced the prospects of publishing houses, it also did much to shape the character of the magazines. Under this sponsorship magazines remained closer to literature than to journalism, to books than to newspapers. Editors tended to think of their audience as the same one which publishers would count on for serious books. Magazine topics were the same ones which publishers stressed in their catalogues. Alden explained that the Harper firm "was eminent as publishers of books on themes especially suited to a popular illustrated periodical—books of travel and exploration, of science popularly treated, of history and biography, and, in general, of the kind of literature best suited to the home, when the practice of reading aloud in the family circle was still a prevalent custom." [8] These remained the chief categories of material in *Harper's* for many years, as in its two chief rivals also.

Magazines of this sort shared other characteristics of the

eminent publishers. They deplored and avoided much of the more ruthless competition prevalent in this era of business. Their editors remained far more interested in the creative side of their publications than in the distributive side. Writing and working with writers remained far more congenial than concocting schemes for expanding circulation. Like responsible publishers, editors carefully avoided shocks to the moral sensibilities of their readers. Magazines, in fact, were thought to need even more caution in this matter than books since, as Alden explained to Henry James in 1890, "Readers choose their books; but the Magazine is pledged against offence to any of its patrons." [9] In all these ways and other more subtle ones the three great magazines of 1893 shared the outlook of the leading publishing houses which through family ownership and long conditioning maintained standards established before the Civil War. It could be said of these magazines, as it has been said of the publishers, that "the traditions for the 'Gilded Age' were set in quieter years, and at a time when literature was identified more with gentility, scholarship, and instruction, than with popular entertainment." [10]

This was the old order which was overthrown by revolutionary changes in the field of general magazines during the decade from 1894 to 1903. In June, 1893, a new magazine appeared on the newsstands. Its name was *McClure's,* and its price was listed at fifteen cents a copy. One month later *Cosmopolitan* lowered its price to twelve and a half cents. In October a third monthly magazine, *Munsey's,* carried the trend further by announcing a rate of ten cents a copy. Within two years all three were selling for a dime, and all three were reaching unprecedented heights of circulation for general magazines. A new big three had been born to seize the lead from *Harper's, Scribner's,* and the *Century* in circulation and advertising and to set new patterns in editors, audience, and contents for the magazine world.

Frank A. Munsey, S. S. McClure, and John Brisben Walker of *Cosmopolitan* were not essentially professional or literary men. Their model was the entrepreneur, the successful business promoters of their own and the immediately preceding generation. Their magazines were their own personal ventures, not connected with and therefore not limited by the traditions of established publishing houses. Their associations had been not so much with the world of books as with the worlds of business and of newspapers. They had virtually stumbled into magazine publishing at just that moment when conditions were making it possible for magazines to become big business.

As a young man in a telegraph office at Augusta, Maine, Frank Munsey had nourished the ambition and confidence of an Horatio Alger hero. "I was so sure of myself," he remembered later, "that I would willingly have given ten years of my life, without compensation, for a chance with some of the big concerns of the country—railroading, steel-manufacturing, shipping, banking or any of the great staple industries." But Augusta at that time was the center for several of the largest mail-order journals. This was the great business of the city, "making vastly more money than anything else." Munsey therefore cast his lot with this most available business: "The publishing germ gradually got into my blood, and as visions of steel-manufacturing, of merchandising in a big way, of banking, and of other alluring enterprises receded, my thoughts focussed more and more on the publishing business, until at last I lived and breathed in the publishing world." [11]

McClure too had fallen almost by accident into magazine publishing and awakened to a sense of the expansive possibilities for a career in that field. Fresh from Knox College in Illinois, he had taken a job with the Pope Manufacturing Company, successful makers of bicycles. Only at the insistence of Colonel Pope did he consent to edit the Company's small magazine, the *Wheelman.*

> The first number of the *Wheelman* came out in August, 1882, within two months after I left college, and, quite by accident, I was the editor of it. I had never expected to be an editor, or planned to be one; but now that I found myself one I was not surprised. . . . I felt now that I had managed to attach myself

> to something vital, where there was every possibility of development. I was in the big game, in the real business of the world; and I began to live in the present.[12]

Though Walker has left no personal statement of his early business ambitions or of his sense of "conversion" to the possibilities of magazines, the facts of his career testify to a similar business orientation. He had made and lost a fortune of half a million in iron manufacturing before he was thirty. He had been a successful newspaperman and gained another even larger fortune from Denver real estate before purchasing the failing *Cosmopolitan.* Even while editor he undertook the manufacture of Locomobile steam cars and became the first president of the Automobile Manufacturer's Association. How sharply Walker's outlook differed from that of the more traditional literary editors was dramatized in 1892 when he attempted to work with William Dean Howells as his joint editor of *Cosmopolitan.* Despite a lucrative salary and original expectations of permanence in the post, Howells resigned at the end of four months lamenting a "hopeless incompatibility" between himself and Walker.[13]

The incompatibility between the new and the old type of editor lay partly in the difference between a business and a professional orientation. It also lay in the difference between books and newspapers. If one could conceive of the contents of *Harper's, Scribner's,* and the *Century* as potential material for books, one could see much of the writing in the new magazines as potential feature articles in Sunday newspapers. Munsey was most explicit about his leanings in this direction:

> We believe that the time has come when it is well to throw conservatism and conventionality to the winds, and to open our eyes and learn a thing or two about publishing from the great daily journals with their marvelous Sunday issues.
>
> An extensively and handsomely illustrated monthly, supplemented by reading of strong human interest and plenty of it—reading as clever, as timely, as juicy as the best work in the

> metropolitan dailies. . . . This is our conception of the *fin de siecle* magazine.[14]

Munsey's Magazine became the closest of the three to the newspaper model. Ironically, though, when Munsey later turned his efforts to newspaper publication itself, he proved a dismal failure. Walker, on the other hand, had been an able managing editor in the newspaper field. McClure's first independent enterprise had been to organize the syndication of articles and stories for newspapers. He had been so successful at this that his magazine was originally designed as a further outlet for his syndicated material. All three stressed the desire for magazines that should be timely, lively, and full of human interest, though only Munsey would call his reading matter "juicy."

In their efforts to challenge the dominant position of *Harper's*, *Scribner's* and the *Century*, the three entrepreneurs were aided by various fortunate circumstances. The depression of 1893 which lingered on for three or four years made their new low prices particularly attractive in comparison with the continued high price of the established monthlies. It also made paper and printing facilities available at low cost. A vast expansion in national advertising came at just the time these new periodicals could offer advertisers a greater audience than ever. Prior to 1885 most advertising had been done by retailers for their local markets in which the obvious medium was newspapers. After that date, and with a great surge in the 1890's, manufacturers themselves began exploiting their trademarks and brand names on a national market which could be reached only by magazines. Within two and a half years after its first issue *McClure's* could boast that "we had, month by month, more pages of paid advertising than any other magazine at any time in the history of the world."[15]

Still another technological development helped the new monthlies to compete with the fine illustrations of the more expensive big three. The recently discovered process of photoengraving made unnecessary the costly investment in illustrations from wood blocks. McClure testified to the importance of the new technique:

> The impregnability of the older magazines, such as the *Century* and *Harper's,* was largely due to the costliness of wood-engraving. Only an established publication with a large working capital could afford illustrations made by that process. . . . Not only was the new process vastly cheaper in itself, but it enabled a publisher to make pictures directly from photographs, which were cheap, instead of from drawings, which were expensive.[16]

The new reliance upon photographs as the basic source of illustrations further encouraged emphasis on the timely and transient. It even made the trivial possible since the cost was trivial. An editor who desired illustrated biographies need not turn to eminent and often dead heroes whose portraits could be copied onto wood blocks by highly trained staff artists. He could turn to contemporary figures whose features and homes might be easily photographed for the purpose of "human interest."

Yet all these circumstances would have been fruitless without the presence of new and wider audiences. Exactly who bought and read these new periodicals we cannot know since even their editors had little specific data about readers. No advertising manager could then hire an elaborate organization for market research to determine the age, income, and educational level, the consumer habits and reading preferences of subscribers. The circulation figures alone had to suffice for advertisers. Beyond that they could employ only their own deductions from a magazine's content in estimating the groups to which it appealed.* The historian must do likewise.

* That advertisers did not depend solely upon circulation in making their choices is evident from the fact that *McClure's,* though consistently lower in circulation, attracted more advertising than *Munsey's.* It had more prestige and undoubtedly was read by a more literate and prosperous element of the population.

Circulation figures were dramatic enough in themselves. Some 200,000 copies of a single issue had been about the top figure for the *Century*, best seller of the previous big three. Within four years after the advent of the ten-cent monthlies, *McClure's* could boast a circulation of 260,000, *Cosmopolitan* of 300,000, and *Munsey's* of 700,000. By the end of a decade in 1903, *McClure's* had risen to 377,000, *Cosmopolitan* to 350,000, and *Munsey's* had slipped slightly to about 600,000. Meanwhile the *Century* had declined to around 150,000.[17]

Losses among the older magazines indicated that they may well have lost some subscribers to their new rivals. Others of the customary audience for general magazines may simply have added a copy of *McClure's* or *Cosmopolitan* to the *Harper's*, *Scribner's*, or the *Century* on the living-room table. Yet the new circulations were too large to be explained satisfactorily in this way. As Munsey boasted in 1897, his magazine alone was selling more than twice as many copies as all members of the older three combined. The new periodicals were obviously reaching entirely new readers for general magazines.

Two educational developments of the period undoubtedly played a role in widening this audience. During the eighties many new high schools had been established, and their enrollments had been expanded in unprecedented proportions. During the nineties a craze for adult education and self-improvement societies impressed many observers. The Chautauqua movement, the lending libraries, and women's clubs flourished as never before. Correspondence schools and university extension, with its evening courses and summer sessions for adults, achieved their first real prominence in this decade. All of these changes not only prepared the way for magazine-reading but testified to an urge for wider horizons, for greater familiarity with the world and its standards, for needed orientation to a rapidly changing society —an urge which could also be met by the more timely concerns of the new magazines.[18]

Examination of the contents of *Munsey's*, *McClure's*, and

Cosmopolitan suggests two further hypotheses about their readers: (1) they appealed by their price and by their style to the middle class rather than exclusively to the upper-middle class; (2) they struck the mood particularly of the generation coming of age in the nineties—they were youthful magazines in tone, in editors, in contributors, and probably in audience too.

The change in class level was most evident in *Munsey's*. Here was the wide-eyed fascination of the country boy or the city clerk for the wealthy mansions, the fashionable churches, the financial leaders of New York. Here was the outsider's curiosity about the athletics and secret societies of Yale and Harvard. Here were the serials by Horatio Alger and the Alger-like fiction of Munsey himself. *Munsey's Magazine* achieved the greatest circulation of all because it alone was aimed at readers of a lower-middle-class level by an editor who shared their interests, their aspirations, and all their limitations except, after the magazine's success, those of personal income and power.

While the other two new periodicals lowered to some extent their class appeal, the change most evident in *McClure's* and *Cosmopolitan* seems a change in generations. *Harper's* and the *Century* had been the great magazines for those Americans who had come of age in the Civil War. The greatest successes scored by the *Century* had been its long series of articles on Civil War battles written by the leaders of both sides and its publication of the Nicolay and Hay biography of Lincoln. *Harper's* and the *Century* were the monthly magazines of the Mugwumps, those high-minded, educated, principled, professional and mercantile gentlemen of old families who looked with considerable distaste upon the political corruption and unscrupled industrial competition of the Gilded Age. Like them the magazines had preferred not to dwell overmuch on the contemporary political and economic scene. Feeling at home in the world of literature and scholarship, among the scenes and ideas of other times and other places—more at home perhaps than in the America of President Grant, Jay Gould, James G. Blaine, and John D. Rockefeller—

the Mugwumps had welcomed magazines which stressed history, travel, and literary reminiscences.

The generation born during and after the Civil War, however, could not find the same personal identification with that struggle, could not feel the same aloofness from the turbulent America in which they were reared. The meaning and drama of their own lives, the insistent demand for success which pervaded their generation even more than others, could be pursued only in the challenging, changing new America of the cities, the trusts, and the mass education whose initial impacts were explored and exemplified by the new magazines. This was the generation whose needs and interests were sensed by McClure and Walker on one social level and by Munsey at a somewhat lower one.

In searching for those models of the successful life which captured the American imagination in the years after 1893, one can turn with some confidence to the best-selling general magazines of each succeeding decade, at least until the end of World War I. During this period magazines, unrivaled by radio, movies, or television, were the only communications medium of national scope. After the magazine revolution initiated in 1893 their audience was not limited to a small upper segment of the population. They could lay claim to fair representation of the standards, assumptions, and interests of the vast American middle class. Ranking the best sellers for each year in the decade from 1894 to 1903 indicates that *Munsey's, McClure's, Cosmopolitan,* and the *Century* (in that order) rated as the top four in circulation for this decade. Such a sample ranged in viewpoint from the lower-middle to the upper-middle class, from a younger to an older generation. Any characteristics which these four shared in common could presume to be central concerns of Americans in those years. From the biographies in these four periodicals can be discerned an image of that decade's hero which may fairly be granted national influence.

Yet to appreciate the contexts in which these biographies appeared, to sense the backgrounds and purposes of the editors who selected and shaped them, to see the differences in each magazine's biographies before noting what they shared, we need to examine more closely the editors and contents of each of these four best sellers. More clearly than their predecessors each of the new popular magazines was a personal expression of an editor's individuality. What distinguished each from another came largely from an editor's peculiar experience and interests. What they shared came from the common questions of the age.

I

The Century Magazine

He desired that the two magazines [Century *and* St. Nicholas] *should be powerful instruments of righteousness. That the tone of them should always be elevated; that nothing impure or unworthy should be allowed to appear in them; that they should never be permitted to assail or undermine genuine faith or pure morality; that they should pour into the community a constant stream of refining influence—this was his central purpose, his lofty ambition.*

Washington Gladden (speaking about Roswell Smith, business manager and part-owner of the Century*)*

The mark of the Mugwump lay clearly upon the *Century*, upon its editors and even upon its business manager, upon its politics and its fiction, upon its reform causes and its moral attitudes. The great decade for the *Century* was the great decade for the Mugwumps, the 1880's, the years of the Civil Service Act, the repudiation of Blaine, the first administration of Grover Cleveland. In these years the magazine severed its connection with the Scribner firm, changed its name, established its own publishing house, printed its great series on the Civil War and on Lincoln, supported Cleveland, and reached a circulation over 200,000.

Richard Watson Gilder, then in his forties, was the *Century's* editor at this time, and the somewhat younger Robert Underwood Johnson was the associate editor. Both men would serve most of their lives in guiding the destinies of the *Century*, Gilder until 1909, Johnson until 1913. Yet neither could forget nor greatly change the form of the magazine in its most illustrious decade. Thereafter the times seemed to be out of joint and the newer magazines to be "straining after effect" and full of "revolutionary madness." [19] The old ways and the old readers were the true ones. Johnson believed it was "a good principle of editing to keep an old friend rather than make a new one." [20] And the old friends were those who had shared in the upheaval of the Civil War, been appalled at the scandals under Grant, supported "principle" with Cleveland, and continuously upheld pure morality, elevated spirituality,* and refinement.

Gilder himself, fifty years old in 1894, represented the best of the Mugwump tradition. His father was a minister and, for a while, head of a female seminary where the boy was the only male pupil. Despite a frail physique and a grieving mother, young Richard enlisted at nineteen with a Philadelphia battery of artillery, gloried under Confederate shell fire on the outskirts of the battle of Gettysburg, wrote and had published a poem entitled "The Potomac-1861," reprimanded some regular troops for swearing in the midst of a battle, and climbed through a window of Independence Hall to view Lincoln's body lying in state. His ambition to write led him briefly into newspaper work and then to editing magazines. When *Scribner's Monthly* started in 1870, Gilder was installed as associate editor. When it was changed to the *Century* in 1881, he became editor-in-chief, after explaining: "Business is not in my line;—I want to devote myself to editing and to a certain unfortunate passion for making words

* Johnson explained that one of the unformulated principles of editing the *Century* was to insist that every issue should contain at least one article, poem or editorial of "spiritual significance." Robert Underwood Johnson, *Remembered Yesterdays*, 113.

rhyme." Though stating his intention to stress "the elaborate discussion of living, practical questions" as "the best of all magazine material," his interests lay strongly with poetry, art, and literature. He made over his house next to the Century Club according to designs by Stanford White with a medallion for the facade by St. Gaudens. It was an appropriate residence for the new arbiter of taste and literature for polite society.

Gilder's political and social enthusiasms fitted well the Mugwump canons. On the national scene Civil Service Reform was his one great interest and Grover Cleveland his one hero. After playing a small part in the convention of 1892 which renominated Cleveland, Gilder wrote a letter of congratulation to the candidate. Neatly, but with unwitting irony, it summed up the Mugwump attitude: "Every one whose heart is in the right place is happy in this tremendous triumph of principles over policy. . . ." In his own city Gilder was a member of the New York Tenement House Commission and a supporter of the Citizen's Union in their efforts to break the power of Tammany.

The year 1896 was a fearful one for Gilder. On the one hand there was Bryan, a "light-weight professional agitator," whose platform promised not only free silver but "free riot, free spoils, and free injustice." On the other hand were the new popular magazines threatening the *Century*'s position. "Between you and me and the barber," wrote Gilder to a friend, "I like it not . . . the vulgarizing of everything in life and letters and politics and religion, all this sickens the soul." There was much to sicken his soul as the decade after 1894 wore on and as the *Century*'s circulation declined, but Gilder did his best to maintain the old ideals while admitting at last more and more discussion of "living, practical questions" to the magazine.[21]

The old fascination with the remote in place and time which seemed a hallmark of the *Harper's-Century* type still could be found as Gilder's magazine strove to keep old friends after 1894. The May issue in 1901, for example, contained no less than six articles on "picturesque" foreign scenes ranging from "A Hamlet in Old Hampshire" and "Along the Paris Quais" to thirty pages on "Out-of-the-Way Places in the Orient" and more on "A Recovered City of Alexander the Great." The Civil War raged on in these years as Horace Porter went "Campaigning with Grant" at serial length and Confederate Generals debated with Union Generals over "Why the Confederacy Failed." The most successful serial fiction was a historical romance of the American Revolution.

Yet even the *Century* showed changes, and it was the war with Spain in 1898 which seemed to awaken its editors to some of the drama of the contemporary American scene. The first reaction of the magazine to the conflict was an interesting adaptation of their fondness for travel and historical articles to the concerns of the moment. In the issue for June, 1898, they paid their respects to the war by printing Stephen Bonsal's travel article on "Toledo, the Imperial City of Spain" together with an historical sketch of "The Spanish Armada." Only months later, when the fighting itself had become history, could they approach the conflict more directly with pieces by General Shafter, Admiral Sampson, and Lieutenant Hobson. Thereafter, from 1900 through 1903, the *Century* printed more and more material on the immediate domestic scene. Andrew Carnegie's correction of "Popular Illusions about Trusts" in 1900 was followed by articles on "The So-Called Beef Trust," "The So-Called Steel Trust" and "The So-Called Sugar Trust." Readers were introduced to "The New New York," to "The Chicago Board of Trade," to "Making Laws at Washington," to "The State Boss and How He May Be Dethroned," as well as to "Midsummer in New York" by Mrs. Schuyler Van Rensselaer. The contagious interest of Americans in their own present institutions and what was happening to them, an interest first sensed and exploited by the newer popular magazines, wrought its effects even upon the *Century*.

With what attitude did the magazine approach these domestic developments as the nineteenth century moved into the twentieth? Unlike *Harper's*, which purposely eschewed all controversial topics, the *Century* had always professed ambitions of leadership on pressing social and political questions. What that leadership meant to its editors can be seen from the list of reforms which in 1929 Johnson proudly set forth to its credit:

> Among the movements of which it was either the pioneer or, among the magazines, the most conspicuous advocate, were International Copyright, Civil Service Reform, Forest Conservation, Free Art, International Arbitration, Kindergarten Instruction, Tenement House Improvement, the Gold Standard, the Australian Ballot, Art in the Home, More Artistic Coinage and many others. It opposed the Boss System in Politics, all forms of Sectionalism and Lawlessness, the Louisiana Lottery, and many other pernicious social influences.[22]

The list was a catalogue of the causes for which good Mugwumps had crusaded in the 1880's and 1890's. Behind these lay their hopes to bring order, peace, and culture to the world by placing men of principle in government, by improving the character of the poor and of the young, by eliminating power struggles among nations through reason, and by promoting the status of art and of literature. Except for adherence to the gold standard and opposition to the lottery, economic questions were of little concern to these editors. Like other Mugwumps their faith lay in character and culture. The yardstick of character was the chief tool of analysis which they brought to bear in assessing the contemporary scene. Not reforms in the political, economic, and social structure but a revitalization of character—of integrity, independence and responsibility—and a greater role for upper-class men of proven character seemed called for by the problems of city bosses, of labor, and of trusts.

The *Century* hailed the Christian Endeavor societies as "A New Force in Politics" in 1896 and concluded: "If all the churches and religious bodies of the country could be induced to preach and practice the same doctrine, the day of our deliverance as a nation from ignorant, corrupt, and often rascally government would be at hand.[23] The doctrine presumably would be "vigorous, robust, muscular Christianity . . . . devoid of all the etcetera of creed . . . that which shows the character and manliness of Christ."[24] Presumably also such Christian character was most manifest in the prosperous business and professional circles who read the *Century* since its "Cure for Municipal Corruption" was to insist that: "Those citizens who are most favorably situated as to the opportunities of education and property, in addition to carrying the heaviest end of the burden of taxation, must attend to the drudgery of politics."[25] Even after the national election of 1896 which saw McKinley and Mark Hanna quell the threat of Bryanism, the *Century* complained that the business and property interests of the nation had separated themselves too much from the legislative process.[26] To shake the hold of "politicians" and bosses over government, to open the way for men of character and business principle, the *Century* felt as late as 1901 that as "the most useful cause now appealing to the support of Americans we should name Civil Service Reform."[27] Gilder's magazine did not see any threat of class legislation or special-interest advantages in a government dominated by businessmen though, of course, it did condemn the "foible" of bribery practiced by some of the new and "vulgar rich, whose dazzling display of luxury is corrupting the young."[28]

While businessmen of character held the *Century*'s hopes for the salvation of government, its concern for labor was that organized unions should not deprive a workingman of his "right" to sell his labor independently and of his opportunity to develop character through hard work and self-reliance. The editors called for the independence of each worker and felt "President Eliot was right when he said that the workingman who resists the tyranny of his fellow-workingman is a good type of the American hero."[29] At a time when steelworkers toiled twelve hours a day at the blast furnaces, the *Century* reiterated the verities of its creed about the relation between work and character:

> In general, work is not a curse, but a blessing—a positive means of grace. One can hardly begin too early to impress upon children lessons of self-help by talks appropriate to their age and forces, and to beget in them scorn of idleness and of dependence on others. To do this is to make them happy through the self-respect that comes with the realization of power, and thus to approximate Tennyson's goal of man: 'Self-reverence, self-knowledge, self-control.' [30]

The ideal of the independent, industrious, self-reliant individual was one all readers of the *Century* could share. Since few steelworkers or coal miners had access to the magazine, they were in no position to question the relevance of such truths in a discussion of labor's problems. The yardstick of character remained the unchallenged criterion for the needs of labor as well as of government.

When the *Century* in 1900 turned its attention to the new trusts, it strove to draw upon recognized experts in the field. Andrew Carnegie, a close friend of Gilder's, explained in orthodox Spencerian terms that the recent consolidation of business "is an evolution from the heterogeneous to the homogeneous, and is clearly another step in the upward path of development." Even more important for the *Century's* concern with character was Carnegie's assertion that "The bigger system grows bigger men, and it is by the big men that the standard of the race is raised . . . dealing with larger affairs broadens and strengthens character." [31] Further articles, aiming "not to present a partizan view of these organizations," set an air of objectivity in their titles, "The So-Called Beef Trust," "The So-Called Sugar Trust." A scholarly Professor of Political Science from Williams declared it to be "no part of the purpose" of his article "to assist in a search for evils the existence of which is often asserted, but which are difficult to define." He went on to liken the steel trust to "an industrial democracy" while his fellow writers repeatedly stressed how the whole development was "a matter of natural evolution." [32] In the effort to achieve objectivity and avoid sensationalism, the *Century's* articles managed to endow trusts with the "scientific" sanctions of economics and evolution.

Though Carnegie also pointed to the broader, stronger character developed by trusts, the editors here experienced some fears. The supreme goal, "independence of thought and action," as well as "the assumption that individuals will act as individuals" both seemed threatened by the new consolidations. Editorial hopes, however, played down the desirability of "concrete legislation" and called for a greater recognition of duties by "the monopolist," in short a more responsible character among the leaders of the new business world.[33] If the danger was to the independent character, the solution lay in the responsible character. The old yardstick was stretched to cover the new size of business.

This emphasis on character, the tendency to see society and social questions in terms of the independent, self-reliant, responsible individual helped to make biography a prominent feature in the *Century.* Along with historical and travel articles biographies had always formed a strong part of the *Harper's-Century* material. But in the 1890's the *Century* printed more studies of individuals than in preceding decades.* In accord with its traditions these individuals often represented the more remote in time and place. About 60 per cent of the persons discussed were dead, while 64 per cent of them were not Americans. Only 14 per cent of the subjects were living Americans, and only one of these appeared before 1899. The articles were usually lengthy, running around ten pages each. Many were serial biographies written by eminent authors, such as William Milligan Sloane's on Napoleon, John Bach McMaster's on Webster, or John Morley's on Cromwell. A high proportion of biographies, 45 per cent, came from the field of the arts, treating writers, painters, sculptors and musicians. The painters and sculptors provided material for the

* In 40 issues of each magazine (a one-third sample) from 1894 through 1903 I found 55 biographies in the *Century,* 45 in *McClure's,* 65 in *Cosmopolitan,* and 50 in *Munsey's.*

costly wood engravings by Timothy Cole which had already brought the magazine great distinction for its illustrations. The *Century* paid little attention to businessmen, Andrew Carnegie being the only one admitted to biographical notice.

In all these respects the *Century* differed somewhat from its more popular rivals. Its heroes were those of an educated class accustomed to draw upon all history and all the Western world for its models, interested in reading about the arts more than about contemporary business or politics, respecting scholarly competence more than colorful style. Its biographies were for a generation, or a small part of a generation, willing and able to read at leisure and at length about figures with whom they were familiar in books or art galleries rather than in daily newspapers. To group these biographies together with those of the newer magazines in an effort to discern a hero-image for this decade seems at first glance a procrustean task. Yet the interesting fact is how much the biographies in the *Century* share with the more contemporary, less scholarly articles in the newer magazines. Much of what *McClure's* saw in a Philip Armour or *Cosmopolitan* in a James Hill the *Century* praised in a Napoleon or a Cromwell. The Mugwump emphasis on individual character was not too far removed from Munsey's obsession with individual success. In the decade from 1894 to 1903 all seemed to agree upon the importance of the creative, productive, powerful individual.

II
McClure's Magazine

McClure's Magazine *is designed to reflect the moving spirit of the time: by portraying in close personal studies the character and achievements of the great men of the day; by reporting . . . the new discoveries, tendencies or principles in science and their application in new inventions; by setting forth, with text and picture, present-day phases of the human struggle for existence and development; by describing great industrial enterprises and their effect upon contemporaneous life; and by giving to its readers the best imaginative literature by living writers—all presented with virile and artistic illustrations.*

Advertisement in McClure's

The key to *McClure's Magazine* was enthusiasm. It was the key quality in Samuel S. McClure himself. His commencement oration at Knox College bore the title "Enthusiasm," and in it the future editor argued that: "It is not the critical, judicial type of mind, but the Garibaldi type of mind, that generates the great popular ideas by which humanity rights itself." He felt that his own qualifications for being an editor were simply that he was "open-minded, naturally enthusiastic, and not afraid to experiment with a new man."[34] All his colleagues on the magazine testify to McClure's amazing and often reckless enthusiasm. Lincoln Steffens described him as "the wild editor of *McClure's Magazine*":

> Blond, smiling, enthusiastic, unreliable, he was the receiver of the ideas of his day. . . . He was rarely in the office. 'I can't sit still,' he shouted. 'That's your job. I don't see how you can do it.' . . . his nerves drove him, too; his curiosity, his love of being in it, his need to wonder and to be wondered about. He

followed the news, especially big, personal news. If a new author rose on the horizon, or an explorer started for it, or a statesman blew in over it, S. S. went forth to meet him and 'get him into *McClure's.'* To Africa he traveled, to Europe often, to the west, south, east, and north of the United States to see things and men, to listen and to talk. . . . He would come straight from the ship to the office, call us together, and tell us what he had seen and heard, said and done. With his valise full of clippings, papers, books, and letters, to prove it, he showed us that he had the greatest features any publisher had ever had, the most marvelous, really world-stunning ideas or stories. Sometimes he had good things.[35]

The verve, the openness to experience, the excitement over new things, and the recklessness of Sam McClure were evident in his magazine and evident too in the whole generation coming into power in the 1890's. The youthful, almost adolescent character of America in these years has impressed many observers. Teddy Roosevelt exemplified it to perfection. The Spanish-American War was partly a result and partly a release of these energies. The times were as suited to the tone of *McClure's* as they were for an awakened hero-worship.

S. S. McClure was one of numerous younger men striving to make their mark in the world during the closing years of the nineteenth century. Thirty-seven years old in 1894, he was a contemporary of Theodore Roosevelt, Woodrow Wilson, and Lincoln Steffens more than of Cleveland, Rockefeller, or Richard Watson Gilder. The romance of his own career, like those of other successful men, continually fascinated him. At his first interview with Ida Tarbell, though pressed for time, he delayed the business at hand to recount "the story of his struggle up."[36] Brought from Ireland at an early age, he had been reared in poverty and in the Middle West. After knocking about at several jobs, he worked his way through Knox College by summers of selling coffeepots all through the area. This experience, he later claimed, "had given me a very close acquaintance with the people of the small towns and the farming communities, the people who afterward bought *McClure's Magazine*." He discovered that they were interested in "exactly the same things . . . that interested me." As an editor, therefore, he felt entirely free to trust his own instincts. "I bought and printed what interested me, and it usually seemed to interest the other Middle-Westerners." [37]

McClure did not share Munsey's scorn for the older, high-priced magazines. When he found himself editing *The Wheelman* for the Pope Bicycle Company, he made it resemble "a thinner *Century*." In the mid-1880's a connection with the *Century* seemed to him "the uttermost limit of my ambition." [38] He did manage to gain a post with Gilder's publication but soon was reaching out with an enterprise of his own, supplying syndicated stories and articles to newspapers, making contacts and contracts with writers who interested him and thus could be counted on to interest newspaper readers. From this syndicate came the idea of a cheap magazine.

The first issue of *McClure's* emerged almost simultaneously with the depression of 1893. Twelve thousand of the first twenty thousand copies were returned unsold. For a year and a half losses mounted at the rate of $5,000 a month for the firm which had begun with only $7,300 of capital. Only McClure's confidence, his friends, and the growing appeal of his magazine pulled him through to the expansive profits of 1896 and thereafter. The whole experience was a heady one, sure to reinforce strongly McClure's faith in his instincts, in his career, and in the future of his world. A man who had thus launched himself upon the full tide of fortune could live with enthusiasm upon "The Edge of the Future," as McClure entitled a leading feature in his magazine. The year which seemed so threatening to Gilder and his associates, 1896, was the first year of McClure's great success. Understandably he plunged with greater verve than Gilder into every aspect of the life about him. Understandably, too, he placed greater hopes upon the people, the people who had responded so favorably to his magazine, than upon the character and culture of the upper class.

It was this enthusiasm, this fascination with the present and the future, this curiosity to examine all aspects of the contemporary scene, this concern for "the real world," and this faith in the people to deal with reality when it was presented to them which distinguished *McClure's* from the *Century*. This was what contemporaries sensed when they called the newer magazines more "timely." Actually *McClure's*, and *Cosmopolitan* too, did not differ radically from their distinguished predecessor. They boasted many of the same authors of fiction who were already prominent in *Harper's* and the *Century*. They ran articles on art, on travel, a few on history, a far greater number on popular science—all themes familiar in somewhat different proportions in the older magazines. In number and quality they strove to rival the illustrations of their established rivals. The high proportion of biographies in *McClure's* was only slightly less than that in the *Century*.[39] McClure had always respected the *Century*. His divergences from it came gradually, at first a product of his own different temperament and interests, then of his increasingly journalistic staff and of the changing times.

Up to 1898 the difference was most noticeable in the concentration of *McClure's* upon science. "The Edge of the Future" seemed to be simply the edge of scientific discoveries and of new inventions. The first issue contained an interview with Alexander Graham Bell and an account of "Unsolved Problems Edison is Studying." Thereafter readers were introduced to endless numbers of new scientific projects ranging from "Criminal Identification" and "Scientific Kite Flying" to "The Roentgen Rays in America," and "The Search for the Absolute Zero." McClure was so eager to keep abreast of scientific advances that he advertised articles on "Discoveries About to be Made." The enthusiasm and optimism which such developments held for *McClure's* could be seen in a New Year's Forecast published in January, 1894, in the midst of the most serious depression known to Americans then living. The piece purported to be "a report on the various problems of modern civilization," but the marginal captions give some idea of the results which were assumed to flow from "inventions of new forms of mechanism in every department of industry": "Wars and Hunger Cease"; "Science Will Win from the Earth Her Abundance"; "Easier Lives in Store for All"; "Psychology to Secure Us Wealth and Art, Wisdom and Happiness." [40] While the *Century* often seemed to ignore problems of the present by dwelling on the past, *McClure's* in these early years sometimes tended to distract attention from the present by anticipating the future.

Yet already there were some signs of a new note of directness, of realism, in examining American institutions. Interest in the violent strike at Homestead led McClure to print a vivid report by Hamlin Garland on "Homestead and Its Perilous Trades." A month later the magazine offered a view of "Homestead as Seen by One of Its Workmen." The next month Stephen Crane, like Garland one of the younger generation of realistic writers, contributed an article, "In the Depths of a Coal Mine." [41] These pieces struck a note of reportorial interest in aspects of contemporary American life which had been largely neglected by the *Century*. So too did an article on Philip D. Armour and his activities, a specific but highly eulogistic account of his achievements and his philanthropies. Several articles on railroading captured much of the fascination which Americans felt for this glamorous enterprise. But before 1898 these were about all. For politics in these clamorous years of the Populists and the Bryan campaign *McClure's* showed little interest. It printed Murat Halstead's recollections of past Republican leaders. It gave some traditional whacks to Tammany and the old Tweed Ring. McClure was too preoccupied with the edge of the scientific future, with adventures among wild animals, with the fiction of Kipling and Anthony Hope, to direct his enthusiastic curiosity toward many of the "present-day phases of the human struggle for existence and development" which had been advertised in his prospectus.

For *McClure's* as for the *Century* the war with Spain served to awaken a new sense of the magazine's role. Ida Tarbell, who turned at this time from her studies of Napoleon, of Lincoln, and of Pasteur to her four years of research into the Standard Oil trust, remembered the Spanish-American conflict as a key influence in the transition:

> The war had done something to *McClure's* as well as to me. In all its earlier years its ambition had been to be a wholesome, enlivening, informing companion to readers, to give fiction, poetry, science of wide popular appeal. . . . It had touched public matters only as they became popular. . . . *McClure's* suddenly (in the war) was a part of active, public life. Having tasted blood, it could no longer be content with being merely attractive, readable. It was a citizen and wanted to do a citizen's part.[42]

There is much evidence that around this time the magazine changed its role from that of entertainer and wholesome companion to that of a monthly journalist. The war certainly helped to make its journalistic function seem exciting, relevant, and popular. Instead of depending upon travel pieces about Spain and historical tales of the Spanish Armada as did the *Century*, *McClure's* in its June, 1898, issue printed no less than eight pieces directly on the war. It boasted that it had "representatives, contributors, artists, and photographers with every branch of the army and the navy." [43] Circulation of its war numbers increased by nearly 100,000. And after the fighting *McClure's* continued to keep on top of the news, especially the debate over imperialism. Kipling's influential poem, "The White Man's Burden," was sent first to *McClure's*. Brooks Adams wrote on "The New Struggle for Life Among Nations." Even in a back cover advertisement Pear's Soap ran a picture of Admiral Dewey washing his hands on shipboard along with the suggestion: "The first step towards lightening the White Man's Burden is through teaching the virtues of cleanliness." [44] From 1898 on, *McClure's* threw itself as enthusiastically into political and economic affairs as it had previously into scientific advances.

Another important stimulus to this transition was the new staff which McClure gathered under him from 1897 to 1899. Men like Ray Stannard Baker and Lincoln Steffens came directly from newspapers and retained the instincts of reporters. When Steffens was hired as managing editor for *McClure's,* he was asked what would be his policy for the magazine. "Put news into it," he replied. His idea was that many stories were too long and complex for newspaper publication but that a monthly magazine could print them complete and point up their significance.[45] Steffens never really performed the functions of managing editor, and he had initial difficulties in finding just this kind of story for the magazine. By October, 1902, however, he hit upon just what he was after in an exposé of conditions in St. Louis. In 1903, with Steffens doing a series on "The Shame of the Cities," Ida Tarbell another on the Standard Oil Co., and Baker writing articles on labor bosses, *McClure's* found itself the pioneer in a new style of magazine writing which Roosevelt soon labeled "muckraking."

The story of muckraking has often been told.[46] It has, in fact, tended to obscure all other questions in the magazine history of these years. All participants agreed that the original muckraking articles in *McClure's* came as the result of no concerted plan to expose evil or call for reform.[47] They seemed at their inception simply the kind of news story which a monthly magazine could best do. What gave them their great impact and their striking style was, first, the specific nature of their revelations; second, the national scope of their findings (something no local newspaper could provide); and, third, the tone of outrage and disillusionment in which they were written. The specific facts came from a staff trained as journalists. The national scope and national audience came from the new status of the popular general magazine. The outrage and disillusionment came from writers and editors who had shared enthusiastically the faith of the 1890's in progress and that decade's admiration for the successful individual life. The essential background of the muckraking story lies in the values and assumptions of the decade preceding 1903. Nowhere are those made more clear than in the magazine heroes of the time.

McClure's had not been a reform magazine in any way. It had not even printed regular editorials. After his own remarkable success, Sam McClure had no reason not to find the world good and most of its men and institutions promising. Science seemed to him an augury of continual progress in all fields. In 1900 Ray Stannard Baker found in "The New Prosperity" much evidence of that progress.[48] The war and the expansion which followed it seemed an extension of our own beneficent institutions to more benighted areas. Yet the main concern of *McClure's* had not been with institutions but with men. The first aim of the magazine cited in an early advertisement was to portray "in close, personal studies the character and achievements of the great men of the day." An early innovation was a series of "Human Documents," pictures of successful individuals from youth to old age in which presumably readers could trace the development of character and personality. Tarbell's serial biography of Napoleon scored the first real gains in circulation for the magazine. Her heavily illustrated life of Lincoln did the most to establish its prosperity. *McClure's* averaged slightly over one biographical article per issue, not counting the numerous "Human Documents." A slight majority of its subjects were living; two-thirds of them were Americans. Articles averaged seven or eight pages in length. Numerous pictures and a sprightly style distinguished them from the more ponderous *Century* biographies. They concentrated upon military figures, the arts (though considerably less than the *Century*), and politicians. Several business leaders were treated. The article on Philip Armour ran to twenty pages and to extravagant tributes. Most of the biographies struck personal, familiar notes which the *Century* would not have countenanced. Their very number testified again to the decade's fascination with individuals and with the successful career. Their contents, as will become evident, glorified the forceful, independent, productive individual who had made his mark on the world.

For nine years of the decade 1894–1903 *McClure's* promoted adulation for the successful individual. Increasingly it turned to contemporary Americans for its examples. There was a direct link between such biographies and the advent of muckraking. As McClure remembered it, the initial step which led to the Standard Oil series was actually the laudatory article on Philip Armour and his works:

> That gave me the idea of having articles written on the greatest American business achievements, and it was suggested in the office that the business achievements and methods of the Standard Oil—more especially the great care that had built up their methods of economical handling and distribution—would afford a very interesting article. Then, as we got into the subject, we saw three or four articles, and planned, I think, to begin about February, 1897. About that time the talk about the trusts had become general—it was an important subject. The feeling of the common people had a sort of menace in it; they took a threatening attitude toward the Trusts, and without much knowledge. So, in our office discussions, we decided that the way to handle the Trust question was, not by taking the matter up abstractly, but to take one Trust, and to give its history, its effects, and its tendencies.[49]

The critical attack on Rockefeller in 1903 thus grew directly out of the uncritical eulogy of Armour in earlier years. An article which started as praise of the economical methods of the Standard Oil Company was transformed by a change in popular feeling, by careful research, and by the early bias of Ida Tarbell (her father had been one of the independent oil producers driven out by Rockefeller's operations) into the first great muckraking blast at business practices. The tone, the style, the impact of this and other exposés would not have been the same without the uncritical eulogies which preceded them and set a pattern for most of the decade. Lincoln Steffens recalled this background as an essential ingredient in muckraking:

> Indeed I think now that my writings of that period were effective because I set out on my search with all the taught ignorance of my day. It was this that put the astonishment, shame, and patriotic indignation into my reports.[50]

When in January, 1903, came the three articles exposing the practices of John D. Rockefeller, of Minneapolis officials, judges, and businessmen, of Chicago labor leaders, *McClure's* was roused to a famous editorial which reached the conclusion that there was no one left to trust, "none but all of us."[51] Historians have neglected a second editorial six months later commenting on the Standard Oil and "Shame of the Cities" series still running. Here McClure made more explicit the shock which these revelations brought to a nation of success worshipers:

> And if we can finally persuade our readers to recognize as traitors some of the great men among us who have succeeded by means of boodling and are excused because of success, we shall have achieved our purpose. . . . A briber is a traitor. He may be a captain of industry, he may be a United States Senator, he may be a philanthropist. If he has won his fortune by bribery, the cost of his success is undermining of the institutions of his country. He is not an 'example to youth,' he is a corrupter of youth. . . . The only force that can stop him is PATRIOTISM.[52]

But an appeal for concern with the nation and its institutions, a recall to the early republic's sense of patriotism, could not overnight divert Americans' attention from the heroic individual figure. It could only alter somewhat the requirements for such a figure. In the last issue of this decade *McClure's,* which had already anticipated other magazines by its entry into muckraking, further anticipated them by outlining the new hero for the Progressive decade to follow. The December, 1903, issue carried an article by Ray Stannard Baker called "The Lone Fighter." Here Baker told how a single individual had reformed a union by capturing it from a "boss" and how a single politician had managed to retain his honesty under pressure. "It has rather an odd sound," commented Baker, "a hero in politics, but I want to tell of just such a hero." "If this republic is saved," he concluded, "it must be saved by *individual effort.*" [53]

As for McClure himself, he undertook no political action, no reform campaign. With the enthusiasm and confidence in himself which had carried him so far, he conceived plans for establishing a gigantic new enterprise, a form of one-man trust to help society and promote the magazine. His scheme was for an expanded *McClure's* distributed from various points in the country, a much larger McClure Publishing House which would also put out textbooks, a McClure Life Insurance Company to secure funds for the other enterprises, a McClure Bank for ready credit, and with the surplus profits McClure Settlement Houses and McClure Housing Projects. When this scheme was broached to his colleagues, the largest and best part of his staff walked out to buy the *American Magazine. McClure's* was never quite as good again.

III
The Cosmopolitan

Magazine-making is not like an ordinary business. It is so mixed up with the business of humanity that after a time the editor comes to learn that other people's affairs are his. . . . The Cosmopolitan *has represented from the beginning the belief that, with the closing of the nineteenth century, the human race is destined to make rapid strides towards a new and higher civilization. Every great periodical, by fearlessly championing the cause of justice and reason, has the power to advance the time when all may enjoy greater prosperity and, with the development of high intellectual powers in the right directions, greater happiness.*

Cosmopolitan, *1897*

Cosmopolitan was the most complex and, in many ways, the most interesting of all the magazines of this decade. It did not in its entirety resemble any one of its contemporaries. Yet it contained distinctive features from each of them and pushed these features further than anyone else. *Cosmopolitan* had more picturesque travel articles than the *Century,* more provocative pictures of women than *Munsey's,* more material on scientific and technological advances than *McClure's,* and much more emphasis on public affairs than any of them. It combined a fascination for war and military matters with an unsurpassed attention to education. It promoted various projects to advance civilization: a Cosmopolitan University headed by a distinguished educator and designed for correspondence courses; a contest for the best automobile in a race between *Cosmopolitan*'s New York office and its suburban printing plant; an offer of one hundred million dollars to Spain for the purchase of Cuban independence (made in person to Spanish statesmen by a *Cosmopolitan* representative); a plan for a credit system to save the nation from depressions;

a commission organized to develop an international language; a proposal for a World Congress. *Cosmopolitan* carried more laudatory articles on contemporary business organizations and more eulogistic biographies of captains of industry than any of its major rivals. Its editor and owner was the only man in this editorial group with extensive prior business experience and the only one with a fortune gained apart from his magazine. Yet *Cosmopolitan* alone called for government ownership of railroads and trusts, alone welcomed a number of socialists to its pages. Historians can find in *Cosmopolitan*'s fiction and articles numerous anticipations of muckraking before *McClure's* ever discovered that phenomenon. Historians can find no easy formula, however, to explain the rich diversity and apparent contradictions which characterized the magazine.

The complexity of *Cosmopolitan* stemmed from the personality and interests of its editor, John Brisben Walker. Educated at West Point, leaving there for diplomatic and military adventures in China, making and then losing a fortune in iron manufacturing during his twenties, working on newspapers in Cincinnati, Pittsburgh, and Washington, ranching and speculating in real estate in Colorado, using his second fortune to buy *Cosmopolitan,* Walker at the age of forty-six in 1894 had direct experience of more activities and more areas of the world than any of his editorial colleagues. Like McClure he lived poised on the edge of the future, though his vision of the future included not only technology and science but war, diplomacy, economic reorganization, and education for the masses. He conceived of the magazine as an instrument in pushing society to meet and conquer all such problems. Utopian fantasies and speculations about the future fascinated him. He crowded the magazine with Howells's "Letters of an Altrurian Traveler," Camille Flammarion's "Omega; The Last Days of the World," H. G. Wells's "The War of the Worlds," and many similar pieces. His own business success, far from making him conservative and cautious, seemed to spur his confidence in change and to encourage his assurance that organization and intelligence could solve all social problems. Admiring the accomplishments of his fellow capitalists in the organization of production, he admonished them to tackle next the problem of equitable distribution. So long as Walker owned the magazine, *Cosmopolitan* was his reflection. He insisted on approving all details of its operation. "He was a czar in his own world," reported one of his subordinate editors.[54] But the magazine was not sufficient for his energies. He became involved in the new craze for "horseless carriages," bought a factory for the manufacture of Locomobile steam cars, became first president of the American Automobile Manufacturer's Association, and in 1905 sold the *Cosmopolitan* to William Randolph Hearst in order to concentrate upon his automobile activities.

Readers who liked the romance and "picturesqueness" of travel articles in the *Century* could find them also in Walker's *Cosmopolitan.* The opening issue of 1894 recounted the "Quaint Customs of an Island Capital" in Sicily. Others followed: "Tunisian Tints and Tones," "From Baku to Samerkand." In the month of the hotly-contested presidential election between Bryan and McKinley, *Cosmopolitan* featured as lead article, "Under the Shadows of Vesuvius," and continued next with a look "Through Oriental Doorways." Closer to home, Niagara Falls appeared repeatedly as the most impressive domestic scene for writers and photographers. Readers of somewhat different tastes, those to whom *Munsey's* appealed with its numerous pictures of the draped and undraped female form, might be titillated by the many similar illustrations in *Cosmopolitan*'s series of art studies, its series on "Great Passions of History" (Antony and Cleopatra, Abelard and Heloise), its "Portraits of Women," or such articles as "The Beautiful Models of Paris." Readers of a more technological bent could find *Cosmopolitan* challenging *McClure's* with a large section on "The Progress of Science," plus articles on railroads, "horseless carriages," and the prospects of aerial flight.

But only in *Cosmopolitan,* among these general magazines, could readers find throughout the decade continual attention to the economic structure of society and radical suggestions about its reorganization. Though such items increased after 1898, Walker did not wait for the Spanish-American War to find dramatic interest in contemporary American institutions. As early as 1892, with the labor violence at Homestead, he had written on "The 'Homestead' Object Lesson":

> . . . in the hope that it will cause my own class, who have power and authority, to stop and reflect that perhaps it will be best to concede something in the way of law, to regulate this one-sided distribution of wealth, lest it should be regulated through bloodshed or, what is more horrible still, should throw into power, through sheer brute force, elements which will bring our Republic to anarchy.

Walker reviewed the process through which individuals, benefitting by laws designed for an agrarian society, had usurped the reward of industrial advance, had controlled the processes of law-making and law-enforcement, and had erected "a divine right of property." He pointed to the vast "inequalities of wealth," to the division whereby "the man who lives in what is known as the world of society has no conception of what the world of labor is thinking." He proposed as remedies the income tax, government control of railroad and telegraph lines, the establishment of postal savings banks, the taxation of speculative real estate, and the government arbitration of labor disputes on the recognized principle that "when men employ labourers their business ceases to be purely a private affair, but concerns the state." He praised labor leaders as "a highly intelligent class." The whole article vigorously propounded the most liberal middle-class doctrines of the day, many of them echoed in the Populist platform of that year.[55]

Aspects of socialism continued to intrigue Walker. He had printed "A Traveller from Altruria," the socialist critique of America by William Dean Howells. After 1894 the theme was continued by another Howells series, "Letters of an Altrurian Traveller." In 1896 appeared a fictional series attributed to "Sir

Robert Harton" on "The Discovery of Altruria or A Brief History of an Ideal Republic." It described a middle-class utopia complete with bloodless revolution, the triumph of intelligence and Christian principles, the leadership of a benevolent manufacturer from the wealthy class, and the establishment of a republic which "reduced government to a scientific basis, where the law of Christ has become synonymous with the law of the land; where the rights of individuals are protected against the strong hand of brute force or the keen devices of mental cunning." [56] On his title page and in small print down the side of the front cover design, Walker ran the slogan, "From every man according to his ability; to every man according to his needs." [57] By 1900 Jack London was writing on "What Communities Lose by the Competitive System," and Richard T. Ely was advocating "Public Control of Private Corporations" and the "Advantages of Public Ownership and Management of Natural Monopolies." Walker himself, while hailing the organizational practices of the trusts, was calling for governmental ownership as the only remedy for their threats to "the many." [58]

Did all this mean that *Cosmopolitan* did not share in the decade's admiration for the successful, forceful individual? Quite the contrary—no magazine except *Munsey's* paid as much attention to the current dream of success. Edward Everett Hale, a regular columnist, advised young men on "The Choice of an Occupation," warning them that failure stemmed only from "a moral lapse or selfish introspection" or laziness, assuring them that promotion by merit "is sure to go forward, and it is because it is going forward in America faster than in any other country of the world that America, on the whole, succeeds as no other country succeeds." [59] Edward Bok provided an inspirational series in 1894 for "The Young Man in Business." Walker contributed to a later series which ran on through 1903 reviewing the opportunities for various careers in "Making the Choice of a Profession." Early in 1897 *Cosmopolitan* began a lengthy series on "Great Business Organizations" which covered everything from the collection of news and of garbage to the making of steel and the conduct of a political campaign. The enterprise and efficiency which masterful executives had brought to these operations were glowingly recorded.

In its biographies *Cosmopolitan* surpassed all other general magazines in glorifying the productive, powerful individual. It printed more biographical articles during the decade than any of its rivals. Nearly half of these portrayed business leaders, mostly in a series on "Captains of Industry" and all in highly favorable terms. Walker published more pieces on Napoleon over a longer period than did his competitors. Despite this obsession with Napoleon, only *Munsey's* showed a greater concentration on living figures. *Cosmopolitan's* biographies gave no reason to believe that its occasional socialist heresies betrayed any lack of faith in the forceful, successful individual. As in the writings of Jack London, socialism proved to be compatible with admiration for the superman.

The truth was that Walker looked to successful entrepreneurs like himself for the leadership in future as well as present society. The guiding genius of the ideal republic of Altruria was a wealthy manufacturer. When the magazine printed an article describing and defending the growth of trusts, Walker wrote marginal comments to accompany it. Here he explained his outlook:

> The field of opportunity in the United States, with its great rewards for able comprehension, has been so inviting, that the problems of production have fascinated and monopolized the minds of our ablest men. The time, however, is not far distant when many of these, satiated with success in the first field, will turn to the broader and infinitely more intellectual field of 'distribution.' . . .
>
> Fortunately . . . it requires only the application of able minds to solve the difficulty. Tired of accumulation . . . the very men who now give their genius in opposition to what seem the best interests of the public, will someday turn their attention to the more intellectual problems of distribution.[60]

Walker and his *Cosmopolitan* had no real quarrel with the activities of Morgan, Rockefeller, and Armour. Certainly he offered no alternative heroes to the public. He simply wished these men of his own type to extend their heroic assets into still wider fields.

For himself, he went back to the production of automobiles shortly after his magazine began praising Progressive political figures like Joseph W. Folk of St. Louis as the new "Men of Honor and Stamina Who Make the Real Successes in Life." [61]

IV
Munsey's Magazine

This was about the way the problem looked to me as I analyzed it. Magazines were in danger of being driven from the field [by Sunday Newspapers]. They were emphatically off the key. They seemed to be made for an anemic constituency—not for young, energetic, red-blooded men and women. Editors edited these magazines for themselves, not for the people. These editors were not men of the world. They didn't mingle with the world—didn't get down to the people and mix with the people. They lived in an artificial literary world, where they saw everything through highly-colored spectacles.

Frank A. Munsey

Frank Munsey was everything that the magazine heroes of the young republic conscientiously were not. Immoderate in his personal ambition, largely uneducated, uncultivated in his tastes, almost without friends, Munsey devoted his life to a single-minded pursuit of what he hailed as "riches, power, position, the world, the great big world!" [62] He accused editors like Richard Watson Gilder of living "in an artificial literary world," but Munsey himself lived all his life in the fictional world of Horatio Alger. He read and printed Alger's stories. He wrote similar ones himself. He placed the Alger stamp on every issue and almost every feature of his magazines. Unlike Alger, however, who never in real life escaped poverty and frustration, Munsey's magazines made him a multi-millionaire, and his wealth won him a measure of prestige and political power. Frank Munsey might be excused for believing that the Alger world was the real world—especially since 700,000 of his fellow Americans in the 1890's seemed to share his fascination for the glamour of success which they found portrayed in *Munsey's Magazine.*

By any standards outside the Alger myth Munsey's career would appear sordid and unattractive. Within the framework of the myth, however, it took on glorious meaning, and Munsey always saw it in that framework. Before his success he wrote fiction about its achievement, *Afloat in a Great City* and *The Boy Broker.* After his success he wrote the actual story in much the same terms[63] and loved to recount his career to any audience. An apocryphal tale was circulated that he had once told the story of his life to an editor of the *Sun* for thirty-eight consecutive day.[64]

Fact really seemed to follow fiction in Munsey's rise to success. There were many of the usual dramatic scenes. First came the young telegraph clerk in Augusta, Maine, son of a poor farmer and handyman, whose "very soul cried out for an opportunity to carve out for myself a bigger life." [65] Inspired by the money being made at Augusta in publishing mail-order journals, the young man spent his modest capital in buying some manuscripts and set out for the big city to start his own magazine.

Next came the arrival in New York, forty dollars in his pocket, the manuscripts under his arm, friendless and without the means to publish anything. The earnest young entrepreneur soon impressed a publisher with his plan, and in time for Christmas, 1882, appeared the first issues of the *Golden Argosy, Freighted with Treasures for Boys and Girls.* On the first page of the first number was the greatest treasure from Munsey's bundle of manuscripts, a serial entitled "Do and Dare, or a Brave Boy's Fight for a Fortune" by Horatio Alger, Jr. Inside was another serial, "Nick and Nellie, or God Helps Them That Help Themselves." [66]

Then followed the long years of struggle with Munsey facing one blow after another, doing most of the work single-handed, staying up far into the night to write *Afloat in a Great City* and other serials of his own, planning and scheming and changing the nature of his magazine continually in the effort to gain circulation. What secured the first great expansion for the *Argosy* was Munsey's simultaneous plunge into extensive debt and into a bold advertising campaign. This move brought him nearly $15,000 profit per week and induced a mood of heady exhilaration:

> Five years of poverty, five years of awful struggle, and now the earth was mine! Rich at last, richer than I had ever dreamed of being—a thousand dollars a week net, and with every week adding to it by leaps and bounds—fifty thousand dollars a year, and all mine—next week sixty thousand, then seventy, and a hundred—a million, maybe—GREAT HEAVENS, AND IT WAS ALL REAL! [67]

This state of "great, dizzy, dazzling, glorious intoxication" very soon ran into some harsh realities. The *Argosy*'s circulation began declining. A juvenile magazine could not count on a stable audience nor could it attract much advertising. *Munsey's Weekly* for an adult audience was therefore launched in 1889. Foundering badly it was changed to a monthly, *Munsey's Magazine,* in 1891. Even this move, however, was not sufficient for a magazine selling at twenty-five cents a copy. Munsey was thirty-nine years old and some $150,000 in debt on what he called "that fateful day," October 1, 1893, when he lowered the price to ten cents and advertised this fact widely in the newspapers. As a result, "that day marked the beginning of real success with me." [68] *Munsey's* spurted ahead of any of its monthly rivals, reaching a peak of 700,000 copies within four years. Its editor's clinching argument that *Munsey's* became "the wonder of the world as a popular magazine" was a statement of its net annual earnings:

$69,000 in 1894; $172,000 in 1895; $250,000 in 1896; over a million dollars a year by 1905.[69] Where McClure, in his reminiscences, primarily remembered the exciting features which appeared in his magazine, Munsey recalled the toil and struggle, the business decisions, and every minute curve of his magazine's earnings record.

After the success of *Munsey's,* its creator proved even more anxious than Walker and McClure to branch out into other activities. He speculated successfully in Wall Street; he founded a chain of grocery stores; he embarked on a frenzied course of buying newspapers, merging them with others, killing many off, and reducing all of them to mediocrity. At his death this newspaper career inspired William Allen White to a famous obituary notice:

> Frank Munsey, the great publisher, is dead.
>
> Frank Munsey contributed to the journalism of his day the talent of a meat packer, the morals of a money changer and the manners of an undertaker. He and his kind have about succeeded in transforming a once-noble profession into an 8 per cent security.
>
> May he rest in trust.[70]

What was the appeal of *Munsey's Magazine* for a vast new body of magazine readers which snapped it up at ten cents a copy? Some of its rivals thought the appeal lay chiefly in its numerous illustrations of "half dressed women and undressed statuary."[71] These appeared in the regular lead article on "Artists and Their Work," in departments on "The Stage" and on "Types of Fair Women," and in articles on "Artists Models." The Wilkes-Barre Public Library refused to take *Munsey's* because of these illustrations, receiving a tart rejoinder from Munsey himself.[72] Munsey took pride in his illustrations. He hailed the February, 1894, issue as "The Most Picturesque Yet" for its illustrations which "are picturesque and attractive—*pictures, veritable pictures*—not indifferent illustrations of barn yard scenes and stone culverts and barren prairies and jagged mountains, and this sort of thing in which there is nothing to awaken a sense of pleasure or human interest."[73] A count of the illustrations in this issue shows what he meant by "pleasure and human interest": 17 pictures of women (6 of them highly idealized paintings of nudes), 19 pictures of men, 12 pictures of dogs, 3 pictures of New York Clubs, and 22 small cartoons. Yet after 1897 the pictorial sex appeal of the magazine declined greatly. One could not accurately point to this as any real explanation for the magazine's continuing popularity.

Sheer quantity of material was an asset of the magazine which Munsey himself stressed. In March, 1898, he ran a comparative count of items in the previous month's issue of three leading magazines:

Comparative Showing on the February Magazines[74]

	Century	McClure's	Munsey's
Serials	2	1	3
Articles	13	5	7
Short Stories	4	2	6
Poems	5	0	19
Topics Treated in Departments	11	4	81
Total Number of Topics	35	12	116
Number of Illustrations	57	63	66
Number of Pages	160	96	160
Price	$.35	$.10	$.10

Such numerical reasoning may have impressed some of the more simple-minded readers of *Munsey's*. Certainly the magazine offered far more Departments than any other.* They provided a cheap means for printing a mass of material on numerous topics

* These included: Artists and Their Work, Literary Chat, The Stage, Impressions by the Way, The Contemporary Press, In the Public Eye, In the World of Music, In the World of Sport, Latest Fads, Types of Fair Women, In Vanity Fair, and others.

which could be written by anonymous hack writers at rates well below those for separate articles. Munsey rationalized this practice "as better journalism, [which] is closer to the people's wants, than the pretentious articles." [75] These chatty, brief, unpedantic comments and gossip on items of contemporary interest may well have attracted readers who would not care for the more scholarly, lengthy articles on more remote topics in the *Century*. But after a peak in 1896 and 1897 the proportion of departments to signed articles dwindled drastically. Again the accent on quantity and on departments is not fully sufficient to account for the continued circulation leadership of the magazine through 1903.

The one theme which remained constant in Munsey's magazine, as in his life, was the preoccupation with success, with the ways by which it could be won, with the men who had attained it, and with the luxurious activities which displayed it. Like his career, Munsey's magazine would have been sordid and boring apart from the glamour with which his generation imbued the successful life. After 1893 only one serial story by Horatio Alger and two by Munsey himself were printed. As Munsey's own fortune began to grow, not fictional accounts of the struggle up but actual reports of the world of the successful filled the pages of *Munsey's*. Rural readers and city clerks could thrill, as did the former farm boy and telegraph clerk who was its editor, to illustrated articles on "Wall Street," on "Two Miles of Millionaires" (about Fifth Avenue), on "Ball Giving in New York," on "The Equipage of the Millionaire," and on "The Palace Cottages of Newport." They could learn all about the Astors, the Vanderbilts, and the Goulds in a series on "Prominent American Families." They could focus on more spiritual things in a series on the fashionable churches of New York which assured readers that: "The rectors of such parishes as Trinity, in addition to their pastoral work, are men of business of the highest class. They are such men as in secular life would be the heads of great corporations, the managers of large enterprises." [76] And, of course, there were articles on "the great secular organizations of the world" from railroads and the collection of New York garbage (". . . and the Money Made from the Rubbish of a Metropolis") to Tammany Hall ("The Most Perfect Political Organization in the World") and the German Army ("The Most Perfect Military Organization in the World").

Munsey's did not look upon the splendors of the rich as reasons for bitter envy by the average man: "If Biltmore and the Breakers and English Duchies grew out of a ferry boat [Commodore Vanderbilt's], what future splendor may not arise from the toil in which the average mind is busied." [77] Nor did it fear that the organization and consolidation of business was lessening the prospects for success. Munsey himself, in response to one contributor who had voiced such a fear, assured readers: "Since the beginning of time there never was a period when genius, or even first rate ability, could command in the business world anything like the salary it commands today." * The distinction between high salary and the opportunity for independent enterprise does not seem to have bothered Munsey's thinking about success at all. How young men might win fortunes in various occupations was explained in another series of articles with such titles as "The Rewards of the Law" or "The Physician and His Fees." Munsey wrote the one for his own field, "Getting On in Journalism," which may have revealed a self-image of the editor in its assertion that "The world's real benefactors are its brave men, the men who have the soul to do and to dare, to risk everything, fortune, reputation, and life itself." [78] For those like himself who could see the establishment of a money-making magazine in such romantic terms, the pages of *Munsey's* were full of fascination.

The result of this concentration upon success and all its attributes was that *Munsey's,* from its very beginning as a monthly

* Frank A. Munsey, "Impressions by the Way," *Munsey's,* XXIV (November, 1900), 308. Later in this confusing editorial Munsey struck a rare note of disillusion by asserting: "As a sure road to happiness, the American habit of getting rich is a delusion."

in 1891, concentrated more exclusively upon the contemporary scene than any of its rivals. In the magazine movement toward "timeliness," *Munsey's* took the lead. Its focus, of course, was a narrow one, largely on life in New York, and its opinions on all passing topics were usually predictable. It was confident that "the majority of Americans who reflect upon the subject are inclined to regard with extreme jealousy all suggestions looking to the extension of governmental control of what are now private concerns." [79] In the tumultuous year of 1896 it hailed "The Reign of the Business Man." When the debate over retention of the Philippines arose, *Munsey's* welcomed "The rich opportunities that will be offered to fortune seekers when the great tropical island group . . . shall be opened as a new field for American enterprise." Munsey himself asked why we should give away Cuba. "I can't see any good business in it. . . . My theory from the first—from the very day war was declared—was to hold all the territory we might get, and to get all we could." He briefly summed up the 1900 presidentail election with its debate over imperialism and free silver: "To me the whole thing is a business problem from first to last." [80]

Munsey's did give space to reformers like Governor Pingree of Michigan to advocate "Municipal Ownership of Street Railways" and to Sam Jones, the Mayor of Toledo, to talk about "Government by the Golden Rule." It did engage in what might be called reverse-muckraking with an article on "The Political Wrecking of Business Enterprises" revealing "How political dishonesty, spreading into business life, threatens to debase our national standard of honor—a danger that honest men must arise to combat." [81] In handling the problem of the trusts, *Munsey's* twice printed debates between defenders and mild questioners of the consolidation movement. On the whole, though, the magazine left no doubt of its general approval. James B. Dill—famous corporation lawyer, framer of the permissive New Jersey Statutes enabling trusts to incorporate, influential midwife to the Morgan steel trust—assured Williams College undergraduates in a speech which *Munsey's* published that "Individualism is not dead. On the contrary, individualism is still more strongly called for in the development of combinations." [82] And in the final year of this decade another *Munsey's* author eulogizing "The Richest Americans" concluded:

> Who shall say that it is less the purpose of the age to unify industries than to unify nations? If it is His hand 'that has made and preserved us a nation,' perhaps it is His hand that works so marvelously in this great economic movement. It were little short of atheism to doubt that things will come out all right.[83]

The biographies in *Munsey's Magazine* were an important part of this total pattern. Despite the heavy emphasis on Departments for part of this decade, *Munsey's* averaged better than one biographical article per issue—and that does not include the many brief sketches of successful lives which appeared in the Departments or in composite articles on "The Richest Americans" or "Prominent Families." The biographies were often relatively brief, running from two to five pages. They were written by staff writers like Munsey himself, Matthew White, and Richard Titherington, all men who had in earlier years turned out Alger-like fiction. If the biographies sometimes sounded like an extension of the fiction, that was understandable. *Munsey's* devoted more attention to living heroes—80 per cent of our sample—than any other magazine. Before 1894 it had been the first to include contemporary businessmen among its heroes, though *Cosmopolitan*'s series on Captains of Industry gave that magazine a higher proportion of business heroes during the decade after 1894. No one, however, surpassed *Munsey's* in its statements of adulation for such figures nor more studiously portrayed men of other occupations in business terms.

The need for illustrations which could awaken "a sense of pleasure or human interest" by reproducing paintings of feminine beauty helped to raise the biographies of artists in *Munsey's* to a high frequency. A similar purpose added a number of articles on actresses who could combine the allure of their pictures with the glamour of a career "From Chorus Girl to Prima Donna." * Throughout ran the uncritical admiration for ambition, for success, and for individual power. Munsey's biographer has pointed out that the editor was easily able to worship J. P. Morgan and Theodore Roosevelt at the same time: "They were the great antagonists of their day, but Munsey felt no struggle between this worship of God and Mammon. Both represented the obvious power which he admired." [84] The most popular of all the general magazines, *Munsey's* embodied the reverence of individual force in its most extravagant and vulgar form.

The magazine revolution of the 1890's was both a symptom and a cause of basic changes in American society. The kind of challenge which Munsey, McClure, and Walker posed for their Mugwump predecessors was one which everywhere since the Civil War had been forcing old established houses and old standards of business to totter. Taking advantage of new technological processes and aggressively employing new business methods venturesome promoters had raised business operations to a new scale. The combination of machine production, rapidly expanding supplies of raw materials and of labor, a developed railroad network, and a permissive political context had opened up a national market for exploitation at new levels. Many types of goods previously reserved for the more privileged classes were coming into the homes of ordinary middle-class citizens. Many firms long entrenched in local markets were facing the competition of national producers and distributors. As the only national communications medium magazines offered an unexcelled access to this enlarged market. Profiting from the needs of national

* The title of an article which actually told of a woman trained at the Royal Academy in London who had stepped directly into small parts with no experience as traditional "chorus girl." Marie Tempest, "From Chorus Girl to Prima Donna," *Munsey's*, X (February, 1894), 480–83.

advertisers the new magazines could lower their prices and become themselves one of the items now available to an expanded segment of the population.

Magazines, however, were different from soap and shoes and sealing wax. While the new periodicals provided access to a national market for the producers of goods, they also created a new form of national marketplace for ideas and for prestige. The local authorities and village sages in every region now had to compare their views on trusts with those of a John Brisben Walker or a James B. Dill. The local leaders of society could be measured against the Astors and the Vanderbilts. The local factory-owner or banker had to be viewed in the shadow of a John D. Rockefeller or a J. P. Morgan. Perhaps more importantly the influence of a local teacher or clergyman had to be assessed against the power of a Carnegie or a Philip D. Armour. Even the hallowed attractions of the local community itself had to be revalued in the face of detailed descriptions of the glamorous features of life in New York. If the new magazines played a part in expanding the scope of business activity, they played a greater part in enlarging the popular imagination and dramatizing new dimensions of the successful life.

Magazine biographies, therefore, took on a new importance and exercised wider functions in setting the standards of success and prestige for the nation. Just at the time when industrial trusts, urban life, violent labor strikes, a severe depression, and new imperialistic ventures might have led Americans to question the adequacy of their cherished individualism, new magazines burst forth with impressive examples of the individual who was the master of his environment. *McClure's*, *Munsey's*, and *Cosmopolitan* hailed with enthusiasm all the technological advances and consolidating tendencies of the age. They professed to see in these only greater opportunities for individual ambition and fulfillment. They proceeded to raise the nineteenth-century version of individualism to a new national scale of force and achievement.

Chapter 4

The Hero as Napoleon

The fact remains that millions still bow down to
Napoleon Bonaparte because he was the greatest embodiment
of physical force in all ages.
Cosmopolitan, 1903

"THE YEAR 1894 was a Napoleon Year," remembered Sam McClure in his autobiography.[1] He might have added that the whole decade from 1894 through 1903 was a Napoleon decade. During those years the masterful French Emperor seemed to symbolize everything that Americans most admired in their image of the successful individual.

Back in the 1830's when romantic individualism first severely challenged the hold of neo-classic standards, Ralph Waldo Emerson had observed that Napoleon was "the idol of common men because he had in transcendent degree the qualities and powers of common men." [2] By the end of the century this idol of the common man had come to seize the imagination of Americans with an unprecedented power. Around his figure seemed to culminate the whole long nineteenth-century drama of individual success. But the very intensity of the fascination with this supreme embodiment of individual force seemed also to betray some of the tensions which a consolidating economic structure was raising for the accepted individualistic view of life. In any case the Napoleonic model of success emphasized how far Americans had drifted from the early republic's idols of dignified, dutiful deportment. The distance could be measured by the difference between a Washington and a Bonaparte.

By 1894 the compulsion for individual success and the tendency to see all of life in its terms had reached a peak. A great variety of influences had worked toward this end. All the prolific priests of the success cult had poured forth a steadily expanding stream of devotional works. Clergymen, journalists, businessmen themselves, and scores of hack writers had labored to spread the gospel of material success in their most urgent tones. Chief among them were evangelists like Russell Conwell, who, after delivering his "Acres of Diamonds" lecture from over 6,000 platforms, had expanded it into a book telling *How Men and Women May Become Rich; The Safe and Sure Way to Amass a Fortune, Be a Benefactor, and Achieve Greatness.* The leading missionaries to youth were William Makepeace Thayer and, of course, Horatio Alger, Jr. Nearly a million copies of Thayer's books had been sold—his biographies of businessmen and politicians who rose from poverty to power, his inspirational work, *Tact, Push, and Principle,* which proclaimed "that religion demands success; that the young man who fails to achieve the highest success does not meet its requirements." Alger was nearing the last of those 135 books which for millions of readers had identified the American dream with the rise of a Ragged Dick or Tattered Tom to fame and fortune.[3] A whole generation of Americans after the Civil War had been converted to the faith with new fervor and were busily engaged in spreading the good news to their descendants.[4]

Over a half-century of teaching and experience had conditioned Americans to accept the doctrines of individual success as the eternal order of the universe. Since 1837 most school children had learned their lessons from *McGuffey's Reader.* McGuffey's carefully selected body of readings emphasized repeatedly that virtue paid, paid quite literally with material rewards, and that vice was invariably and quite materially punished. The virtues stressed in McGuffey's readings were noted for "their suitability to their economic climate. The virtues which they preach are either the virtues necessary for acquisition—industry, thrift, sobriety, perseverance—or those which are, like honesty and respect for the property of others, indispensable accessory conditions to its maintenance." [5]

At higher levels of education the classical economists had elaborated upon the prevalence and the necessity of individual acquisitiveness. The conditions of American life before and after the Civil War seemed to bear out their teachings. The opportunities for entrepreneurial success proved abundant, and the national economy expanded rapidly under a system of individual exploitation. Everything had conspired to make the tenets of economic individualism plausible. Everything induced in Americans a compulsion for individual success and led them to view their leaders primarily as examples of individual success. In 1898 "An Up-to-Date Journal of Inspiration, Encouragement, Progress, and Self-Help" began monthly publication. Its attention was fixed exclusively upon the requirements for success and upon the individuals who had achieved it. Its title was simply *Success.*

Yet by the 1890's a new note had begun to intrude upon the basic themes of the success literature. The older patterns had emphasized character. They had invoked industry, thrift, honesty, responsibility, piety, and philanthropy. The new note was one of power. It called for strength of will, forcefulness, and what the period termed "animal magnetism." * It was a change of emphasis not of ideology, but it betrayed some of the tensions beginning to tug at traditional individualism.

Horatio Alger, after all, died in 1899 having lived out a life of

* In 1898 the magazine *Success* printed the results of a questionnaire which asked "What is the most desirable single quality one can possess in the battle for success?" The replies showed a clear preference for forcefulness rather than the more traditional virtues of the Protestant ethic: Inflexible Will (8), Perseverance (8), Courage (3) as opposed to Good Character (4), Honesty (4), Industry (2), Thrift (1).

frustration and penury. William Makepeace Thayer died a year earlier. The conditions of society were changing rapidly before everyone's eyes. The proliferating trusts and the multiplying millionaires were raising the stakes of success to new levels. They were also threatening to close off many avenues of opportunity for ambitious youth. Frederick Jackson Turner reported that the frontier had closed in 1890. If he was not entirely correct about the frontier, he did voice the suspicions of many that America was entering a new stage in its development.[6] Far from being "gay," the nineties were a decade of depression, labor violence, strong political protest, and radical intellectual questioning. The homilies of the past were not entirely adequate to explain the realities of the present or to provide reassurance about the possibilities of the future. Character alone could scarcely account for the power of a Rockefeller or a Morgan. Character alone could scarcely hope to win recognition in a world of ruthless organizations, large cities, and new magazines for the masses.

In the brutal "realities" of social Darwinism men could find a more elemental rationale for the new order of individualism than the classical economists or the Puritan ethic had provided. Theodore Dreiser would capture forever the fundamental fascination of this dramatic view in his image of the lobster eating the squid. A success conceived in terms of "the survival of the fittest" allowed more play for elements of force and power than had the older pattern of "industry, thrift, sobriety, perseverance." Harsher analogies often seemed necessary to describe the new mettle of success. Where businessmen in the popular fiction of the 1880's had been portrayed as men of character, in the novels of the nineties they became men of force with iron jaws, steel wills, and magnetic personalities.[7]

Some hopeful acolytes of the success cult found a remedy for the new conditions in a fresh approach to the coveted goal. If industry, honesty, and persistence no longer seemed sufficient guarantees of success, they would reach it through the "power of thought" or the "power of will." The New Thought movement was one distinctive form of response to the tensions of the time. Beginning in 1890 it rapidly gained adherents among hopefully-minded but still unprosperous citizens in a number of cities. Intellectually it stemmed from transcendentalism and was closely related to Christian Science. Its central ideas were that material things could be spiritualized and brought under the domination of thought while thought in turn could become material. In practice most of its concern and most of its literature dwelt on the way to achieve material success. The secret lay not in character but in power. *The Power of Will, The Power for Success,* and *The Culture of Courage* were typical titles in its *Power Book Library.* It stressed personal magnetism as the means to control others and win success. Whitney Griswold has written a fascinating account of this movement in which he identifies New Thought with "the traditional American philosophy of success." [8] His approach, however, misses the more interesting question of how this movement differed from the previous success writings.

The significance of the whole approach of the New Thought movement lay in its essentially desperate and unrealistic character. People who had lost any rational hope or conception of the way to succeed in their society were falling back upon mental suggestion and dreams of wish fulfillment. Its importance here is to demonstrate that much of the new talk about "power" and "will" and "personal magnetism" in the 1890's was also in part a rather desperate effort to cover over the widening gap between the ideology of individualism and the changing conditions of society. The vast power of accumulated millions and of a Standard Oil had to be explained in individual terms. Therefore the successful millionaire and trust-builder had to be endowed with vast personal powers of will and magnetism. The increasing difficulty a white-collar employee, however earnest his character, faced in achieving independent status and entrepreneurial rewards also had to be explained in personal terms. What he lacked must be personal force, indomitable will, and that mysterious quality of magnetism.

If it was a time of triumph for individualism, it was also a time of challenge. The pressures from both directions demanded heroes of masterful proportions. The cult of Napoleon in the 1890's and the cult of the Superman which followed it in fiction around 1900 were responses to frustration and doubt as well as to the actual, unprecedented power of the new tycoons.

Speculative as it may be, some such explanation seems required to account for the particular features of magazine biographies in the decade from 1894 through 1903. Their heroes were not simply individualists. Their model of success included not only the virtues of the Protestant ethic. It encompassed a strength, a force, a will which had never been envisioned in a *McGuffey's Reader*. The comments of biographers reflected not merely a fundamental conviction to individualism. They betrayed at times some anxiety about the possibilities of individualism in their changing society. During the last few years of the decade a number of biographies explicitly began to revise the accepted model of success. Several pointed in the directions which Progressive heroes would follow after 1903. Despite all the general unity of this decade's hero-image, despite all the assurance with which it hailed the masterful individual, the decade cannot be understood apart from the tensions which pervaded it.

The Napoleonic hero of the McKinley era was an exaggerated model of the individualism which Americans had learned to cherish. Like any youth in a strange environment, Americans responded initially to changing conditions by reasserting more vigorously the values on which they had been reared.

I
Standards of Success

The great aim of the successful individual portrayed in this decade was Personal Fame. This standard of success was explicitly applied to nearly 70 per cent of the heroes of biographical

Table II

Standards of Success, 1894–1903

The frequency of appearance of five categories of terms used to describe the nature of the hero's success in a one-ninth sample of biographical articles from four best-selling magazines.

Category	No. of Articles in Which It Appeared	Per Cent of Total Articles*
Personal Fame	50	69
Social Contribution	29	40
Achievement in Field	22	30
Monetary Standard	19	26
Personal Happiness	6	8
Total	126	173

* The total adds up to more than 100 per cent since various standards were often applied to the same hero.

articles (see Table II) and was assumed or implied in many other cases. To grasp the meaning of this requirement is to understand the mainspring of the inner-directed character and to find a main clue to the psychology of the period. It might be expressed in simple references to "the career in which his name and fame were made," to the hero's "decisive prominence in all men's minds," or to the hero's possession of "those qualities which carry one to fame." [9] Its more distinctive flavor was best expressed in frequent tributes to the hero who had "made his mark," had "made an impress on the world," or had "made his individuality felt." One author described it as the "commendable desire to be honored and envied, to make one's mark in the world and leave a respected name as an inheritance to one's children." [10] For a generation under compulsion of the drive for individual success it was natural to honor heroes who had forced the world to recognize them as individuals.

Biographers who were interested in subjects chiefly for their individual fame and individual careers could range far back into history and far from the American scene for examples of heroic individuals.* Even the great number of heroes who were dead (40 per cent of our sample) and the greater number who were not Americans (45 per cent) could hold immediate contemporary importance for individualistically-oriented readers. According to the biographers of this decade history was primarily a matter of individuals,** and history in the broader sense was necessary chiefly to measure out the exact degree of fame due to the heroic individual.[11]

This persistent concern with measurement of the hero's rightful fame revealed a conception of the world in which individuals struggled up a competitive ladder of power and influence to reach the highest possible rung of fame. The hero must be measured in terms of his own historical or social environment,[12] but still he was considered in competition with the individuals of all ages and of all the world. Has Lincoln, asked a biographer, "any claims to rank beside the heroes whose fame, far from being provincial . . . is swept up into the loftier glory that belongs to

* The presence of so many historical and foreign personages in the biographies was also, of course, an inheritance from older magazine traditions. The newer, low-priced periodicals were beginning to devote more attention to the contemporary scene in biographies as well as in other areas. This is apparent in our sample where the older, conservative *Century* ran biographies 60 per cent of whose subjects were dead and 64 per cent foreign. But even the newer magazines retained a high quota of biographies in these categories.

† "The story of the great Macedonian's life," stated the biographer of Alexander the Great, "inseparable as it is from history in its widest range stands none the less in stubborn protest against that view of history which makes it a thing of thermometers and the rain-gage, of rivers and mountains, weights and values, materials, tools, and machines. It is a history warm with the life-blood of a man. It is instinct with personality, and speaks in terms of the human will and the soul. History and biography blend." Benjamin I. Wheeler, "Alexander the Great," *Century,* XXXV (November, 1898), 1.

the great men of all time and all ages and all races?" The writer, of course, answered his own question by ranking Lincoln "side by side" with famous Greeks, Romans, and Englishmen.[13] Contemporary American businessmen, it was explained, ranked with the empire-builders of other nations: "The railroad builders of America, for example, would have been in England, Germany, or France, prime ministers, leaders of parties, makers of states, governors of empires." [14]

Since everyone in the world, including presumably the reader of the articles, was engaged in this same competitive struggle for personal recognition, the heroes were presented as examples of the possibilities for and the means to individual success. Scattered references throughout the biographies to their "lesson for young men," their "example to youth," or their proof of the power of the individual testify that a chief function of biographical articles for their readers in this decade was to serve as inspiration for emulation of their subjects.[15]

Into this perspective the Napoleon cult of the 1890's easily fitted. No other individual, at least none other in the nineteenth century, had so dramatically achieved personal fame, had so thoroughly made "an impress on the world," or had demonstrated so completely the "forcefulness" possible in an individual's rise from poverty to power. The author of *Cosmopolitan*'s serial biography of the French Emperor explained most fully Napoleon's fascination for Americans of this decade:

> Mean and bad as he certainly was, his strong personality, immeasurable genius, and, if you will, his restless, gnawing hunger for undying renown, will never fail to fascinate men of every nationality and of all creeds and all classes. There was, after all, something grand about his desire for fame, for it was not vulgar ease, or comfort, or riches, or even personal enjoyment he sought after; his 'immortal longings' were for the fame that should never perish, and in its pursuit he was prepared to violate, and did violate, every recognized law, human and divine, ignoring all right and justice.[16]

Fascination there undoubtedly was. Three of the four best-selling magazines ran serial biographies of Napoleon.* The fourth ran a single article on him and felt obliged also to comment editorially on "the secret of his success" that could be drawn from "the new Lives of Napoleon" which "are so fashionable." [17] An article on his descendants was explained by the comment: "Everything that recalls Napoleon from the smallest trifle to the greatest memorial of his career arouses curiosity and stimulates thought." [18] S. S. McClure credited Tarbell's "Napoleon" with doubling the circulation of his magazine during the precarious early months[19] after he had wisely refused to print an anti-Napoleon article which had been submitted.†

The figure of the triumphant emperor so captured the imagination of magazine biographers that he was repeatedly used as a standard of comparison. Heroes were endowed with "Napoleonic characteristics." They sat "motionless with head bowed as we are told was Napoleon's manner." A businessman was "The Young Napoleon of Finance." [20] Napoleon's image was the single most common stereotype in magazine biographies of this decade, and an historian conscious of its significance can find its imprint throughout the thinking of leaders of this generation. It is re-

* William M. Sloane's "Life of Napoleon Bonaparte" began in November, 1894, in the *Century*, Volume XXVII. Ida Tarbell's "Napoleon Bonaparte" also began the same month in *McClure's*, Volume III. Not until the end of the decade in January, 1903, did *Cosmopolitan* (Volume XXXIV) run its serial on "The Young Napoleon" by Viscount Wolsely at the same time when it was featuring an extensive series on "Captains of Industry."

† Ida M. Tarbell, *All in the Day's Work, an Autobiography* (New York, 1939), 148. In Chapter 8 of this book Tarbell discusses "The Napoleon Movement of the Nineties" with the advantage of her experience in France: "I had seen the Napoleon movement start and grow in Paris in 1892 and 1893 . . . but I looked on the Movement as political, an effort of the Bonapartists to revive the popular admiration for the country's most spectacular figure." She does not here explore the social and economic causes which led to the widespread growth of the Napoleon cult in America.

ported, for example, that when Frank Munsey was asked why he always undressed for his before-dinner nap, he replied, "I do it because Napoleon always did." [21] C. Vann Woodward has commented perceptively on the fact that even the Populist leader Tom Watson was fascinated by Napoleon and wrote a favorable biography of the great conqueror in 1902. Woodward notes that the same image of the forceful individual apparently appealed to Americans of diverse social groups:

In a different connection Watson once wrote:

> 'There is not a railway king of the present day, not a single self-made man who has risen from the ranks to become chief in the vast movement of capital and labor, who will not recognize in Napoleon traits of his own character, the same unflagging purpose, tireless persistence, silent plotting, pitiless rush to victory. . . .' Precisely. But what was a Populist doing celebrating the virtues of the self-made railway king? What was Tom Watson about in erecting an image of capitalist acquisitiveness for his people to worship? Could it be that Israelites worshipped the same gods as the Philistines? Could it be that the only quarrel between the two camps was over a singular disparity in the favors won? [22]

It was not merely, as this quotation indicates, Napoleon's "hunger for undying renown" which made him the stereotype of the period's hero-image. It was also his embodiment of supreme individual force and his self-made rise from obscurity which fitted him for the role. Nor was Napoleon alone among the figures of the past who could be made to demonstrate the power of the individual. Our sample biographies for this decade include a series on Alexander the Great and two serial biographies of Oliver Cromwell. Alexander, too, was a man who had "made it evident that he was either to be 'The Great' or nothing." [23] It was "probably true that among the great Englishmen of history no other is comparable to Napoleon in so many respects as Oliver Cromwell." [24] These three made a strong trinity for the worship of a decade preoccupied with the question of individual human force. "The names of Alexander, Cromwell, Napoleon," noted the *Century* editorially, "pass on the tongues of men as symbols of tremendous human power—in the case of Napoleon, at least, of almost superhuman power." *

Personal Fame achieved by powerful individuals who "made an impress" on their environment emerges as the dominant goal for these years. Other success standards were applied less frequently (see Table II) and often seemed subordinate or merely contributory to establishing the hero's fame. If in his pursuit of "the fame that should never perish" Napoleon was excused for violating every law and "ignoring all right and justice," it is not surprising that biographers generally paid far more attention to the Personal Fame of their heroes (in 69 per cent of all articles) than to their Social Contribution (40 per cent). Where reference was made to the social value of the hero's activities, his Social Contribution was usually portrayed as the natural, incidental result of the hero's drive for individual success. As one biographer remarked: "When a man's ideas have been proved good enough to make millions for himself, there is a fair prospect that some of them may be useful to the community." [25]

Increasingly, however, by the end of this decade appeared signs that some of these easy assumptions about the inherent social values of heroic individualism were being questioned. The same social tensions which by 1902 were leading *McClure's* into muckraking produced occasional new notes in our biographical sample. The traditional Christian values were reemphasized in

* Editorial, "An Old Story with a New Moral," *Century*, XXXIX (February, 1901), 634. This editorial was prompted by the *Century*'s life of Cromwell by John Morley which began in that issue. Interestingly enough, despite this editorial comment, Morley protested in his "Prologue" to the biography against "those impatient and importunate deifications of Force, Strength, Violence, Will, which only show how easily hero-worship may glide into effrontery." John Morley, "Oliver Cromwell, Prologue," *Century*, XXXVII (November, 1897), 375.

various biographies.[26] A *Century* editorial of 1903 commented on a current biography of John Wesley:

> It is interesting to note that in the same summer when is begun the celebration of a world-influencing act of empire, there have been two very notable personal celebrations, neither being of men connected with governments or exercising power through legislation or warlike conflict [John Wesley and Ralph Waldo Emerson]. . . . It shows . . . that the physical, the sordid, the external do not entirely dominate these times of rush and strain, of vulgar distraction and unsavory success. . . .[27]

Lincoln Steffens in *McClure's* that year turned to a contemporary figure in paying tribute to Jacob Riis as "the most useful citizen of New York" and one who "does not care for fame." [28] In the *Century* by 1902 Andrew Carnegie was still hailed as "one of the first to acquire a fortune so great that its possession gave him historical prominence"; but with a new requirement that "every success ought to be interpreted in terms of social service," his biographer hailed Carnegie's "greatest service" as "not his vast beneficence, but his attitude toward his success, his recognition of the social element in great enterprises, his return in kind to the community which made his rise to affluence and power possible." [29] In *Cosmopolitan* by the opening of 1903 J. P. Morgan's rise to power was not wholly sufficient unto itself. "Extraordinary power has been given this man," concluded *Cosmopolitan's* editor. "He will be judged in the future not by its acquisition but by the use he makes of it." [30] Popular thought as revealed in the magazines was in process of transition to a decade when readers would be asked to judge the heroes rather than simply to emulate them and when that judging would be done once again chiefly by the standard of Social Contribution.

Even the much debated Monetary Standard of success appeared of secondary importance to the ideal of Personal Fame in the biographies from 1894 to 1903. Contemporary critics and later scholars have assailed this generation for measuring the man by the dollar. Certainly unabashed tributes to money were uttered as in *Success* magazine's statement on "Wealth and Its Blessings":

> Fanatics may pile up their anathemas against the accumulation of wealth, the clergy may denounce it yet the most eloquent sermon in praise of poverty provokes but a smile.
>
> Never before in the history of the world was poverty so hard to bear as to-day, when life has grown so rich in possibilities and grand opportunities . . . we would teach that, in this land of opportunity, it is a disgrace for the average man or woman to live in continual poverty.
>
> We believe with Horace Greeley, that every healthy young man in this country ought to be ashamed of being poor. We would like to fill every young man and woman who reads *Success* with an utter dread and horror of poverty. We would like to make them so feel its shame, its constraint, its bitterness, that they would vow to escape its thraldom. . . . No; more men are ruined by underestimating the value of money, than by overestimating it.[31]

The Monetary Standard was used in a quarter (26 per cent) of the sample biographies but never so frequently as the standard of Personal Fame (69 per cent).

It is necessary, also, to realize what the acquisition of wealth signified in the hero of this generation. In the words of Napoleon's biographer, "it was not vulgar ease, or comfort, or riches, or even personal enjoyment he sought after." It was personal power and the exercise of his forceful abilities to the utmost.

> Next to the love of man for woman comes the love of man for power. In the vanished centuries 'power' was attained by physical or, later, by military prowess. . . . To-day, he has the greatest power who commands the most dollars. The acquisition of financial power, therefore, must necessarily occupy in men's thoughts the same place that the acquisition of military power did in the military days. He who wins financial duels is a great potential hero.[32]

"What is the meaning of money after it has reached a few millions?" asked a Morgan biographer, "—power! This is the modern attribute at least of possession." [33] Morgan, explained another writer, "works not merely for money but for the sense of power; probably most of all for the intellectual exercise which is afforded by moving the world's greatest interests." [34]

The millionaires of the day were not worshiped for their money itself, for the luxuries it provided, nor for the philanthropy it made possible. If popular biographers are to be believed, the millionaire was valued primarily as a man of great ability:

> Take the case of a nineteenth-century man, who, born poor, becomes a great millionaire, in control of a great railway system, the founder of a financial dynasty, lord of the destinies of a great army of men who are fighting for him and his courtiers—the stockholders—fighting to make him ever more powerful. It is, after all, the *man* that counts; it is the exercise of certain gifts and abilities that makes the interesting reading.[35]

The supposed ability demonstrated by millions of dollars was sufficient to canonize any kind of millionaire in this decade. "But whether a millionaire be of good or of evil nature, of broad or of narrow mind, infused with public spirit or warped by private greed," stated Philip Armour's biographer, "this fact remains, that the great millionaires—those, I mean, who have carved out their fortunes for themselves, or who have successfully developed inherited wealth—are men of very great ability." [36] Rather than damn this decade's worship of the dollar, critics of its standards would be more pertinent if they condemned its glorification of irresponsible power and of certain limited human abilities.

It should be noted also that respect for the wealthy in this decade did not appear as homage paid to a class set distinctly apart from the readers of these articles. Here too the pattern of emulation was assumed by biographers. "So the world, full of folk with fortune still to achieve," wrote one, "looks with eagerness upon all that concerns the family with fortune achieved . . .

[displaying] an interest not in the least servile which fortunes in the process of making pay to fortunes made." [37]

One persistent fear about great wealth pervaded the magazines of these years. More than anything else, perhaps, it proves that the ideal of the decade was not wealth itself but the power, the ability, and the competitive achievement which its acquisition symbolized. Biographers did not express fear of the undue political or social influence of wealth. They were concerned only that the possession of millions might weaken the forceful character of their owner or might not give the second generation of a wealthy family the chance to prove itself in the struggle for individual fame. One spokesman for the decade expressed a commonly-voiced opinion:

> I would say that it is a distinct disadvantage to be born rich. . . . [The wealthy heir] cannot certainly know whether he was born man enough to win a prize in the struggle for life. . . . No man can reach the highest development of his powers except under the spur and pressure of necessity.[38]

So eminent an authority as J. D. Rockefeller was quoted as believing that "Sons of wealthy parents have not a ghost of a show in competition with the fellows who come from the country with a determination to do something in the world." [39]

Once again occasional evidence appeared after 1900 indicating that these dominant conceptions about the money standard did not fully satisfy all the tensions produced by the accumulating fortunes of a few. In the early years of the decade only Walt Whitman had been noted as "indifferent to financial considerations." [40] In the new century there appeared within our sample a serial life of Christ and one of John Wesley. Steffens portrayed Jacob Riis as extremely careless in his personal finances. Carnegie's biographer in 1902 stated: "It is probable that the severest test to which society is to be subjected lies before it in the opulence of the near future . . . [with the threat that] in the greatness of their material fortunes the spiritual fortunes of men will suffer permanent eclipse." [41] A still recessive attitude toward wealth which was to emerge into dominance in the next decade of biographies was revealed in a 1903 article on "Unavailing Wealth" in the *Century*. Here the author bewailed the waste of life spent in money-making and significantly hailed Theodore Roosevelt, who was to be the outlet for so many unresolved tensions of this decade, as the symbol of a new outlook:

> The really great rewards, the splendid and lasting prizes worthy to crown a life of effort and abnegation, have never yet been accorded in any land or by any race to mere wealth, not even here in this money-loving continent and in our material age . . . few people will deny that the most admired man today in this country, the most respected and the most loved, is our young President, whose mind and thoughts have ever been fixed as far above financial ambitions as that of a Cromwell or a Washington. It is for this, as well as for his brilliant statesmanship, that our Chief Magistrate's name today has the power to thrill the nation's blood and make the pulses beat faster.[42]

Even at the peak of national admiration for the millionaire it was not Midas but Napoleon who was the popular idol. Wherever you touch the success standards of this period's biographies, you find the picture of a world devoted to the individual who could make his mark. Achievement within a particular field (30 per cent of all articles) as engineer, artist, financier, or soldier was merely contributory to the grand general purpose of making one's mark in competition with men of all time and all places. Success in any one field presumably proved a man's inherent capacity for reaching the top in any competition. "Chance," wrote the biographer of James A. Bailey, the circus magnate, "made him a showman, but he would have been equally great in whatever place his lines might have fallen." [43]

The course of the nineteenth century had brought a marked revision in American standards of success. "Publick usefulness," though still an attribute of the hero, was now generally assumed to be a product of the drive for individual fame and power. A romantic age had come to look at society through the eyes of the individual and to prize individual fulfillment and expression which had made an impact on society. If that fulfillment was sometimes measured in millions of dollars, it was nevertheless the individual and not the measure which remained central.

II
Description of the Hero

To those who look for it, the uniqueness of every man is first apparent in his face and form. Interest in the individuality of their heroes led the biographers of the 1890's to emphasize physical appearance far more frequently and more extensively than writers had in the neo-classic biographies. More than a majority (60 per cent) of the articles made some effort to distinguish the appearance of their subjects. Descriptions varied almost as widely as the range of persons and the use of clichés permitted, but wherever possible biographers dwelt on the physical force and power of the hero.

The most frequently favored type was the hero who "is in every way a large man—large in build, in mind, in nature. He is nearly six feet high, and with a kind of stately bulk which turns the scales at something like 250 pounds." He had "steel blue eyes," a "prominent chin showing his aggressive spirit," "jaws wired with steel," and the "shoulders of a Hercules." In "the full flush of strength" with "intense animal vitality" he demonstrated "tremendous even gigantic physical endurance." [44]

The mentality of the hero which emerges from the descriptions most frequently applied is one admirably adapted to getting ahead in the world. The primary quality was "foresightedness" (or "vision" or "imagination").[45] Cynics might denote this quality simply as an eye for the main chance when they observed

Table III

Mental Description, 1894–1903

Those terms most frequently used in describing the mental characteristics of the hero in a one-ninth sample of biographical articles from four best-selling magazines.

Term	No. of Times Used
"Foresightedness" ("Vision" or "Inspiration")	16
"Shrewdness" ("Canniness")	10
"Judgment"	8
"Force of Intellect"	6
"Common Sense"	5

its application to a man who was purportedly endowed with "the imagination of the born real-estate speculator." [46] But biographers *demanded* that imagination and vision have a practical slant, be combined with "shrewdness," [47] "judgment," [48] and "common sense." [49] Otherwise the hero might suffer the fate of James G. Blaine who "had the caprice and high color in his imagination that produce schemes too fine for success." [50] The ideal was a Cromwell whose "imagination never got the better of his judgment" or a financier who "appears the sublimation of common sense yet has vision twenty years ahead like a dreamer." [51] "Perception" and a "knowledge of human nature" were other valuable mental assets for a hero out to make his mark in the world.[52] Direct, practical mental qualities which could aid in a man's work and career were the only ones out of a fairly wide range described which were repeatedly emphasized by biographers. In a career-centered decade Mark Hanna was fortunate in possessing "the intelligence which makes work easier and increases the capacity for work." [53]

The qualities of character with which these heroes were endowed also fitted them for success in a competitive world. Biographers gave to them twice as many character traits (50 per cent of all traits described) which were adapted to the mastery

Table IV

Character Description, 1894–1903

The relative frequency of appearance of four categories of qualities of character ascribed to the hero in a one-ninth sample of biographical articles from four best-selling magazines.

Category	No. of Traits	Per Cent of All Traits	No. of Qualities	Per Cent of All Qualities
I Qualities Directed Toward Mastery of Others or of the Environment:			255	50
Forceful Traits	183	36		
Business Traits	72	14		
II Qualities Directed Toward Cultivation of Self:			130	26
Personal Traits	110	21		
Individualistic Traits	20	5		
III Qualities Directed Toward Consideration of Others:			104	20
Social Traits	104	20		
IV Qualities Directed Toward God or Ultimate Values:			18	4
Religious or Idealistic Traits	18	4		
Total	507	100	507	100

of other men and of their environment as fell into any other single category (see Table IV). Above all, the hero of this decade possessed the Forceful Traits (36 per cent) and to a lesser extent the Business Traits (14 per cent) which could aid him in the assumed struggle for power and fame.* Showing "cour-

* Typical Forceful Traits (and the number of times they appeared) were: Courage (31), Strength or Power of Force (28), Energy (12), Earnestness (10), Indomitable Will (8), Persistence (7), Ambition (7), Masterfulness (4). Typical Business Traits (and the number of times they appeared) were: Industry (13), Practicality (7), Thrift (6), Skill or Efficiency (6), Executive Ability (5), Honesty (4), Prudence (3).

age," "power," "industry," and "energy," he acted "with that power of concentration and enduring application without which nothing great can be achieved." [54] Biographers explained: "He possesses, too, in rare degree the forceful qualities that turn ambitions into realities—the executive powers . . . the patience that waits for opportunities and the boldness that strikes a clinching blow when they come." [55]

The second most-frequently-applied category (26 per cent) was composed of those character traits which bore primarily upon the hero as an individual, which described his personal nature or emphasized his "unique individuality." These, of course, were extremely diverse. Individualistic Traits (5 per cent) with which he was endowed included his "self-possession," his "self-reliance," or his noticeable "individuality." But what is here called his Personal Traits (21 per cent) may appear simply as a convenient catch-all for terms which do not obviously fall into other categories.* They include a wide range of descriptive terms from "romantic sentimentalism" and "poetic temperament" to "refinement" and "dignity." Certain characteristics, however, were repeatedly stressed. "Simplicity" was the most frequent Personal Trait required by the hero and less often "modesty," "originality," and a "sense of humor."

Traits indicating the hero's consideration for his fellow men were apparently of lesser importance to this inner-directed character type. Such Social Traits as "tact," "generosity," "kindness," "sympathy," and "unselfishness" appeared as a group less frequently (20 per cent) than the traits which emphasized his masterful and self-oriented characteristics.†

Least significant as a requirement for the hero seemed to be any elements of character which denoted the hero's religion or

* Typical Personal Traits (and the number of times they appeared) were: Simplicity (11), Modesty (6), Originality (6), Sense of Humor (6), Sweetness (4), Naturalness (3), Purity (2).

† Typical Social Traits (and the number of times they appeared) were: Tact or Diplomacy (11), Generosity (10), Geniality (10), Kindness (7),

idealism (4 per cent). "Piety," "faith," "religious fervor," or "moral vision" were Religious or Idealistic Traits with which biographers equipped only a small number of their heroes.* Mark Hanna might be "not a man of exalted ideals," but "only a man like Hanna could have acted in the time of stress so wisely." He had "saved the nation from calamity," and he represented the forceful characteristics of its dominant hero-image. "The remedy for Hannaism will be found," wrote William Allen White in 1900, "when Hanna's critics give to the exemplification of high civic ideals the force of unqualified success and the charm of virile personality."[56] If this sounds like a prescription for Theodore Roosevelt, it was. An understanding of the character type praised in this decade affords an insight both into the popular support accorded the masterful builders of trusts and at the same time into the popular appeal of the most conspicuous reformer who rose to challenge them. In neither case did Americans look for the moderate, dutiful, principled model of character which had been admired in the early republic.

III
The Hero's Personal Habits

"When great capitalists began to appear," complained Carnegie's biographer, "there was a great deal of idle and, in many cases, of vulgar curiosity about their habits of life, their amusements and occupations."[57] In the magazine biographies, however, the striking thing was how relatively little interest appeared in the personal life of the hero and how negatively writers treated anything which distracted from his career. Various disparaging re-

---

Sympathy (5), Courtesy (5), Unselfishness (4), Humanity (4), Fairness (2).

* Typical Religious or Idealistic Traits (and the number of times they appeared) were: Piety (4), Faith (3), Moral Vision (3), Religious Fervor (2), Ideals (2).

marks were made about this whole area of life. "To the truly great," stated one biographer, "life is full of work. There is little time for recreation, for repose, for giving away to others." [58]

Napoleon was said to have despised all pastimes and to have cared nothing for "art, music, etc." [59] Like him the hero of this decade seemed to have little use for recreations which did not in some way contribute to the heroic career. Justice Holmes was reported to approve rough outdoor sports for this reason: "If once in a while a neck is broken, I regard it, not as a waste, but as a price well paid for the breeding of a race fit for hardship and command." [60]

Though the current idols were imperial in their achievements, they proved to be extremely frugal and middle-class in their tastes. More than half of the references to consumption habits (10 out of 18) were negative in tone. They emphasized that for the Idol of Power, "the quality of the meal was a secondary consideration to him, provided it afforded sufficient brain-fuel." This ambitious, abstemious hero might well have "never tasted tobacco or used spirituous liquours." He "drank sparingly of champagne caring only for the flavor." A multi-millionaire would be called "hopelessly 'middle-class.'" by "the Newport Set" because "He liked pie, and there are awful indications that he has not entirely outgrown the fried steak habit." Even the Czar of Russia was reduced to middle-class terms by a biographer who portrayed him as a very quick eater who liked simple food and who abominated banquets.[61]

Why philanthropy is here rated as a personal habit rather than one of the Success Standards for this period is best explained in a quotation from an 1893 biography of Collis P. Huntington:

> Collis P. Huntington is one of the great men of our times. He is inherently great. Nature cast him in a big mold. He has done something—has left his impress upon the history of our national development. That man who has the power within him to do great things and does them, is great—great in the direction in

> which he works. What Huntington might have been as a theologian is of no consequence. What he has done in the way of philanthropy is not the test. His achievements are the measuring sticks by which he must be measured, and by which honest intelligence will measure him.[62]

The achievements of a man in his individual career were sufficient to lift him to heroic status. But it cannot be denied that philanthropy was an important asset for the hero. Mention of it appeared in a majority of the biographies of businessmen. What was its function? First, perhaps, it appeared as a safeguard against class rancor:

> America is the land of wealth and its social conditions are such as to multiply millionaires; there need, however, be no class prejudice or jealousy of wealth, if every millionaire will be animated at least in some measure by the public spirit of the greatest philanthropist that America has yet produced [Stephen Girard].[63]

Secondly, the practice of philanthropy could serve to enhance the importance of the individual. If the hero were regarded as a trustee of his wealth, not only did it become "a man's duty to make all the money he can, keep all he can, and give away all he can," [64] but the welfare of society would presumably be in the hands of its most able individuals. Private philanthropy rather than public social action meant that the social concerns as well as the economic affairs of the nation would be in the hands of those who could manage them in the same business-like, creative, inner-directed fashion in which they managed their own careers. "If my wealth is a trust," Philip Armour was quoted as saying, "I propose to work as hard as a trustee as I do at selling meat and grain." *

* *McClure's* (February, 1894), 260. See also Samuel E. Moffett, "John Arbuckle," *Cosmopolitan,* XXXIII (September, 1902), 542–44. Arbuckle's

A final element in the personal life of the hero was his religion. Though mentioned in a significant number of articles (18 per cent of the non-clergy articles), religion obviously formed neither so frequently cited nor so important a part in the hero's life as it had in the 1790–1820 biographies. The religion of these work-centered individuals at the close of the century was a formalized, institutionalized religion. Seldom was a biographer concerned with whether his hero had met the terms of salvation. It was a secularized, this-worldly religion which drew attention primarily in terms of church membership, church attendance, or financial contribution to the church. Of President McKinley, for example, it was mentioned only that he had joined the Methodist Church and remained a member throughout his life. Rockefeller was noted for giving regularly to his church every Sunday. "It is a good habit for a young man to get into," he had observed, along with similar advice to be thrifty and persevering.[65] Apparently it was necessary to explain away any strong evidences of piety displayed by a secular hero. "There is nothing strange in Cromwell's piety," explained his biographer. "It was but the natural outcome of the times he lived in and the training he had received. . . . The practice of religion evidently became a habit with him."[66] That was it in a nutshell. Instead of the central explanation of man's place in the world, instead of the final seal upon the successful individual, religion had become a habit. It was a good and useful habit for the young man to cultivate along with the other habits necessary to his advancement in the world.

---

particular "creative" contribution in philanthropy might serve as a classic example of the fallacy of the idea that millionaires were necessarily the fittest leaders for remedying social ills. He was cited for having spent $300,000 in organizing a system of "poor men's yachts" whereby workers in New York would have the chance to spend one night apiece out on the ocean during the hot summer months.

IV

The Hero's Relation to Others

The basic pattern of human relations for the individualistic hero is easily understandable. His parents gave him certain inherited traits, a desire to succeed, a training in hard work, and then as soon as possible faded from the scene to throw him upon his own resources. Rising to power by seizing or creating an opportunity for himself, he defeated his rivals, dominated his partners (if any), and controlled with a firm hand his employees or subordinates. Once established he was generous to his inferiors who might come to love him for his firm-handed justice and his generosity. His colleagues respected him for his ability. The public awarded him recognition and fame for his masterful achievements.[67]

Lincoln's biographers explained that: "The only unbroken outside influence which directed and stimulated him in his ambitions was that coming first from his mother, then from his step-mother." Neither "persuasion of friend or threat of foe" could sway him from his determined aims. Like Napoleon, the hero as a child might have few companions except those useful to his ambitions. An actress, for example, was interested in "only the few playmates who submitted to being used as stage trees or lay-figures." Like Napoleon also, the hero might boast: "Nothing awed me; I feared no one. I struck one, I scratched another, I was a terror to everybody." Men of principle like the abolitionist John Hale would not sacrifice their principles for popularity or peace: "He loved the approbations of his fellows and would have lived in peace with all men, but he had convictions and followed them." It was assumed that the successful career involved placing ambition before popularity: "All successful men are hated by somebody." As a natural consequence the hero's "swift rise begat a host of enemies."[68]

Not all biographies in this period, by any means, followed this pattern in all its stages. But enough articles clung to most of it and enough others revealed parts of it so that even in our statistics its influence is apparent. The specific persons most frequently mentioned in connection with this decade's hero were those who played a role in his career rather than in his personal life. The Colleagues or Rivals with whom he competed (in 36 per cent of the articles), the Parents who prepared him for his career (29 per cent), the general Public who awarded him fame (29 per cent), the Inferiors who were his employees or subordinates (28 per cent), these emerged as more important figures to the hero than his Friends (28 per cent), his Spouse (26 per cent), or his Children (15 per cent). Where the nature of his relations with other persons was explicitly described, he was overwhelmingly a man who could dominate others (in 50 per cent of the articles). In other relationships the hero took or he gave. Only rarely did he cooperate with others (8 per cent).

The most striking feature of this masterful hero was his ability and need to dominate. As one biographer put it, "He can no more follow than a fish can walk." In the words of another, "To make others obey him is his breath of life."[69] In the competitive ideology of the day it was, of course, particularly important to dominate one's supposed equals, one's colleagues, whether they were partners or rivals. Hence stemmed the primary attention paid to colleagues. Hence stemmed the repeated stories of how Alexander had defeated the rivals to his throne, how James Bailey's circus had won victories over P. T. Barnum, how Jacob Schiff had triumphed over Morgan and Hill, how Philip Armour had crushed the rival who tried to "squeeze" him.[70]

Just as necessary was the hero's domination of his inferiors. The soldier exercised severe discipline over his troops. The public executive was a "rigid disciplinarian" of his subordinates. The businessman kept a close watch on his department heads and maintained undisputed control over his labor relations:

> Where there was labor trouble the contest was short and decisive. . . . Either things were right or they were wrong. If he

thought they were wrong, he fixed them on the spot. If he believed they were right, the work went on.

Even the religious leader might hold "absolute sway over all who believe in him," and the pioneering medical scientist might consider his "patients not persons just experiments." [71]

The harshness of this treatment of inferiors was often mitigated by the hero's generosity. Both because of that generosity

Table V

The Hero's Relation to Others, 1894–1903

Others Mentioned in Articles

The frequency of appearance of ten categories of people other than the hero in a one-ninth sample of biographical articles in four best-selling magazines.

Category	No. of Articles	Per Cent of All Articles
Colleagues (or Rivals)	26	36
Parents	21	29
The Public	21	29
Inferiors	20	28
Friends	20	28
Spouse	19	26
Children	11	15
Superiors	9	12
Teachers	7	10
Siblings	7	10

Nature of the Relations

The frequency of appearance of six categories describing the nature of the hero's relation to others in the same sample.

Category	No. of Articles	Per Cent of All Articles
Dominate Others	36	50
Loved by Others	12	17
Aid Others	12	17
Aided by Others	12	17
Respected by Others	9	12
Withdraw from Others	6	8
Cooperate with Others	6	8

and because the hero was an "inspiration" to them, his followers frequently were portrayed as loving the man who dominated them.[72] Ten of the twelve heroes who were said to be loved by others were loved by their inferiors. The hero's spouse, who might have been expected to show the greatest affection for him, displayed her love in only one biography. Possibly this was retribution for the attitude of the heroic John Wesley who had laid down two requirements for a wife: (1) that she must be inferior to her husband, (2) that she must so behave.[73]

These masterful individuals were not particularly lovable nor popular figures. They did not need to be, apparently, to win praise in a decade devoted to power and individual achievement. True, biographers endowed them with a fair number of friends. But that friendship was occasionally described in strange terms. Mark Hanna was said to have "learned the business of friendship . . . as thoroughly as he learned the iron and coal and steel and ship and railway business." In his friendship with McKinley he had "grappled it to him as he grappled his business ambition—with all his heart and mind." [74] Here was an inner-directed friendship based on the hero's personal determination rather than on any reciprocal affection.

Nor must the hero necessarily have friends. If they interfered with his career, biographers lauded him for his withdrawal from others. The "really delightful intimacy" between the inventors Nikola Tesla and Thomas Edison had to be broken for the sake of Tesla's career: "Even the most cometic genius has its orbit. . . . Mr. Tesla must needs draw apart; and stimulated by this powerful spirit, he went on his own way for his own work's sake." [75]

If friends could be disregarded when they stood in the hero's way, so too could the general public. To be sure, the public was "the great jury which gives a man fame," at least eventually, but the hero was not to be castigated if he violated public sentiments in the pursuit of his own goal. The public, apparently, did not always know what was good for it and set up obstacles to real individual achievement. "Instead of being hailed as a public benefactor," the pioneering hero might too often be "a target for scorn and contempt." In this kind of a world real advances might be delayed while the hero "combated political onslaught and conciliated public sentiment." Hence it did not really matter what the immediate public reaction to the hero's action was. "Had he been of another sort very likely he could have conciliated public opinion," but in that case he might never have been the man to accomplish his great feat. It did not even particularly matter that "Hanna's solicitude for the people is as tender as that of the late William H. Vanderbilt. He believes in every man for himself and the devil take the hindmost." It was still men like Hanna who had "saved the nation from calamity." [76]

Not until 1902 did biographers endow any hero with a particular concern for the feelings of the public. It was then found in a biography of the Standard Oil Executive, H. H. Rogers, that at least one member of the industrial elite was not content to pursue his creative way in silence:

> Some men who have won great success are indifferent to public opinion. Mr. Rogers . . . is sensitive on that side. He knows that Standard Oil methods are not popular and he is restive under that consciousness. You may be a person of utter financial insignificance, making less in a year than he can make in an hour, but if you happen to be thrown into contact with him under favorable conditions, he will devote two hours of argument to an attempt to convince you that the recording angel would be wasting time in inspecting the books of the Standard Oil Company.[77]

Whatever the verdict of the recording angel, this article, published one month before Ida Tarbell launched the muckraking movement in *McClure's* with her series on Standard Oil, betrayed no doubts about the validity of Mr. Rogers's argument. Its only variation from the usual pattern was this somewhat surprised recognition of a new sensitivity to public opinion. It was the first crack of what was to become a major breach in the wall erected in popular biographies between their heroes and the general public.

For this decade, however, the wall generally remained firm. In his relations to others the hero was unmistakably the inner-directed ideal following his personally determined path with slight regard to the feelings or demands of his fellows and dominating his human environment with his forceful character and masterful tactics.

V
The Road to Success

"How he did these things, how he became a great American millionaire, how he developed from a country lad to what he is to-day: that is the fascinating romance."[78] Americans in the McKinley era seemed to have an insatiable interest in accounts of the heroic Road to Success. Nothing more clearly marked the change from the early republic's view of life. Then the route to success had been passed over hastily, and the question was how well the hero filled his "appointed station." Now the major part of every biography was devoted to the Road to Success, and the heroic rise to prominence seemed to embody the ultimate meaning or at least the ultimate drama in life.

"How did he get his money and his success?" repeated another biographer. "This is always an interesting question, especially in this good country of ours where we are all ambitious, and where the race for glory is said not to be a handicap event." The process of identification with the hero and the hope of emulating him focused upon the course of his career far more than upon his character or his personal habits. If it was Napoleon's "gnawing hunger for undying renown" and his "embodiment of physical force" which fascinated Americans, it was "the unparalleled rise of a poor and foreign adventurer . . . to a European greatness unknown for many centuries" which made "his story peculiarly dramatic." [79]

When an American felt he must "certainly know whether he was born man enough to win a prize in the struggle for life," the only meaningful success was one achieved in spite of obstacles. Consequently the childhood environment of the biographical hero was usually a picture of many hardships. "Miss Nethersole's early life was paved with struggles and disappointments and unsatisfied yearning to accomplish something great but indefinable," wrote the biographer of an actress. Presumably, also, the real hero (or heroine) would have surmounted the handicaps of any childhood environment. "From whatever environment she might have sprung, to whatever obstacles," continued the same writer, "she would have conquered." [80]

In those biographies where class origins were suggested the heroes came most often from middle-class and lower-class homes. Out of thirty-one cases where the father's status was mentioned six were definitely upper-class, thirteen definitely middle-class (mostly professional men), and twelve bore lower-class connotations. Actually, however, of these dozen "lower-class" figures nine were farmers and one a carpenter. By any objective standard only the father of that rather dubious "hero" Richard Croker would clearly be rated below the middle class. In Alger novels, in *Success* magazine, and in these biographies a rise from the status of a farm boy was regularly credited as a rise from "the bottom." It seems clear, in retrospect, that the traditional success story cherished by middle-class Americans was actually conceived as operating only for the middle class itself. The "bottom" from which the individual was to rise was in reality only the bottom of the middle class.* It seems clear also that these biog-

* There is evidence for such a conclusion in the articles themselves. Lincoln's biographer, for example, seemed anxious to point to middle-class elements in the pioneer environment of her hero's youth: "It was rude, but it was only the rudeness which the ambitious are willing to endure

raphies, either by omission of heroes with upper-class origins or at least by omission of reference to the upper-class origins of their heroes or even by distortion of the actual facts,[81] stressed modest origins for the hero far out of proportion to any objective accounts of the origins of the period's leaders.[82]

The biographies also stressed, wherever possible, the advantages of a rural upbringing for the hero. Some struck a note of primitivism in referring to "many of the great men of America who were reared far away from cities and in close contact with the mysteries of forests and streams, of night and seasons."[83] Others found in country life a better grounding for the Puritan ethic of sacrifice and hard work. John D. Rockefeller was quoted as believing:

> There is something unfortunate in being born in a city. . . . Most young men raised in New York and other large centers have not had the struggle which comes to us who were reared in the country. It is a noticeable fact that the country men are crowding out the city fellows who have wealthy fathers. They are willing to do more work and to go through more for the sake of winning success in the end.[84]

Coming from a man who had moved at the age of eleven to a community of nearly 8,000 population and at the age of fourteen to Cleveland, this statement suggests that in these years there were some fundamental reasons for distorting or suppressing the actual facts about the relative superiority of an urban youth for the would-be successful.*

---

in order to push on to a better condition than they otherwise could know. These people did not accept their hardships apathetically. They did not regard them as permanent. . . . It is worth notice, too, that there was nothing belittling in their life, there was no pauperism, no shirking. Each family provided for its own simple wants, and had the conscious dignity which comes from being equal to a situation." Ida Tarbell, "Abraham Lincoln, Part II," *McClure's*, VI (December, 1895), 3.

* See Erville B. Woods, "Heredity and Opportunity," *American Journal of Sociology*, XXVI (July and September, 1920), 1–21, 146–61. Basing his

If the image of success which emphasized modest origins and a rural childhood was not consciously an attempt to relieve social tensions in a period of increasing urban dominance and decreasing opportunity for the old, independent middle class, certainly it was well adapted to supply consolation at just those social and geographical points where tensions were the greatest. In the study of primitive cultures Malinowski has found myths emerging to meet social tensions:

> It is clear that myth functions especially where there is a sociological strain, such as in matters of great difference in rank and power, matters of precedence and subordination, and unquestionably where profound historical changes have taken place.[85]

If there was an element of myth in the widespread assertions about the farm as a nursery of success, perhaps this was a clue to the strains of profound change in an America where city life was rapidly overshadowing the traditional rural past.

Modest origins and a rural rearing were only two of the four prerequisites to success which biographers of the 1890's preferred to find in the childhood environment of their heroes. A third desirable element was some specific youthful hardship. Some thirty-nine hardships were mentioned in the childhood of twenty-three different heroes (32 per cent of the sample). Nine of these "Algerian" heroes had suffered poverty in their youth. In sixteen cases the hero had begun work at a very early age "being anxious to relieve the family of the burden of his support." Three young

conclusions on statistics in *Social Environment* by George R. Davies, Woods states: "Contrary to a popular impression it is the cities with the regions immediately surrounding them which have produced eminent men out of all proportion to their population." This, he continues, has been shown to be true on both sides of the Atlantic. See also: Roy H. Holmes, "A Study in the Origins of Distinguished Living Americans," *American Journal of Sociology,* XXXIV (January, 1929), 67–85. Holmes emphasizes particularly the reasons for the low proportion of farmers' sons in the ranks of *Who's Who.*

heroes had wrestled with poor health. Four had been compelled to support their families when their fathers lost health or money or life itself.[86] In the context of the articles these seeming hardships were often the blessing in disguise which set the youth on the proper path to greatness. When Mark Hanna's father sickened and the management of the store fell on the boy, "the responsibility put iron into him, and gave him the luck stone of his life—the habit of industry. It schooled him, as no university can, in the uses of grit and self-reliance and courage. It made a man of him." [87]

Even for those eleven heroes (15 per cent of the sample) whom biographers recognized as having exceptional advantages of inheritance or training,[88] it was customary to assert that the hero's individuality had emerged *despite* these advantages. Theodore Roosevelt, despite his descent from a line "whose lives were closely interwoven with the aristocratic and blue blooded portion of our population, is a self made man." [89]

The fourth and final element in the childhood of these inner-directed heroes was the process by which their goals and standards were implanted at an early age. Thereafter they could follow these "directions" unswervingly without much regard for the approval or disapproval of others. A regular feature included in one-sixth (16½ per cent) of the sample biographies was some account of how the pattern and drive for success was initially established in the hero. Webster's father had urged the young Daniel: "Exert yourself, improve your opportunities, learn, learn." In another distinguished case:

> The elder Roosevelt knew the secret of bringing up boys. It may be summed up in a single word—work, plenty of work, hard work. Although the family was considered wealthy, he taught his boys . . . that the most despicable of created beings is the man who does nothing.

Abraham Lincoln was all the greater because he had learned the pattern of "inner direction" without benefit of his father's guidance: "In spite of the fact that he had no wise direction, that he was brought up by a father with no settled purpose, and that he lived in a pioneer community, where a young man's life at best is but a series of makeshifts, he had developed a determination to make something out of himself, and a desire to know, which led him to neglect no opportunity to learn." From his mother and stepmother, from the responsible leaders of the community, and from his reading, Lincoln absorbed the proper goals:

> The ideal they held before him was the simple ideal of the early American, that if a boy is upright and industrious, he may aspire to any place within the gift of the country. . . . Everything he read confirmed their teachings and he cultivated, in every way open to him, his passion to know and to be something.

Along with modest origins, a rural upbringing, and youthful hardships the individualistic hero was expected to learn early in life to chart his course for success. Napoleon's example again confirmed the pattern and inspired his biographer to comment: "But the more we know of psychology through autobiographies, the more certain it appears that many a great life-plan has been formed before ten, and carried through with an unbending rigor to the end." [90]

Formal Education was a part of the hero's experience, but biographers did not seem to view it as a very necessary or important step on the Road to Success. Although it was mentioned in many (39 per cent) of the sample biographies, writers referred to it in simple, objective terms. They did not endow Formal Education with the same significant meanings which they attached to rural environments or to youthful hardships. Nor were the heroes, as revealed in these articles, a particularly well-educated group. Only two (3 per cent) were associated with any advanced graduate training, and only ten (14 per cent) were described as reaching college. There were, on the other hand, three heroes characterized as "self-taught," and five were commended for leav-

Table VI

Road to Success, 1894–1903

Formal Education

The formal education of the hero as it was mentioned in a one-ninth sample of biographical articles from four best-selling magazines.

Nature of Education	No. of Articles	Per Cent of All Articles
Graduate School	2	3
College	10	14
Military Academy	3	4
High School	8	11
Country School	2	3
Parents Tutored	2	3
Artistic Training	1	1
Total	28	39

ing school early to go to work. Formal Education seemed to have little essential relevance to the heroic career in the success mythology of the McKinley era.

Important as it was for the hero to get an early and proper start upon his career, most biographical attention still focused upon the Means to Success, upon the tactics required for climbing the "ladder of fame." Most biographers spelled out admiringly and at length the essential Individualistic Tactics which the decade approved in its heroes.

The great glory of the nineteenth-century view of life was its emphasis upon the creative individual. Whatever may be the dangers of "rugged individualism" in an interdependent society, it should not be forgotten that the primary features of this ideology at its peak in the 1890's were creativity and originality (see Table VII). Along with his "all-absorbing" aim "to be a brilliantly successful man" Alexander the Great was honored for his "love of action and creation." The successful artist was "a man with a new way of looking at the world" or one who possessed "great creative vision." The heroic businessman made "innovation the order of the hour" or established a "kingdom" which was "founded on an idea." [91]

In carrying out his creative vision the hero demonstrated prodigious industry and a dauntless perseverance. Biographers dwelt upon the accepted moral value and practical necessity of hard work.[92] With it they coupled the determination of the inner-directed character to pursue its own will or purpose over all obstacles, human or material. Rockefeller testified: "There is no other quality so essential as perseverance. It overcomes almost

Table VII

Road to Success, 1894–1903

Means to Success

The frequency of appearance of certain types of activity displayed by the hero in his career as described in a one-ninth sample of biographical articles from four best-selling magazines.

Activity	No. of Articles	Per Cent of All Articles*
I Individualistic Tactics		
Creativity and Originality	30	42
Hard Work	24	33
"Inner Direction" (Following Principle, Purpose, or Will)	23	32
Siezing Opportunity	14	19
Executive Ability	13	18
Fighting His Way	12	17
Self-Made Achievement	11	15
Accepting Responsibility	6	8
Thrift	4	6
II Social Tactics		
Winning Trust of Others	6	8
Total	143	198

* The total adds up to more than 100 per cent since various types of action were often displayed by the same hero.

anything even nature!" An actress's "determination was a torrent no one could check." [93]

A third group of characteristics filled out the essential tactics of the individualistic hero's Road to Success. These were the forceful, masterful activities whereby the hero imposed his will on his environment and made his individual mark in the world. Biographers recounted how their subject had seized his opportunities.[94] They dwelt on his executive ability.[95] They told how he had fought his way up.[96] They emphasized the self-made character of his achievements.[97]

Relegated to a minor role amongst the heroic tactics were several habits long recommended to young men as the foundations for advancement in the world. *McGuffey's Reader* and other more explicit writings on success from the time of *Poor Richard's Almanac* had consistently advised youths to accept their responsibilities faithfully and to practice thrift. It is not surprising, therefore, to find these attributes included in the biographical Road to Success. What is surprising is the relatively insignificant place given to them in the heroic career of the 1890's. These more pedestrian qualifications for success were completely overshadowed by the emphasis on creativity, work, will, and forcefulness which pervaded the Napoleonic model of success. It was another measure of the extent to which individualism had come to signify power and force rather than the more sober qualities of the Puritan ethic.

All the major means to success in this decade remained individualistic ones. Only infrequently was the hero pictured as going beyond these to a more democratic form of leadership in winning the trust of others. Even in those cases he usually seemed to win support on his own terms for the benefit of his own career rather than as a champion of other people's interests.[98] The accumulating emphasis on his quest for Personal Fame, on the forceful character he displayed, on his domination of others, on the childhood obstacles he overcame, and on the masterful tactics he employed all centered attention on the individual himself. He was apparently the self-made master of his environment, and the important purposes of his society were his own purposes and his own advancement.

Yet one nagging question remained. Around it clustered many of the tensions of the period. If the hero were to become the master of his environment by forcefully seizing his opportunities, somehow the environment would have to provide the opportunities. Was the environment actually more important than the individual?

Ideally the completely masterful individual should make his own opportunities, but it was granted that, "Of course, in a certain sense no man can absolutely make an opportunity." At best a hero like Admiral Dewey had "partly grasped and partly made his opportunity." He could not have achieved his brilliant success without a war and without "the forethought, energy, courage, and capacity of countless other men." Even for the greatest heroes certain circumstances were necessary if they were to act with the "qualities which carry one to fame if opportunity be given." *

Here was a dilemma. On the one hand was the ideal of the self-made master of his environment. On the other hand was a clear recognition of a certain environmental determinism. For this decade at least the ancient question was resolved with very little diminution of the importance of the individual. The answer was that everything "will be wasted unless at the supreme moment some man of the heroic type arises capable of using to the best advantage the powers lying ready to hand. . . . At the crisis a great triumph can be achieved only should some heroic man appear." Even Cromwell had not wholly made his opportunities, but he was the indispensable individual: "To be sure, circum-

* Theodore Roosevelt, "Dewey," *McClure's,* XIII (October, 1899), 483. It is interesting to note the emphasis placed on the forethought and courage of "other men" by this biographer who had himself, as Assistant Secretary of the Navy, given Dewey his assignment and prepared his orders.

stances had much to do with Cromwell's advancement, but he was the one man among millions who was capable and daring enough to seize and utilize every opportunity as it presented itself."[99] The focus remained clearly on the individual and his forceful will.

Under the assumption that all possibilities would "be wasted" unless "some man of the heroic type" emerged to capitalize upon them, obviously the all-important factor was the heroic individual. Nothing should be allowed to hamper his exploitation of the social potential. The millionaire, who by definition had proved his ability "of the heroic type," could be relied upon to make maximum use of the environment. Society would presumably gain by encouraging his individual seizure of opportunities. He could serve also as an example for the next generation from which must come a supply of heroic individuals capable of exploiting the social potential to the full. So long as it was believed that widespread opportunities for the individual existed and so long as the multi-millionaire seemed an example of those opportunities rather than a threat to them, this resolution of the dilemma could be accepted.

As the decade wore on, however, occasional notes of concern for the social environment began to appear in biographies alongside the paeans to individualism. The most dramatic example came in a 1902 biographical article on Carnegie. Here the writer first hailed Carnegie's achievement in clear terms of orthodox individualism:

> His success was the more dramatic because it was achieved by the use of so few tools at the start; it had no visible foundations of inherited capital, organization, or opportunity; it rested solely on the character and force of the man; on his insight into the possibilities of the means, the openings, and the men about him; on his courage, steadiness, power of combination, and sustained force of intellect. . . . The foundations of Mr. Carnegie's work were laid in his personality. He is often spoken of as the conspicuous example of the self-made man. . . . Mr. Carnegie

> made his fortune by virtue of qualities in his own nature and with little aid from without.

Yet within a few pages this same biographer was speaking about the same man in radically different terms:

> To the making of every powerful man many agencies contribute: ancestry, racial tendencies, general conditions, local opportunities. No man succeeds without help from others; no man becomes great in any field of endeavor by isolated growth; all development is aided by cooperation; every success is social in its conditions if not in its origins; and therefore every success ought to be interpreted in terms of social service.[100]

These were strange-sounding phrases amid the biographies of this decade. They indicated that changing ideas were beginning to overlap the traditional views. To intimate that development was fostered by cooperation rather than competition, to suggest that success was social rather than individual, this was going far beyond the admission that opportunities had to be provided by the environment.

This decade was neither the first nor the last to struggle with questions of free will and determinism, of the individual and society. In its magazine biographies, however, it placed far greater reliance upon the will of the individual than Americans have in other periods. It clung to the assumption that the Road to Success could be found by the forceful man who formed his determination before the age of ten and who persevered industriously until the almost inevitable opportunity presented itself. Reiteration of the persisting presence of opportunities served to quell any doubts of the value of this formula for the individual. Reiteration of the creative activities of individuals generally served to answer questions about the formula's value to society. Biographers could assume that readers were anxious to find this road for themselves. All seemed to assume that it was the only road worth travelling.

VI
The Heroic Occupations

The leading occupations of the heroes from 1894 through 1903 very neatly met the needs of this particular model of success. They were the fields of activity in which an individual could most readily make his mark through creative, forceful exercise of his will and his vision. The great majority of heroes in this decade were creative artists, captains of industry, empire-builders, pioneering scientists and inventors, or the founders of religions.

Perhaps the most surprising aspect of the hero's occupations in the 1890's was the great numerical supremacy held by the arts (33 per cent of all biographies). Magazine biographers in the early republic had virtually ignored this field. Popular magazines in the twentieth century would pay only passing respect to it. Yet here in the McKinley era biographers turned their attention to writers, artists, musicians, and figures from the serious theatre twice as often as to the captains of industry and finance.

The reasons were partly technical ones connected with magazine publishing. The older traditions of cultural concern established by *Harper's* and the *Century* still influenced their more popular rivals.* Editors were not averse to publicizing the authors whose work they printed. And the biographies of painters and sculptors made possible the copious use of illustrations from their works by the new, cheaper process of photo-engraving.

Still, this concentration upon the arts was not dictated by technical reasons alone. Creative artists were also perfect examples of the hero-type honored at this peak of individualism. They were creative writers, painters, sculptors, and composers far more

* In the years 1891–1896, 60 per cent of the biographies in *Harper's* and 63 per cent of those in the *Century* had been in the field of the arts.

Table VIII

The Heroic Occupations, 1894–1903

The occupations of the heroes in a one-third sample of biographical articles from four best-selling magazines.

Category	No. of Articles	Per Cent of All Articles
The Arts	72	33
Business	34	16
Foreign Rulers	32	15
Politics (American)	25	12
Military	21	10
Science and Invention	10	5
Religion	7	3
Education	3	1
Judges	2	1
Bureaucrat	1	0.5
Reformer	1	0.5
Miscellaneous (Spiritualist, Magician, Explorer, Aristocrat, Pocahontas, Photographer, Indian)	7	3
Total	215	100

often than actors or singers who performed the works of other men. They were serious artists concerned with their work rather than entertainers concerned with their public images and their private lives. They demonstrated the inner-directed pattern of determination, perseverance, and hard work. The career of Hall Caine, it was said, "shows how, by firmness of principle . . . a man of undoubted genius has been enabled to raise himself." They possessed the accepted forceful character. F. Marion Crawford was described as "a virile, strong, intellectual man, whose imagination and emotions are the obedient servants of a dominating will." The artist mastered his environment. Even James Whitcomb Riley was hailed for dominating and transforming his surroundings in "the most remarkable exemplification of the power of genius to transmute plain clods into gold that we have seen since the time of Burns." "Most of us must be content with being . . . only results," but the French writer de Blowitz seemed a true hero:

> A chief reason why Monsieur de Blowitz is worth considering is, that he is and always has been a producer himself, a fact pregnant with a thousand others, rather than the resultant of many vague facts that have gone before. . . . Monsieur de Blowitz, prodigious result as he is, is even more striking as initiator, as himself the creator of a special environment, as himself in his own way a 'final cause.' [101]

Despite their number and despite their congruity with the decade's general model of success, biographies in the arts clearly did not make the artist into *the* American hero of the period. Biographers, in fact, paid relatively little attention to contemporary Americans currently pursuing any of the arts. The total of seventy-two articles on artists in our sample included only forty whose subjects were alive and only twenty-three whose subjects were American. Only sixteen biographies were devoted to living Americans in any of the arts. Six of these, moreover, described their heroes as living abroad "where there were artists enough to create an atmosphere of their own." [102] American artists made up less than a third of the painters and sculptors appearing in the magazines. More English writers (12) than American (11) were honored. American actors and actresses were in a minority, and no Americans at all were considered worthy of biographical attention in the field of music (see Table IX). Readers of these biographies could not help being impressed with the derivative nature of American culture, with its inferiority to European artistry, and with the superior advantages of the European environment for the artist.

For once in American history creative artists admirably fulfilled most of the requirements of the popular model of success.

Table IX

Heroes in the Arts, 1894–1903

The number of biographical articles in the field of the Arts (72) from a one-third sample of four best-selling magazines arranged to show the number of heroes from each category of the Arts and the number of heroes who were American or foreign, dead or alive at time of publication.

Total Dead	32	Total Foreign	49
Total Alive	40	Total American	23
	72		72
Total Living Americans in the Arts	16		

Category	Total				
Painting and Sculpture	31				
		Dead	15	Foreign	22
		Alive	16	American	9
Literature	28				
		Dead	14	Foreign	17
		Alive	14	American	11
Stage	7				
		Dead	0	Foreign	4
		Alive	7	American	3
Music	6				
		Dead	3	Foreign	6
		Alive	3	American	0

But young Americans anxious to make their marks in American society were scarcely encouraged to find in that society promising opportunities for a career in the arts.

The real contemporary field of promise and of performance for the heroic career was, as every American knew, in business. The magazine biographies of the McKinley era provide one further measure of the dominance which business enjoyed at the end of the nineteenth century. The Napoleonic model of success offers some further insight into the nature of the hold which business exerted over the American imagination in those years.

Despite depression, strikes, agrarian protest, war, and attacks from scattered intellectuals, the masters of American business managed to extend their sway dramatically in the decade following 1893. While critics railed against "the trusts" for dangerously augmenting the threat of wealth against the commonwealth, industrialists and financiers proceeded freely to organize a record number of holding companies between 1897 and 1904. They induced the government to break the Pullman strike, raise tariffs, and promote foreign markets by the novel acquisition of overseas territory in Hawaii and the Philippines. They succeeded in avoiding any real interference from legislation designed to curb trusts, regulate railroads, and impose income taxes. How could the business elite exercise such power in a decade of depression, war, and protest—conditions which often have seriously weakened the position of dominant groups?

Accounts of railroad and trust influence in executive agencies and legislative bodies, analyses of conservative preconceptions among Supreme Court justices, exposure of the threats brought to bear upon employees at election time do not fully answer this question. This was no narrow conspiracy. The triumph of business was too complete to be explained simply as the result of coercive economic power and class position. In the most dramatic instance of business victory over rival groups Mark Hanna saw his presidential candidate elected in 1896 by the largest absolute margin of popular votes in twenty-four years. By 1900 the margin for McKinley had nearly doubled. Clearly the phenomenon of widespread popular acceptance of business leadership at this time requires some understanding of the contemporary image of businessmen in the popular mind.

Magazine biographers left little doubt that business was the true field for the modern American hero. More living American heroes of biographies (34) came from the ranks of business than from any other occupational group. In contrast to biographical subjects in the arts only two business heroes within our sample were dead and only two were foreigners. Any young American calculating his chances for personal fame in various occupations could thus conclude from the magazines that business offered the greatest opportunity for making a mark in his world.

Such a conclusion would find further reinforcement in the contents of the articles themselves. The American business elite was hailed as the modern successor to the prestige of the older military, political, and artistic elites:

> The time was when the soldier, the poet, the orator, the jurist, the sculptor, the painter were almost alone endowed with genius. That was before the day of the financier. In this country of ours . . . genius asserts itself in the financier and becomes most forceful and most dramatic. The most dramatic spot on this earth today is Wall Street.[103]

Without criticism or qualms biographers noted the tremendous powers possessed by individual businessmen and treated these not as threats to the public but as proof of heroic capacities and reason for public interest. "Because around him revolve such tremendous plans and forces," J. P. Morgan was singled out as "the most interesting figure today before the public." [104] In the context of this attitude toward business leaders, hostile charges that economic developments had placed excessive social powers in the hands of industrialists and financiers served only to enhance their prestige. When "the supreme type" of greatness for an individual was defined as "the greatness that leaves its mark on history, that moves the destinies of vast territories and of important races," [105] the logical conclusion followed that the increasing power of businessmen was simply proof of their heroic stature.

Biographers particularly took pains to note that in America business provided a far wider field for heroic action than did politics:

> In America the greater part of our highest ability is attracted into business life. It is one of the chief respects in which our

civilization differs most widely from the civilizations of the old world. There the ablest brains are usually to be found in the service of the state; here they interest themselves in commerce and finance. The railroad builders of America, for example, would have been in England, Germany, or France, prime ministers, leaders of parties, makers of states, governors of empires. Different conditions have turned to other uses the conspicuous genius, the constructive minds of our country. The great public problems in this country are municipal rather than national, local rather than imperial; and so the men of imperial minds have been turned into those fields of action from which they are not excluded by the narrow traditions of our public service. Armour is an imperialist in his ideas and in his acts.[106]

The secondary position of politics in America was reemphasized by the repeated claim that a successful man of business could secure and capably fill any political position he might desire. Even with the austere and forbidding personality of a Russell Sage, his biographer confidently asserted that "a man of his boundless energy and tireless pertinacity, of his consummate shrewdness, of his wonderful judgment of men and of things, might have reached almost any prize in the absorbing game of politics; but he deliberately turned away from it." [107]

Politics might be an "absorbing game," but business provided the true test for heroes. Readers were assured that "the American business men" were

. . . the men who fight the battles of life where they must now be fought, in the markets of the world, not in the fields or forests, and among whom real progress can be made only by manly and moral qualities. Financial exigencies try a character today not less than did the test of fire in more martial times. He who lives a modern business life with unblemished honor throughout, has had quite as much of the reality of struggle, if less of the romance, as had the soldier in earlier days. They who would be leaders in commerce must be fit to stand anywhere.[108]

Not only, then, was business presumed to provide the scope for heroic action lacking elsewhere in America. It also offered the definitive test of the heroic character. The man who had won success in business, the assumption ran, had thereby proved his worthiness to be ranked with Napoleon, Cromwell, and Alexander.

The parallel which Americans felt between their own masters of business and the empire-builders of foreign nations was emphasized also in the occupational statistics. Almost the same proportion of biographies focused upon imperial foreign rulers (15 per cent) as upon the domestic business leaders (16 per cent). And there could be no question that what attracted American interest in these rulers was force rather than humanitarianism, individual power rather than democratic representativeness. The admired foreign ruler in this decade was one who demonstrated "the supreme passion for bringing his environment under the control of his personality." [109]

Less than one-fourth of the foreign leaders in magazine biographies held elective positions. They were instead emperors, czars, kings, or sultans. Napoleon, Cromwell, and Alexander were the great prototypes, the subjects of the serial biographies and of the most frequent references. In the contemporary world biographers paid most attention to the flamboyant figure of the Kaiser and to Li Hung Chang, the new Premier of China who was prematurely given credit for single-handedly imposing a modern order upon the chaos of that ancient empire.

An editorial in the *Century* introduced its serial biography of Alexander the Great and made clear some of the relevance which Americans felt in 1898 between their own situation and that of the great conquerors:

> The new life of the Macedonian hero which *The Century* is to print will appeal with special timeliness to the American people, on account of a correspondence of conditions and results

> which the recent war helps to enforce. In the same way Macedonia was despised by her enemies older in the practice of nationality, for her newness was taken as the sign of semibarbarism, and her aptitude for material success was looked at askance, as implying coarseness and greed. But wherever she met her enemies in the clash of brain and brawn, the victory was so complete and on her side so bloodless, that a miracle seemed to have been wrought—the miracle of courage, intelligence, and discipline.[110]

In historical perspective it may seem as far-fetched to talk about intelligence and discipline in connection with our confused operations against the dispirited Spanish forces in 1898 as it does to see meat-packers and railroad presidents in terms of Napoleon. For Americans in the 1890's, however, the only meaningful analogies for their national experience and for their view of the individual came from the romantic empires and empire-builders of the past and present. Strangely enough, the once-dominant images from a republican Rome and a democratic Greece (both of which had also experienced the spell of imperialism) no longer held any place in the American imagination. Perhaps these remained too intimately associated with a very different conception of life and of the American republic.

Before Theodore Roosevelt's appearance in the White House, domestic politics seemed a rather unlikely field for the heroic career in contemporary America. Senator Foraker explained this general feeling in 1897:

> Many think and say that the day of heroic questions is past; that it is now too late to make great names by the doing of great deeds. . . . The leaders of the last generation were exceptionally favored in having slavery, the Civil War, reconstruction, and kindred questions to deal with. . . . The problems they solved could not be dealt with, either in the field or in the forum, without developing all that was greatest and noblest. . . . The thirty years that have since passed, although covering a most

> thrilling material progress, appear tame and insipid by comparison. . . . The souls of men are not stirred by tariff schedules or rates of duty, whether specific or ad valorem; and important as all monetary questions are, there is but little opportunity for inspiration in their discussion.[111]

Biographers in search of Napoleonic heroes found little inspiration and few subjects among the active politicians of the 1890's.

Before 1900 only one currently active politician appeared within a one-third sample of all biographies. This was David Bennett Hill, the Senator and Democratic boss of New York state. The magazine preferred to concentrate upon the great figures of the past—Lincoln, Webster, Grant, Washington, Aaron Burr, and others. As the election of 1900 approached, articles began to appear on more of the active political bosses, on Hanna, Platt, and Richard Croker. It took the dramatic assassination of McKinley, however, and the sudden elevation of Theodore Roosevelt to the presidency to lift the attention of biographers from their concern with past statesmen and present bosses. After his death McKinley became the hero of three magazine biographies though none had appeared within the sample during his administration.

In Theodore Roosevelt biographers found at last the real contemporary hero in politics. Foraker's lament over the insipid state of politics in 1897 had pointed to the prospects of overseas expansion as the "new and stirring questions" which would revitalize statecraft. It had concluded that "we must look to the vigorous and spirited young men in American politics, who are full of aggressive determination to work out for the American people that manifest destiny of which we hear so much, rather than to the older men who, as a result of these long years of peace and prosperity, have grown unduly conservative." Now one of the young American empire-builders had emerged in the presidency. The *Century* hailed Roosevelt as "an expansionist" and said his presidency "seems to mark the dawn of a new era in our public life."

The dynamic young President fulfilled many of the requirements of the existing hero-image. *Cosmopolitan* compared him with Napoleon and exulted that his success "affords the most encouraging lesson for men young or old who have intelligence sufficient to lay out for themselves definitely outlined careers." *McClure's* denied that this native of New York City was properly "a city boy." It quoted him as asserting, "I belong as much to the country as to the city. I owe all my vigor to the country." It found him the embodiment of individual force: "His training as a soldier in Cuba increased what his life in the West had already given him . . . the love of direct, individual action." *Munsey's* pointed out that "the whole force of his nature has been directed towards the accomplishment of self-elevation . . . he has toiled with restless and ambitious determination to succeed." [112]

But Roosevelt also seemed significant for the ways in which he resolved some of the decade's anxieties about wealth and about the intrigue or corruption of politics. "In this day when the cities are filled with rich young men leading uninteresting and stupid lives," observed *Cosmopolitan*, "it is worthwhile to give an analysis of such a career as that of Theodore Roosevelt." His achievement provided the answer to a nagging question. "At the end of a hundred years we had begun to ask: Is the wealth so abundantly showered upon the individuals of the nation never to produce a class of men who will regard money simply as a permission to high accomplishment?"

As he had removed the curse of idleness from inherited wealth, so Roosevelt had dispelled the dirt and dishonor too often associated with politics. He was a remarkable study "for the young men of the country who may ponder upon this extraordinary exemplification of the fact that there is a place in American politics for clean, fine-minded men who refuse to trample upon their personal dignity or sacrifice their honor and who determine in entering politics to devote their highest talents to the success of the public interest, themselves profiting only secondarily by the part which they play." William Allen White explained in *McClure's* that Roosevelt was "essentially" not a politician and in the denial went on to illustrate what contemporaries felt to be the essence of politics. Roosevelt, said White, "did not get these offices because he was a good 'mixer' . . . or because he was a manipulator of men, or yet because he had 'pull' or influence. . . . He was reelected because of his capacity to accomplish things." [113]

Thus far Roosevelt appeared simply to satisfy the period's demand for the creative, forceful individual and to dissipate some of the more common Mugwump fears. Only one article, a brief biography by Lincoln Steffens in 1902, noted any need for reform and found in Roosevelt the required type of reformer: "The reform must be established by the will of a strong man who is truly democratic and not afraid of a fight." [114] But neither reform nor even politics became a major element for this decade's heroes. Until the end of 1903 Richard Croker remained the only example of a city or state politician in the biographical articles. At the same moment when *Cosmopolitan* burst forth with its enthusiastic response to Theodore Roosevelt, the magazine began its extensive, eulogistic series on Captains of Industry. Business clearly was the true testing ground for the Napoleonic hero under American conditions.

Other occupations which appeared with any frequency provided further fields for the forceful, productive individual. Though a military life was seldom creative, it still offered magnificent opportunities for personal fame or masterful action, and the analogies with Napoleon were reiterated in numerous biographies of generals and admirals. Scientists and inventors combined their obvious creativity with the admired concentration upon their individual work in an age when science was still popularly conceived as an individual rather than a cooperative enterprise. Even the religious heroes bore out the emphasis on creative Idols of Power. They were predominantly the great founders of religions or churches—Christ, Mohammed, Zoroaster, John Wesley—rather than contemporary clergymen in established churches. Beyond that a fairly random scattering of occupations in the biographies demonstrated the decade's interest in a diversity of individuals and individual pursuits. The common factor in almost every case was the focus upon the individual career more than upon its significance for society.

From 1894 through 1903 the newly popular general magazines purveyed their portraits of the Napoleonic hero to a national audience. The impressive individual accomplishments of these heroes, their tremendous powers of will, their dominance over the human and material environment, their spectacular triumphs over obstacles and adversity in the climb to success, all these seemed to prove the continuing vitality and even wider scope for individualism. Biographers could assert that the Napoleonic hero disproved "the fallacy that multitudes and not individuals shape affairs and give direction to the currents of human life; the fallacy that the individual does not count." [115]

Yet the very need to make this assertion betrayed a certain uneasiness about its contemporary relevance. The very extravagance of the Napoleonic individual betokened some anxiety about the changing world. Harold Lasswell, referring to an earlier period of industrial transformation in England, has noted the emergence of "the exaggerated picture of the omnipotent leader drawn by Carlyle." Lasswell tried to explain the popular appeal of the superman in a certain stage of historical development:

> . . . the popularity which this exaggeration enjoyed among certain classes of English society was due to the dislocation of older economic institutions and the rise of threatening collective ideologies. The new business enterpriser felt the intoxicating vanity of the self-made man, and the decayed landlord felt the necessity of individualistic protests against the age of cities and machines.[116]

Though America had fewer decayed landlords than England, Americans had a still deeper commitment to an individualistic order which by 1900 cities, machines, and the new trusts were radically transforming.

Whether the glorification of trust magnates as modern Napoleons would be sufficient to preserve Americans' sense of individualism was still an open question in 1903. Already the biographies of Theodore Roosevelt, one of Carnegie, and one of Jacob Riis had begun to sound several new notes. Scattered demands for a more social-minded individualism were beginning to overlap the decade's concentration upon the forceful individual model of success. Yet the Napoleonic image held firm with remarkable consistency throughout these ten years. Few magazine readers could have foreseen the abruptness and the vehemence with which Progressive magazines would attack the Napoleonic Idols of Power in the decade after 1903.

Part Three

THE IDOLS OF JUSTICE

1904-1913

In which our hero dons

some social garments to protect his individualistic

frame in magazines at the peak of their power

Chapter 5

Progressive Publishers

It is the desire of Collier's *to be in national journalism what a good citizen is to his community.*
Collier's, 1909

THE MAGAZINE MOOD of the Progressive decade after 1903 was distinctive. Nothing quite like it has been experienced in American publishing before or since. Robert Underwood Johnson of the *Century* could not attune to it at all. He described it as a "straining after effect," a "simulated robustness," a "cock-sureness." He deplored the "writing in so many magazines that spoils one's repose by making a problem of everything and by tearing everything up by the roots to see how it is growing." Reared in the graceful, leisurely traditions of the *Century*, Johnson was perturbed by the strenuous tone of the Progressive magazines: "I find this modern type of magazine fatiguing by the very brilliance of its method, as though the peace of the world were banished forever. It reminds me of the remark of an Italian lady, who recently said, 'In America you are always for or against something.'" [1]

His very aloofness from the contagion of the times lent a certain perceptiveness to Johnson's account of its symptoms. Magazines of this decade were more robust and more sure of themselves and their worth than ever before (or since). They were written more dramatically and achieved more obvious effects than at other times. They did leap with vigor from one social problem to another. They did strive to get at the facts of their world, to discover the roots of its evils. Above all, they were preoccupied with questions about what Americans should be for and what they should be against. Biographies in Progressive magazines became a very conscious means of weighing individuals in the scales of popular judgment. For the first time magazine biographers dealt extensively with villains as well as with heroes. The question was how to distinguish one from the other—a vital question for a generation of hero-worshippers.

Many circumstances combined to give the editors and writers for the new magazines an enhanced sense of power and importance during these years. At a time when the independence and prestige of many middle-class occupations seemed threatened by the trusts and the plutocracy, careers on the magazines actually gained in both status and autonomy.[2] As the *Saturday Evening Post, Collier's, Everybody's, Success, Hampton's,* the *American* and others joined the ranks of *McClure's, Munsey's,* and *Cosmopolitan,* the demand for writers increased rapidly. McClure, Collier, and Lorimer of the *Post* were continually active in the search for talent. As the new magazines prospered and competed against one another, salaries and rates rose. In 1890 top editors like Gilder, Alden, and Bok had received $10,000. When *Collier's* made its bid for prominence after 1900, Norman Hapgood was offered a beginning salary of $25,000 as editor, and the young Mark Sullivan joined the staff initially at $7,500. *McClure's* poured from $1,000 to $4,000 into expenses for each of its muckraking articles.[3]

But job opportunities and monetary rewards were not the only attractions magazine journalism offered. For a while magazines seem to have been remarkably free from the kinds of pressures which in later times would curtail their sense of independence. Many publishers gave their editors a free hand.[4] When differences did develop over magazine policy, other opportunities were open. McClure's staff could walk out in protest and buy another magazine for themselves. Norman Hapgood could leave *Collier's* when business office pressures began to mount and find himself an editorial job on *Harper's Weekly*. Lincoln Steffens could cut loose, loaf for a while, write for newspapers, and take a part-time job for $10,000 with *Everybody's*.[5] Advertisers could not easily dictate to magazines. The whole business of national advertising was still fairly new and not thoroughly rationalized. Magazines were the only national medium available. If a periodical offered a large circulation and the respect of the public, advertisers followed along. In the magazines' approach to their readers and in writers' approach to their subjects, both editors and writers had an independence which would be later curtailed by increasingly rationalized procedures. No "scientific" surveys of readers' preferences guided or limited the instincts of editors in choosing and slanting their materials. Few public-relations managers existed in businesses or government agencies to hand information and publicity to journalists.[6] Writers were on their own to develop leads and dig out stories. The magazines also had a remarkable record of success in defending themselves against libel suits in this period, a record dramatically capped by Brandeis's defence of the account by *Collier's* of the Pinchot-Ballinger feud before a hostile congressional committee and against all the resources of Taft's administration.[7]

Along with the many opportunities, more money, and relative independence of a magazine career in this decade went a real sense of power and influence. The War of 1898 had turned magazine attention to contemporary topics, and the war correspondents headed by Richard Harding Davis had helped to glamorize the profession of journalism. When *McClure's* in 1903 and other magazines in the two succeeding years turned to exposés of business and politics, the articles attracted national attention and their authors gained national fame. Writers like Steffens, Tarbell, and Sullivan were hailed as experts on matters of major importance. They were invited to lecture, to examine conditions all over the country, to offer their remedies. Under Theodore Roosevelt they had unprecedented access to the White House. Steffens talked back to the President.[8] Sullivan was excited and somewhat appalled when a casual suggestion of his to Roosevelt started "the turning of mighty wheels" in the government.[9] Magazine campaigns seemed to have observable effects in municipal elections, in national legislation, in breaking the hold of Speaker Cannon over the House and Aldrich over the Senate, in forcing the resignation of Secretary Ballinger. The sense of power which was fed by access to President Roosevelt was maintained by successful criticism of President Taft. Muckraking was not just the story of corruption. It was a search for power in America. In that sense it was simply an extension of the previous decade's obsession with the powerful individual and the great organization. Magazines and all those connected with them sought to penetrate to the power centers of their world, and in doing so they seemed to become powers themselves. For many reasons Mark Sullivan could remember the period as "a happy one for a person of journalistic taste and aptitude." [10]

The dramatic story of this decade was, of course, the story of muckraking.* Historians have tended to divide the magazines into muckrakers and non-muckrakers and then to concentrate almost exclusively on the articles of exposure. Louis Filler, in his admirable book on muckrakers, claims that with the January, 1903, issue of *McClure's* which carried three exposés by Tarbell, Steffens, and Baker, the "middle-class and working-class people . . . cleaned the newsstands of *McClure's* and clamored for more. And the other magazines, startled, hastened to try to understand and follow this new path which McClure had blazed." [11] This

* The immediate source of this term which Roosevelt employed in a speech on April 14, 1906 may well have been a brief notice in *Collier's* on February 10, 1906 about the magazine's attack on a society scandal sheet. The item was headed "The Man with the Muckrake Improved" and referred to the quotation from Bunyan. It is more likely that Roosevelt had been reading *Collier's* in the months before his speech than that he had been reading John Bunyan in the original.

exclusive focus and comments like these tend to obscure some facts about the magazines of the Progressive decade which are relevant to determining the popular heroes of those years.

In the first place, after 1903 *McClure's* did not rank among the top four best-selling magazines. From the circulation figures compiled for advertisers' information in *Ayer's Directory* it appears that the thirty-six muckraking articles by Steffens, Baker and Tarbell which *McClure's* printed in the months of 1903 and 1904 did not bring any dramatic rise in circulation. *McClure's* in fact did not pass the 400,000 mark until 1906, the year when all three of these writers left its staff to found the *American.*

From the same figures it is apparent that only two of the four best-sellers in the heyday of exposure were muckraking magazines. *Everybody's,* which rose rapidly on the appeal of Tom Lawson's series, "Frenzied Finance," barely managed to nose out *Munsey's* for second place throughout the decade. Fourth place was held by *Collier's,* a magazine which embarked on muckraking with some expressed misgivings in 1905.

Most importantly, the great popular success among magazines of the Progressive decade was the *Saturday Evening Post.* This non-muckraker held its new leadership in every year of the period. It achieved a circulation over one million by 1909 and by the end of 1913 was approaching two million. The *Post* and *Munsey's* together, two magazines which eschewed muckraking, far surpassed in circulation any two of the journals of exposure.

Having said all this, however, it seems clear that the distinction between muckraking and non-muckraking magazines is of only secondary significance in gauging magazine attitudes and magazine heroes of this decade. The *Saturday Evening Post* and even *Munsey's* played their parts in the Progressive movement. A reader familiar only with the reactionary orientation of the *Post* during the 1930's and 1940's would be startled at many elements in the magazine during the Progressive years. Though *Munsey's* was least sympathetic to many Progressive attitudes, it did not wholly escape nor set itself against the Progressive movement.

Table X

*Circulation (in Thousands) of the Leading General Magazines from 1900 Through 1913**

	1900	1901	1902	1903	1904	1905	1906	1907	1908	1909	1919	1911	1912	1913
S. E. Post	250	331	375	512	656	728	705	747	886	1,247	1,425	1,739	1,885	1,986
Munsey's	590	623	576	634	627	611	698	698	618	500	500	500	400	400
Everybody's	100	150	150	250	500	700	600	550	500	500	508	632	600	600
Collier's	170	260	321	400	528	568	568	568	531	500	571	520	500	562
McClure's	369	360	377	370	375	375	414	472	440	425	450	450	400	500
Cosmopolitan	350	350	350	300	300	400	450	450	400	425	440	750	750	800
American						300	250	280	267	287	313	275	300	320

* From *Ayer's American Newspaper Annual and Directory.*

Frank Munsey himself, to the consternation of many Bull-Moosers, joined the ranks with Roosevelt at Armageddon in 1912 and provided funds for the Progressive Party campaign. At the same time, the two best-selling muckraking periodicals themselves contained much material which was anything but critical of the existing order. *Everybody's* continued laudatory success stories on captains of industry while *Collier's* printed columns of advice on investments. These years, more so than most, were ones of confusing, often conflicting pulls on American loyalties. They saw a mingled fascination and contempt for material success, an exultant pride in the new industrial, urban America combined with a pervasive nostalgia for its rural past; and they gave rise to strong individuals preaching collective action for the sake of preserving individualism. The dominant style of the magazines as elsewhere was captured in the balanced polarities of a Roosevelt speech. The danger of using too simple categories in describing any aspect of the period is that these may miss the basic tensions which produced its mood and its standards.

The magazines provided the foremost arena for the nation's questioning of its institutions. In their pages went forward the popular search for the meaning and evaluation of the new developments. Muckraking was only one means to this end, though it seemed the most dramatic and stimulating one. Observers have noted the preoccupation of the muckrakers, of the journalists, of the historians, of the younger generation of novelists with "reality." In this concern the Progressive magazines seemed to contrast with the older Mugwump journals which had dwelt so strongly on the "ideal." This distinction underlay Robert Underwood Johnson's uneasiness with the new magazines. He missed the "level quietude, in which was seen the hopeful blue sky and the cheerful sun and, by night, the spiritual suggestion of the stars." [12]

Yet it would be a mistake simply to state that the Progressive magazines were concerned with the "real" as opposed to the "ideal" which had inspired so much of the contents in *Harper's* and the *Century.* The new concern was with the question of relevance. How relevant were the old ideals to the new realities? The previous generation had generally managed to keep the two in separate compartments. Lincoln Steffens tells of seeing Grover Cleveland after the exposé by *McClure's* on conditions in Missouri had appeared. Cleveland, who knew at first-hand much of the corruption in business and politics, wanted to speak of "democracy as an ideal." He asked how Steffens could believe all that the article revealed " 'with'—he pointed out the window—'with the sun shining like that.' " Cleveland did not doubt anything Steffens had written. " 'I have seen it myself in office. I simply cannot make my imagination look at it as it is.' " [13] The Progressive imagination, however, delighted in facts, in "the inside story," [14] in seeing things as they were. Occasionally, as in much of the *Saturday Evening Post's* realistic business fiction and in the naturalistic novels of Norris and Dreiser, the "reality" seemed fascinating in itself. But most of the time in magazine stories, articles, and editorials, as in the social novels of authors like White, Phillips, Churchill, and others, the dramatic question was the one of relevance between ideals and the reality exposed.

The result was that magazines, as seldom before or since, set themselves up as judges of contemporary men and institutions. This function gave much of the zest to magazine careers in this decade. The rewards and relative independence of editors and writers lent them a security and confidence in the assertion of their judgments. The increased circulation of periodicals among the middle classes gave writers a sense of speaking for "the people" at a time when "the people" were assumed more than ever to be the only true guardians of the national interest. More than entertainers, more than straight reporters, magazines shared in the desire which *Collier's* expressed "to be in national journalism what a good citizen is to his community." [15]

In these circumstances magazine biographers could approach their job with increased enthusiasm and seriousness. They concentrated overwhelmingly on living Americans. They could view their task as that of passing "the people's" judgment upon the leaders of the day. They could also grapple with the pressing questions of how "success" should be defined under the new conditions and of whether the heroic individual had any place in an increasingly corporate society. Tensions and attitudes which had been hinted at in some of the final biographies of the previous decade now emerged openly. The magazine biographies became a focal point for many of the major Progressive concerns. They certainly reflected and probably helped to shape Progressive attitudes on key questions.

Again there was a measure of variety within the Progressive consensus about the heroes of the day. Some of the variety sprang from the different outlooks of the four leading general magazines. Examination of their editors and their contents reveals much about the dominant themes of interest in the Progressive decade and about the range of attitudes which clustered under the general head of Progressivism.

I

The Saturday Evening Post

American life is business, not as so many people regard it, an affair of musty ledgers and sordid haggling, but a big, active drama of romance and achievement.

George Horace Lorimer

All historians agree that Progressivism was a middle-class movement. Its idealism sprang from middle-class conceptions of democracy and of social justice. More importantly, perhaps, its strength stemmed from middle-class fears of plutocracy on the one hand and of socialism on the other. All observers of American life in the first half of the twentieth century agree that the

Saturday Evening Post was the preeminent magazine of the nation's middle class. The *Post* began its new career almost simultaneously with the Progressive movement and became the country's best-selling magazine by 1904. The themes stressed in the *Post* and its judgments on contemporary developments evidently appealed to more readers during the Progressive years than those of any other magazine. Yet historians have generally passed hastily over the *Post* during their examinations of Progressivism in the magazines. Such neglect may be justified for those whose interest lies entirely in muckraking or in the campaigns for social justice to underprivileged groups. The *Post* had little part in these aspects of Progressivism. As a reflection of middle-class fears and interests, however, and as a guide to the attitudes which gave widespread strength to the Progressive movement, the *Saturday Evening Post* deserves more attention than it has yet received.*

As it emerged in its new form after 1899, the *Post* was largely the product of two men, Cyrus H. K. Curtis and George Horace Lorimer. Its publisher, Cyrus Curtis, resembled Frank Munsey in many ways. He too had been reared in Maine under humble circumstances. He too had nourished an early ambition for financial success, originally planning to be a merchant. He had struggled up from errand boy and sales clerk and then stumbled into publishing through experience soliciting advertisements. He had kept two successive publications painfully alive before hitting upon the great magazine success of the 1890's, the *Ladies' Home Journal,* and then repeating that triumph a decade later with the *Saturday Evening Post.* His own chief gifts lay in promotion

* Further reasons for the relative neglect of the *Post* may be the general distaste of intellectuals for its complacent Americanism and the fact that its complete opposition to the New Deal as well as its ardent isolationism from 1939 to 1942 seemed to indicate its separation from dominant national attitudes expressed in the election returns. Later distrust of the *Post*'s significance may have been projected back upon the *Post* of 1904–1913.

and advertising. Like Munsey he became attracted by newspapers, bought several, and achieved for them only disastrous failure through what Oswald Garrison Villard termed "faulty and inefficient management and reactionary, uninteresting, and visionless editorial direction." [16] Like Munsey too he believed that "The chief interest in a man's life is the fight for a livelihood; in other words, business." His biography was written by his son-in-law, Edward Bok, in the traditional success terms which Bok employed for such inspirational tracts as *Successward* and *Why I Believe in Poverty.* Curtis probably agreed with his biographer that ". . . his own life demonstrated the marvelous adventurous and romantic elements in business." [17]

Unlike Munsey, however, Curtis never wrote for his magazines or attempted to edit them personally. His success lay in picking able editors, supporting them handsomely, and giving them an entirely free hand. The pattern began when his wife started as editor of the *Ladies' Home Journal* and continued when Edward Bok replaced her. In 1899 Curtis faced the problem of finding an editor for the feeble weekly family magazine, the *Saturday Evening Post,* which he had purchased for $1,000 in the fall of 1897. Whether the publisher had any clear idea of what he wanted the magazine to become is uncertain. In later years Bok wrote that Curtis bought the magazine because of its descent from Benjamin Franklin and because he wanted to establish a magazine for men which would contain authentic business stories and articles.[18] The *Post's* claim to a connection with Franklin has proved to be tenuous at best.[19] The issues of the *Post* for the first year and a half under Curtis's ownership show no particular plan or pattern, and Curtis's own conception of it may have been as vague as was the descent from Franklin.[20] But when Curtis left for Europe in the spring of 1899 to meet with an experienced editor whom he wanted, he left a young man, George Horace Lorimer, in temporary charge of the new magazine. Returning empty-handed from his trip some months later, the publisher was so delighted with the changes Lorimer had made that he gave the editorial post to him immediately. From that date until 1936 Lorimer was the dominant figure on the *Post,* and it was he who made the *Post* into a magazine which dramatized contemporary American life, especially the life of business.

Thirty-one years old when he gained control of the *Post,* Lorimer could draw upon a varied background: a Middle Western boyhood, a year at Yale and another at Colby, three or four years in Philip Armour's meat-packing business, an unsuccessful flier in the wholesale grocery business, and a stretch of newspaper reporting in Boston. Lorimer's turn from business to writing indicated no disillusionment with the life of commerce, only a desire to portray in print the "big, active drama of romance and achievement" which he conceived business to be.[21] The young editor himself did much to boost the early circulation of the *Post* by writing for it a fictional series called "Letters From a Self-Made Merchant to His Son." In book form it became a minor best-seller. Upton Sinclair considered it a work of "commercial depravity," but the Eastman Kodak Company distributed it to all employees.[22] Two other books followed in the same vein. Lorimer's father had been a noted evangelical minister. The son, in his writings and in his editorship of the *Post,* became the nation's leading evangelist for the business life and for salvation through business virtues.

As much as any man could be, Lorimer seemed a composite figure of the American middle-class tastes and attitudes of his generation. He had a partiality for blueberry pie and ham and eggs, a preference for Gilbert and Sullivan, and a love for the outdoors. He liked attending conventions, collecting antiques, and "partying with the boys," while he disliked the trips to Europe on which his wife dragged him.[23] Thus equipped, he edited the *Post* for an audience which he thought of as "the men and women from seventeen to seventy who are growing": in business they were "the gray-haired President with young brains, the never-say-die salesman, and the up-and-coming clerks, the get-ahead cubs"; in law, medicine, journalism and public life they were "the men who win cases and save lives, who fight for clean politics, and a better America"; rural readers were "the farmer who goes to town in his automobile [said in 1917] and the young man who goes to the State College of Agriculture"; in college they were "the boy who has more than the batting averages in his head, and the professor who can interest his classes in a dry-as-dust subject"; women readers were those "clear-eyed upstanding ones who think in terms of something besides cup custards and sex stories." In view of these categories it was interesting that Lorimer hated the term "middle class." [24] Perhaps his aversion to it was based on its necessary implication that there were also other classes worth considering.

The outstanding characteristic of the *Post* during the Progressive period was, in fact, its pervasive and often explicit class-consciousness. Never since the days of the early republic had a general magazine in America so clearly reflected and so frankly commented upon the life and interests of a single class. *Harper's* and the *Century* had represented the outlook of the Mugwumps but had rarely discussed directly the contemporary life of that group. *McClure's* and *Cosmopolitan* had turned more frequently to contemporary issues but had not treated these explicitly in terms of middle-class interests. *Munsey's* had catered to the dream life of the lower-middle class, but this had meant a coverage of the fantasies of its readers not of their actual life. The *Saturday Evening Post* filled its pages with fiction and articles describing current experience in business and the professions. It printed articles on particular middle-class problems. When it recounted the activities of the very rich or of the poor, readers were left in no doubt of the superiority of middle-class existence. Its editorial judgments frankly assessed how political, social, and economic developments affected the status, the standards, and the career chances of the middle class.

This persistent orientation could be seen most clearly when *Post* writers discussed groups above or below the middle class. David Graham Phillips began an attack on "Swollen Fortunes" with an analysis of the class origins of distinguished men whose names appeared in dictionaries of biography. "You find, first," he reported, "almost no sons of rich men; second, many sons of families that were extremely poor; and third, the overwhelming majority—in all ages, all countries—come of parents able to bring up their children without real hardship, but giving them no real luxury, either, and leaving them nothing that could be called an inheritance."[25] Here was a social Darwinism which, instead of hailing millionaires as the "fittest," attacked the rich while boosting the middle class as the source of leadership and distinction. Swollen fortunes emerged as a danger to the development of successful careers desired by individuals and needed by the nation.

Condescension or ridicule directed toward either end of the social scale was a more frequent *Post* device for reassuring middle-class readers. Phillips was also skilled at this technique. He contributed a pair of articles on "The Penalties of Poverty" and "The Penalties of Plutocracy," in the latter of which he claimed, "The plutocrat . . . is to be pitied." He wrote "The Millionaire's Art Primer" in which he demonstrated "How the European Expert Flim-Flams the Rich American." In a piece on "Kitchen Aristocracy" he revealed how imported foreign servants tyrannized the plutocracy. Meanwhile other writers treated high society as a life apart, a pleasant but somewhat ridiculous existence, in articles on "Slumming Among the Four Hundred" or on "Social Veneer; How the Rich Young American Girl Is Given a High Finish." Further articles on "A Modest Home for Five Million," "The Rich Man as Farmer," or "Funny Little New York; The Sufferings of Its Rich During the Late Unpleasantness" (a description of the economies of the wealthy in the Panic of 1907) derived their humor from the application of middle-class standards to the homes, farms, and economies of multi-millionaires.

Clearly superior to these rather un-American circles was "The Real Leisure Class" discovered by Harrison Rhodes. This he found "in its most characteristic condition and in its greatest numbers" to be those elderly middle-class citizens of the Middle West who wintered in the small towns of Florida and California. "They are, in a singularly American way, a solider and pleasanter proof of the real prosperity of the country than all the millionaires of Pittsburg and New York combined." He dwelt on the social function of this group: "Its service is to be a tranquil oasis in a roaring desert, also a kind of a symbol that we are still a democracy with ideals of simplicity and frugality." [26]

The expansive life of the new millionaires raised a threat to the relative prestige of middle-class living standards, a threat which might be dissipated by ridicule and reassurance. Other pressures, however, threatened actually to undermine those standards and could not be so easily dismissed. The high cost of living emerged in a number of *Post* articles as a serious concern for many segments of the middle class, most graphically perhaps for teachers in a harrowing account of "The Pressure on the Professor." A particular source of status anxiety appeared to be what was repeatedly referred to as "the servant question." An article on "The Servant in the House" explained the range of society within which this problem was most acute:

> There are two classes of people untroubled by the servant question: the very rich, who deal with it vicariously through housekeepers whose business it is to see that the problem is kept out of sight, and the very poor, for whom it does not exist, since they wait on themselves. The people most deeply affected by it are those belonging to the various strata of the middle classes—from the wife of the hundred-dollar-a-month man, who tries to get a young girl to work for a home and a very little money, up to the woman whose husband can allow her a cook, a second girl, and a laundress.[27]

The limits of those affected by "the servant question" also defined pretty well the social range of readers to whom and for whom the *Post* spoke. It was a class whose traditional style of life was being most seriously affected by rising prices, rising expectations, and an increasing emphasis upon money as the basis for personal relations with groups above and below them on the social scale. After reading the magazines of the nineteenth century where specific sums of money were scarcely ever mentioned, one is struck by the very frank and frequent references in the *Post* to actual amounts of salary, of wages, of property holdings, of prices, and of costs.

To stop here, however, would be to imply that the major concern of the *Post* was with the consumption activities of the middle class, with its home life and its leisure time. The truth was exactly the reverse. Cyrus Curtis had argued that, "The chief interest in a man's life is the fight for a livelihood; in other words, business." Lorimer asserted, "The struggle for existence is the loaf, love or sex is the frosting on the cake." [28] As a result the *Saturday Evening Post* in this decade was heavily oriented toward description, explanation, editorial defence, and fictional glorification of the middle-class career, particularly a career in business. Lorimer himself had contributed his "Letters of a Self-Made Merchant." Edward M. Woolley revealed in autobiographical form "The Inner Secrets of a Merchant's Rise" as well as those of a manufacturer and a railroad executive. "I have not given this in any sense as an autobiography," he emphasized, "but merely as a sort of formula through which any man of sound commonsense and ability can achieve success." [29] James H. Collins produced numerous articles on such subjects as "Tales of the Road—First Experiences in Selling" or "The Buying End." Will Payne added a series on "Modern Business Practices," a theme which was even extended to cover "The Business Side of a Church." A varied assortment of columns in the back pages of the *Post* kept alive hope and faith in financial aggrandizement. The list ranged from a column on "Just Finding Money; How Some Men Have Recently Made Fortunes Out of Little Things" to Isaac Marcosson's regular column of advice on "Your Savings." It included such titles as: "Getting On in the World; Steps and Missteps on the Road to Fortune"; "Failures of Forty; How Some

Men Start Afresh and Succeed"; and, in order not to discourage any readers, a column on "Getting a Start at Sixty." Business careers received the overwhelming bulk of the *Post*'s attention, but supplementing these were scattered articles on the professions, "The Young Lawyer; Starting in and Building up a Practice; What It Means and How It Pays," "The Young Doctor," and others.

The *Post* shared strongly in the Progressive concern for "reality." Where this concern led other magazines to muckraking, it led the *Post* to a new realism in its business fiction and in its description and advice on business careers. Curtis had been disgusted with the "inaccuracy" of previous business stories.[30] In an advertising brochure Lorimer explained:

> The *Saturday Evening Post* does not make a practice of printing deliberate and deadly, 'inspirational' articles, so called, because they are usually a compound of hokum and bunkum. . . . The *Saturday Evening Post* is trying to do something that it believes is more genuinely useful than these one-sided 'success' and inspirational articles. It is trying both in autobiography and short stories clearly to reflect the facts of life.[31]

Post writers, therefore, did not conceal the sharp practices of the business world. Instead they seemed to take considerable delight in these as an exhilarating part of "The Great Game." The elements of conflict in the *Post*'s business fiction included struggles between business rivals, occasional struggles between a hero's acquisitive instincts and his conscience, and also the conflict between generations each with its own social ideals and commercial ethics. Where other popular writers like Winston Churchill used the conflict between generations to dramatize a dichotomy between business values and human values,[32] *Post* authors generally staged their struggles well within the limits of business values. A typical serial like Edwin Lefevre's "Sampson Rock of Wall Street" involved the efforts of a stockbroker's son to prove himself as masterful as his father in the world of finance though by somewhat less ruthless methods. Revealing the techniques of stock market manipulation as clearly as any muckraker, Lefevre nevertheless managed to cast a veil of glamor and power around them. The climax of the serial saw the son in an emergency prove himself the equal of his father in controlling the ticker tape. Even the "frosting" of love and sex fell into the commercial scheme of values since the hero's motivation in his maneuvers was "to earn this girl!"

A similar realism and unquestioning acceptance of business values pervaded the *Post's* multifarious articles describing business activities and advising incipient capitalists. One striking instance of the *Post's* frank shrewdness and of its class blindness occurred in a column headed "Thrift—Incubating the Nest Egg," which was designed to counsel young men on the best roads to fortune. Here the ambitious youth was urged as his best possible investment to purchase a tenement building. Such a property, he was assured, would yield a 19 per cent return since "properties of this character are seldom empty" and "Very little money is spent on repairs with property of this sort." He need, in fact, spend no money on maintaining the building since in case of its collapse he could almost certainly sell it at a profit for a factory site.[33] These certainly were "the facts of life" without "hokum and bunkum" and without any recognition of the current campaign being waged by humanitarian reformers against the slums and against those who profited from the slums.

At times Lorimer used the *Post* for explicit defence of business elements which were under attack in other magazines. When the "Beef Trust" was being exposed by the muckrakers, the *Post* ran a series of articles defending the packers purportedly written by Lorimer's friend and old employer, J. Ogden Armour. When the stock market was suffering from the revelations by Thomas Lawson and others, the *Post* carried a symposium on "Wall Street Views of Speculation" which presented the social ideas of James Keene, Thomas Fortune Ryan, and other notorious market manipulators. The magazine even seemed to border on "deliberate and deadly" inspirational writing when it printed the unanimously affirmative replies of sixty eminent business leaders like Standard Oil's Archbold and a DuPont to a *Post* questionnaire on "The Golden Rule in Business; Can Commercial Methods Be Squared with Honesty?" But platitudes from practicing business men were somehow accepted as more realistic than platitudes from inexperienced hack writers. Despite these moral justifications of business practices the general attitude of the *Post* toward business seemed largely amoral. It was far more concerned with the drama of the spectacle than with its ethics. Business was "a big active drama of romance and achievement." [34] The *Post's* attitude was best expressed in an editorial on "The Great Game" which concluded:

> In any event, and without regard to ethical values, the practice of modern business has a side not altogether without picturesqueness. Modern business contains more interest for more people than any other field of human activity.[35]

The old middle-class career in business and in the professions, however, was being threatened during these years not only, the *Post* thought, by the specific attacks of muckrakers but by more general developments in the nation's society and economy. The *Post's* recognition of these threats and its response to them aligned it for a decade very closely to many Progressive reforms. Most of the dominant themes in the magazine which appeared alongside its predominant emphasis on business can be understood as concern for the changes currently overtaking middle-class Americans.

The increasing hegemony of the city was one of the most inescapable of these changes. The center of operations for the middle-class career was obviously shifting from the towns and villages of America to the big cities. This shift promised greater financial returns and a greatly expanded scope of activity and influence for some. It offered a far more intense and demanding competitive arena for all ambitious individuals. But in the process the quality of middle-class life underwent some disturbing transformations. The delightfully free and varied activities of a small-town boyhood which had stimulated the imagination and tested the physical skills of a Tom Sawyer and a Penrod, these seemed a grievous loss to the generation which moved to the cities. The relative individualism, democracy, and equality of adult life in the smaller community were fondly recalled by the new urban dwellers. Perhaps the greatest loss felt by middle-class citizens in the city was not so much the imagined *equality* of the towns as the unchallenged eminence and independence which the local judge, the village doctor, the town banker, the country merchant, and the prosperous farmer had enjoyed in a predominantly rural nation.

The *Saturday Evening Post* played upon these ambivalent emotions of its readers with a constant stream of nostalgic small-town reminiscences which accompanied its glorifications of business and its half-humorous, half-envious treatment of millionaires. Edwin L. Sabin recalled "A Dip in the Old Swimmin' Hole as You Used to Take It With Hen and Billy and the Other Boys." He recaptured the atmosphere of old-time Sundays in "A Leaf From a Diary of Used-to-be." Rebecca Harding Davis praised "Religion in the Days of Our Fathers" in an article which claimed that "Religion then possessed every man's thoughts, partly because there was not much else to possess them. . . . The struggle for a living was not then breathless and cruel as now." [36]

William Allen White became something of a folk hero for the generation caught in this conflict of loyalties. He represented a remarkable synthesis of two American ideals then in tension. His writings for the *Post* included "a series of sketches of the types and characters of a small Western town." In his person he became a living example of the "simpler," more traditional life of the small towns where men such as he and his father could consider themselves "the ruling class." [37] He remained the village sage, the eternal boy, the owner of the big house on the hill, and the first-name intimate of all his neighbors. But White proved himself able to combine with all this the prestige of worldly success in urban circles, in national magazines, and in national politics. It would probably have been difficult to determine whether Americans admired him more for having refused a $25,000 job in Chicago[38] or for having been offered the job in the first place.

The two sides of this ambivalence over desirable patterns for life emerged repeatedly in the *Post.* The older pattern of values was supported in a fictional series of "Letters to Unsuccessful Men by a Failure," the plot of which was thus summarized by the editors:

> A half dozen men left a small Middle West town and started out in different directions to find success. All but one of them achieved what the world branded as success. That one came back in the end to edit a small country newspaper, interested himself in local politics and spent the rest of his time getting acquainted with Nature on a twenty-acre farm.[39]

Against such paeans to the simple life, however, must be set all the stories, articles, and columns elsewhere in the magazine which augmented the pressure for "what the world branded as success." Probably the solution which Lorimer, commenting on these divergent life goals, envisioned as most practicable was set forth in an editorial on "The Business of Living":

> At this writing an army of youths . . . is marching from college to join the ranks of the fortune-hunters.
>
> Very many of these youths came from country towns where life has a wide and pleasant margin, and is still democratically conditioned with one honest man that can earn a living as good as any other. . . . Most of them will go to the city, where existence has some ginger and there are prizes worthy the beneficiary of higher education.
>
> There they will live in hall bedrooms up dingy streets. . . . They will find that the city knows democracy no more, but is a

> place of classes that fight one another over the spoils. . . . Many times they will yearn for the shade of the oak in the yard at home and a taste of mother's pie.
>
> [After success] they will find that their measure of success is this: to be able to go back to the country and live where they might have been all the time.[40]

This comment pretty well reflected the particular nature of the *Post*'s response to the dichotomy of values between town and city. *Munsey's* had unquestioningly accepted the superiority of city life and continually presented this in its pages. The muckraking magazines generally spoke for the preservation of the traditional values. Much of their appeal sprang from indignant exposures of the ways in which city politics and urban-centered business violated the small-town canons of democracy, individualism, and public knowledge of all essential operations. They often strove to make the old standards relevant to the new life of large communities and organizations. The *Post,* however, recognized the differences but accepted each pretty much on its own grounds. Lorimer's magazine did not strive in tones of high moral purpose to reconstruct the new in terms of the old. The *Post* lived with this tension in middle-class experience by adopting the half-humorous, half-cynical attitude apparent in Lorimer's editorial. Perhaps the popularity of the *Post* indicates that this attitude was more widespread among Americans than either the wholesale capitulation of *Munsey's* or the outraged reaction of the muckrakers. It seems, in any case, a more tenable position than that adopted by the *Post* in the 1920's and 1930's when Lorimer attempted to defend an overwhelmingly urban America and a heavily bureaucratized business structure against government intervention by invoking the irrelevant images of small town America and nineteenth-century business as true models of twentieth-century reality.

The other great change affecting middle-class careers in the Progressive decade was, of course, the consolidation of business in "trusts" and the concentration of wealth in the hands of multi-millionaires. The *Post* could not look upon these developments with the same humorous detachment which characterized its outlook on the encroachments of the city. They seemed to threaten the middle class in ways which could not be laughed off, and the *Post* aligned itself firmly with Theodore Roosevelt's measures to curb these dangers. The greatest impetus for its support of Rooseveltian reforms, however, came from its fear that the growth of trusts and "swollen fortunes" would swing the nation to socialism. Against these twin perils from above and from below the *Post* clearly set forth its editorial class consciousness:

> The crux of the Socialist position, ever since Karl Marx announced it, has been that the big capitalists would swallow the small ones, that the 'middle-class' would disappear, leaving society composed of great capitalists and wage-earners, when the latter, by virtue of immense numerical superiority, would calmly appropriate the state.
>
> The Rooseveltian measures have been solely by way of checking the swallowing process. The motive has been to protect the little capitalist from the great, to conserve small, 'middle-class' business—which the rebate-giving railroads and the trusts that used cutthroat methods of competition were actually destroying at a rate that made Marx look like a prophet.[41]

Here was the basis for the *Post*'s Progressivism. No longer could the monopolizing millionaire be regarded as the ultimate example of the success of middle-class business virtues. He had actually become a threat to that way of life, a precursor to "Socialism" and a barrier to "Opportunity." The people, according to the *Post*, were not disturbed by envy; rather, "it is the feeling that the diversion of so much of the nation's prosperity into the hands of a few is establishing injustice, is discouraging manly and womanly independence, is narrowing the gateways of opportunity." [42]

In the face of these threats even the magazine dedicated to "the romance of business" freely opened its pages to praise of

Progressive politicians. The *Post* printed a special "Roosevelt Number" at the time of his 1905 inauguration. It played up the various facets of his "strenuous life" in articles on "Roosevelt's Ranching Days—The Outdoors Training of a President as a Man Among Men" and "Having a Bully Time; The Minor Activities of a Major President." It defended him against criticism from the right. During the Panic of 1907 Edwin Lefevre in "Wall Street and That Man Roosevelt" accused "the Street" of stupidity in abusing the man who was saving business. In November of that year the *Post* offered to pay for letters on the question, "Is Roosevelt a Menace to Business?" A month later the magazine reported that thousands of letters had been received which "with few exceptions" dismissed the idea of the President as a menace to business.

More accurately, perhaps, than the more militantly Progressive magazines the *Post* saw Roosevelt's role to be that of a conservative:

> The President is the best friend of these privileged industries if they had but the sense to know it. All his moves since he assumed office have been in the direction of conservatism, of patching up the present machine of society, cleaning the wheels, regulating it so that it may run along on the old lines with less danger of a general smash. For the President is the most conspicuous Individualist this country has ever seen: any form of Socialism is repugnant to him. He sees, however, that the present system of industry is absolutely conditioned on the 'square deal'. . . . If they [the Corporations] want the good old times to keep on they must consent to a little regulating of their privileges here and there, so that the great public that makes up society will be content with it as it is.[43]

Only Alfred Henry Lewis in the *Post* went slightly beyond this conservative basis for support of the President, and Lewis was advanced more in the exuberance of his language than in the substance of his argument. Emphasizing in 1906 "Why Roosevelt

Must Run Again," Lewis painted a background in which "The powerful forces of a malignant predatory wealth were abroad" and conflict raged "between the Man with the Dollars and the Man with the Hands." In this situation Lewis observed that the people resolved upon reform. "And what was that reform? Nothing astounding, nothing hideously revolutionary, surely! The people merely demanded that existing laws be enforced. . . . It is because he enforces the laws, and sees to it that other public officers do their duty in the same behalf, that Mr. Roosevelt, in the eyes of the people, is the President *par excellence*." [44]

Other Progressive leaders themselves wrote articles for the *Post*. Albert J. Beveridge, the young Insurgent Senator from Indiana, contributed regularly and became a close friend of Lorimer. La Follette and even Bryan were admitted to the *Post*'s roll of authors. What Lorimer printed from these men, however, tended to be rather technical articles on a relatively safe topic like railroad rate regulation or very general, very vague effusions like Bryan's "The Moral Awakening." Even so, it was a considerable change from 1896 when none of the best-selling magazines had ventured to print an article about Bryan, let alone one by him.

The most remarkable feature about the *Post* in this decade was that it did not yet reiterate nor even apparently yet believe in the political formula with which it would approach all questions of government in the 1920's and 1930's: "Let us have more business in government and less government in business." Both ends of this verbally balanced if socially unbalanced shibboleth were violated by *Post* editorials during the Progressive years. As early as January, 1905, Lorimer printed an editorial on "Corruption by Intangible Means" describing how a local board of public commissioners chosen for "integrity and business capacity" had failed to serve the public good because they were "themselves, by years of training, in the habit of looking at matters from the point of view of private rather than of public interests." [45] Elsewhere the *Post* observed that, "There have been business mayors and business governors and—almost without exception—their administrations have been as bad or worse than those that preceded and followed them." [46] When Woodrow Wilson became a candidate for Governor of New Jersey in 1910, taunts of "academic" and "impractical professor" stirred the *Post* to comment:

> This college president has probably had as large an experience in dealing with men as any lawyer, brewer or grocer who might have been nominated; but their implication is that dealing with men except in the way of trade—that is, for the purpose of making something off them—doesn't give one any valuable experience of human nature. 'Academic' used as a taunt, means that the person so taunted is not experienced in overreaching.[47]

Despite the *Post*'s preoccupation with the life of business, the Progressive period was a time when the magazine was apparently willing to recognize competence and worth in non-business elements of the middle-class community. This was a key characteristic in the mood of Progressivism.

Nor did the cry for "less government in business" appeal to Lorimer in the Progressive decade. In 1908 the *Post* ran an editorial on the contemporary version of that plea, "Let Us Alone," which concluded:

> And all this immense waste is simply a logical, automatic result of 'Let Us Alone.' It is the ripe fruit of that grand old policy of non-interference by society collectively with business affairs—a policy which many people still pretend, strangely enough, to admire.
>
> Let everybody slash and burn at his own sweet will without the control of a social conscience—and see where you come out. 'Let Us Alone?' We are always sorry to see business men approve a motto which belongs properly to porch climbers.[48]

To be sure, Lorimer was here speaking chiefly of the conservation of natural resources. His tone might have been different, even in those days, if the context had been a discussion of the conservation of human resources. But the *Post* did clearly recognize a need for government regulation of "the trusts." It printed an article on "The Business Man's Bogey Man; How Fear of Trusts Gags and Shackles the Average Business Man" and supplemented this with another asking, "Do the Trusts Own the Capital? How Their Hands Reach Into the Departments and Throttle the Ideal of Civil Service."

In 1912 Progressive citizens were asked to decide on methods of trust control between Roosevelt's "New Nationalism" and Wilson's "New Freedom." Roosevelt's program accepted a concentration of power, contended that some forms of trusts were necessary and desirable, but proposed to regulate them by government commission. The rhetoric of Wilson's speeches on the subject seemed, on the other hand, to call for a diffusion of power, for the dissolution of the larger existing trusts, and for government action to maintain free competition as itself the best guardian of the public interest. The *Post* gave a hearing in its pages to spokesmen for both alternatives. Lorimer left no doubt, however, that his sympathies lay with the "New Nationalism." He gave that program his editorial blessing and invoked impressively safe and respectable business figures to endorse it. George Perkins, a Morgan partner and a financial mainstay along with Munsey of the Progressive Party, was author of the major article explaining a moderate version of the Roosevelt policy. Editorially Lorimer cited the conservative names of Nicholas Murray Butler and Andrew Carnegie to support the inevitability of business consolidation accompanied by government regulation:

> No one whose views are worth considering doubts the economic advantages both of grand-scale production and of restriction of competition; but a great many who see that industrial combination is inevitable refuse to see that regulation of the combine in the interest of the public is equally inevitable. As President Butler of Columbia recently said: 'The era of unrestricted individual competition has gone forever. No president, attorney-general, court or congress can restore it.' . . . Indus-

> trial combination will go on, compelled by the law of economic development. Government regulation will go hand in hand with it, likewise compelled by the necessities of the case. Perhaps this will eventually mean an industrial commission, with the power even to fix maximum prices in certain cases, as Mr. Carnegie suggests; but no one can turn back the hand of the clock which has marked the irrevocable passing of unrestricted combination.[49]

The tone of the *Post*'s Progressivism remained cautious and moderate. It always seemed to be defending itself against possible criticism from the right. Its Progressive suggestions were justified as a recognition of "reality" not as the means to ideal goals or utopian visions.

The limits to the *Post*'s willingness to be critical of existing institutions were apparent in its attitude toward muckraking. Like Coolidge's preacher it did talk about sin, and it was against sin. But it talked about sin in general not about particular sinners. Where David Graham Phillips in *Cosmopolitan* exposed the "Treason of the Senate" by spelling out the specific financial interests behind particular senators, the *Post* printed Beveridge's general disapproval of "The Rich Man in Public Life" and William Allen White's criticism of "The Dollar in Politics." Likewise Phillips himself, when writing for the *Post,* stuck to a general critique of "Swollen Fortunes" and a general review of "The Trail of the Serpent; America's Clamor of Corruption and What It Really Means." Criticisms of business, though obviously well-informed, did not mention specific names in such articles as Henry Hyde's "Graft in Business" or his "Railway Rake-Offs; How Purchasing Agents Shake the Tree and Pocket the Plums." When the *Post* did actually name specific corporations, it was in articles defending them, as in J. Ogden Armour's defence of the meat-packers or in Archbold's defence of his own Standard Oil trust.*

* Four exceptions to this policy might be noted. In 1904 A. H. Lewis exposed "Tammany: Without and Within" and Edwin Lefevre wrote on the "Use and Abuse of Inside Information; The Loaded Dice and the

Not only did the *Post* defend businesses which were under attack in the muckraking magazines; it also ridiculed the muckrakers themselves. Samuel G. Blythe, the *Post*'s rather cynical Washington correspondent, wrote a caustic series in 1908 which purported to be advice for the would-be "conscientious young muckraker." "What you are striving to do," counseled Blythe, "is to help the reformers who are out and want to get control. Bear in mind that every man who is out is a reformer. Only the ins are corrupt." Blythe went on to give parodies of Lincoln Steffens and Upton Sinclair which he entitled "Contaminated Constantinople by Blinken Biffens" and "Orgies and Ogres by Sinton Eclair." [50] Wallace Irwin added to the *Post*'s derogation of its colleagues with a mocking piece on "The Shame of the College's" in which he reported:

> I have investigated Harvard University. It took nearly three hours to do the job; but I do not begrudge the time, because the scandal I unearthed is among the fifty or sixty Greatest Crimes of the Century. I am about to prove that, by educational collusion and brain-rebates, the institution at Cambridge has formed a monstrous monopoly which is today cornering and controlling one of the most useful products of our fruitful land. Harvard University—let her deny this if she can—is the Amalgamated-Gentleman Trust.[51]

The most devastating of the *Post*'s comments on muckraking appeared at the close of the year 1905 when several magazines were exultantly summing up the part they had played in bringing about exposure and reform in various fields. The *Post* too added

Men Who Use Them in the Wall Street Game" in which his chief criticism was directed at J. P. Morgan for not making U.S. Steel as sound industrially as it was financially. In 1910 S. G. Blythe blasted Senator Aldrich for his methods, his philosophy, and his financial connections. In 1913 Will Payne described "The Bossed Railroad" in an article on the New York, New Haven, and Hartford Railroad. In spite of these exceptions Lorimer's general policy was to avoid specific muckraking.

its conclusion on "The Lesson of Exposure" with an editorial which remarked: "The 'exposures' are teaching the people how to make and to save money. Who gets tired of going to a school where these exceedingly useful things are taught?" [52]

The *Post's* Progressivism, then, attempted to be a more cynical, more "realistic," more defensive brand than that displayed in some of its rivals. It particularly avoided any of the humanitarian concerns which appealed to some Progressives. The problems of labor, the evils of the slums, the conditions behind prostitution—all those matters which touched the sympathies of many middle-class citizens in this decade were ignored by the *Post*. Lorimer's magazine stuck directly to questions which obviously affected the lives and careers of the middle-class itself. The main concern remained for the preservation of "opportunity"—the opportunity to get into the great game of business, to secure independent capital, and to be all that was implied by an "individualist." James H. Collins was assigned to a series of articles on "Opportunity—Is It All Gone?" His findings indicated how "the trusts" had imposed limitations in various fields but concluded that opportunities remained abundant, particularly in the West. The columns of advice on investments and careers, the fictional tales of business success, the articles on the secrets of a merchant's rise, all these hammered home the lesson that despite the trusts and the plutocracy opportunity still existed. On this subject the *Post* displayed no cynicism and tolerated no ridicule. Yet the fear for "individualism" persisted and lay back of the magazine's receptivity to many Progressive measures.

Further to dispel that fear, the *Post* selected Alfred Henry Lewis, himself an arrant individualist and sometime muckraker, to write a series of articles on "The New Young Man." The series was designed to illustrate those fields in which individuals were finding outlets for self-expression and achievement and to prove

> The lie that a young man has no chance in these days of vast combinations of capital is nailed every time another leader

> appears. If there's any one thing that is not listed among antiques it is opportunity.[53]

By his third article in the series Lewis was vigorously asserting the preordained conclusion that, "The career of each of these is a refutation of the whining complaint, lifted up so frequently by a whimpering mediocrity, that victory of the individual, for the individual, by the individual, is no longer possible in this land." [54]

Ironically for the *Post,* however, none of the new young individualists portrayed by Lewis had made his career in business. They began with Judge Gaynor whose achievement lay in attacking a political machine. Next came Glasgow, the attorney who had won fame by attacking the Pennsylvania railroad. Included also were the first construction manager of the Panama Canal, a crusading district attorney, the young millionaire reform mayor of Milwaukee, and the reform mayor of Cleveland. These were strangely new versions of the success story, and Lewis was anxious to point new lessons. "For years," he protested, "we have taught that money is the one victory in life." If individualism were to survive, he claimed, we must break the restraining influence of "a nobility of gold":

> Everybody has struggled to get into their caste—the caste of the millionaire. It couldn't be done by prudent accumulation; no honest profit would serve. The one chance was to speculate —to gamble. . . .
>
> We should have a revival of the simplicity of the fathers! a moral awakening!—a return to old ideals. Somewhere between the preacher and the prosecuting attorney will lie the way. The preacher should thunder, the prosecutor indict. The one must lift up the work where the other lays it down.[55]

These were the roles of Roosevelt, of Bryan, of Hughes, of the new Commissioner of Corporations, James Garfield, of the New York District Attorney, William T. Jerome, and of "Moran of Massachusetts," another District Attorney. These were the functions of all the Progressive political preachers, investigators, and bureaucrats whom the *Post* praised in its biographical articles. Like Roosevelt, "the most conspicuous Individualist this country has ever seen," these men would ward off socialism, would "patch up the machine," would hold in careful check both organized plutocracy and organized labor, and above all would preserve a middle-class conception of individualism.

It was indeed surprising how completely this magazine dedicated to "the romance of business" found the heroes for its biographical articles in the ranks of Progressive politicians. The *Post* did not publish biographies as frequently as had the magazines of the previous decade. It averaged only one biographical article in every four or five issues.* Another major change was that a full 95 per cent of these articles were about Americans. The *Post* was already more isolationist in its concerns than any other national magazine. Among these American heroes businessmen took only a small part (five out of the forty biographies), and only one of these businessmen (Harriman) was still alive and active. In contrast to this neglect of contemporary business the *Post* gave nearly two-thirds (62.5 per cent) of its biographical attention to politicians, and nearly three-fourths of these were living, active candidates or officeholders.

What is more, the *Post* no longer found the achievement of high political office unquestioned evidence of a "successful" career. Biographers passed critical judgments on the activities of their subjects. Speaker Cannon had undoubtedly established his personal mastery over the House of Representatives. Senator Aldrich had clearly exercised influence over the Senate. Yet *Post* biographers described the careers of these conservative leaders only to bury them under ridicule and criticism not to praise them. In this decade the *Post*'s heroes were the Progressive politicians. Its villains were the stand-patters.

The overwhelming Progressive emphasis of the biographies in

* In our sample of 173 issues there were 40 biographical articles.

the *Saturday Evening Post* was a remarkable testimony to the strength of Progressivism in this decade and to the essentially middle-class character of its appeal. Even the magazine which spoke most admiringly and most realistically for the values of the middle-class business community found its actual contemporary heroes to be in government. Even the magazine which disdained any "Great Moral Purpose" hailed the political preachers of Progressivism. This orientation of the *Post's* sympathies from 1904 through 1913 was understandable only in the context of the *Post's* fears. At a time when great wealth seemed to threaten the living standards of the middle class, when urban conditions seemed to diminish its status in the community, when the unchecked sway of trusts seemed to curtail the possibilities for middle-class careers and to raise the spectre of socialism, at such a time as this the magazine of middle-class business could find common cause with Progressive politics and could find the exemplars and defenders of "individualism" among politicians and bureaucrats.

II

Munsey's Magazine

The biggest business organization under God's blue sky is the United States government. Beside it . . . every other corporation in America is but a pebble to a mountain. . . . I repeat, therefore, that we need a leader at the head of such an organization, the best man, the biggest man of all the men of the nation. It is not a question of what his politics is, but of what he is—what he can do.

Frank A. Munsey, 1908

The paths which led to Progressivism in this decade were multiple and diverse. The publisher of *Munsey's Magazine* found his way into the inner councils of the Progressive Party in 1912 by a shortcut which bypassed many of the usual Progressive concerns, most of the fervent Progressive rhetoric, and almost all of the distinctive Progressive reforms. The peculiar course of this path has often been lost sight of in general accounts of the movement, yet it formed an interesting part of the Progressive terrain. Perhaps too it was a fairly significant part since *Munsey's Magazine* averaged throughout the decade a circulation superior to all but one of the muckraking magazines. In any case, because that path was blazed with the marks of hero-worship for the powerful leader, its direction does help to locate the traces of the Progressive hero.

Frank Munsey was a strange figure in the ranks of the Bull Moose Party. He had little in common with those whom William Allen White remembered as the heart of the movement: "little businessmen, professional men, well-to-do farmers, skilled artisans from the upper brackets of organized labor . . . the successful middle-class country-town citizens, the farmer whose barn was painted, the well-paid railroad engineer, and the country editor." [56] He had nothing in common with the reformers who made the Progressive Party's convention resound to the strains of "Onward Christian Soldiers": the settlement-house workers, the municipal reformers, the opponents of child labor and of other abuses. He did not even fit in comfortably with the sophisticated George Perkins and the Ivy League group from Wall Street "who," White said, "had known Roosevelt in Harvard, loved him and misunderstood him." [57]

Despite his apparent incongruity it was Munsey as much as any other single supporter who made the Roosevelt campaign of 1912 a practical, feasible possibility. His biographer reports that the wealthy publisher contributed over a quarter-million dollars to campaign funds. In addition Munsey threw his newspapers and his magazine actively into the fight. He bought the *New York Press* for a million dollars in order to have a Roosevelt paper in that metropolis. He kept unprofitable papers going in Boston and Philadelphia as useful Roosevelt organs. His partisanship was said to have cost his various periodicals about a half-million-dollar loss in advertising revenue.[58] Although this may be an exaggerated statement of the actual expense of the campaign to Munsey, there is no doubt that his role was important or that he paid heavily for his support of T. R. The puzzling question is why this multi-millionaire spent anything at all in such a cause. The pages of *Munsey's Magazine* during the ferment of the Progressive years after 1903 demonstrate how many of the Progressive concerns were not shared by this man whose wealth had brought him into a state of "great, dizzy, dazzling, glorious intoxication." They do provide some clues, however, to the mood and the motivation which brought him to support Roosevelt in 1912.

No sense of any loss of status for the middle class ever influenced Munsey's responses or found its way into the pages of *Munsey's Magazine*. The publisher himself had never really known any of the security or satisfactions of middle-class life. From an impoverished boyhood and a desperate struggle for success in early manhood he had leaped to the ranks of the plutocracy. After 1900 only the rising returns on investments, not the higher cost of living, stirred his interest. As a bachelor who lived in a New York hotel suite he had no concern for the "servant question" or for any other pressures on the middle-class family. For him and consequently for his magazine the world seemed to be divided between those who had gained access to "riches, power, position, the world, the great big world" and those who still yearned for such good fortune. Middle-class consciousness in *Munsey's* was remarkable only for its absence.

Nor did Munsey look back nostalgically from the towers of New York to his rural origins in Maine. The magazine continued to dwell upon the sights and society of the big city. Its only glance at the life of an older America came when it raised the question, "Is the Country More Moral Than the City?" *Munsey's* answer was clearly negative.[59]

No sign of anxiety about the perquisites, privileges, or influence of great wealth was betrayed in the pages of *Munsey's*. On the contrary, the magazine extended into these Progressive years its unabashed admiration for the millionaire and his life. Readers were still exposed to accounts of "A Millionaire's Paradise," which described an exclusive island club for the very wealthy, and "Our Fleet of Floating Fortunes," which spoke glowingly of the most luxurious private yachts. A whole series of articles reported on "The Millionaire Yield" of Boston, of Cleveland, of Denver, and of other cities. An analysis of "The Progress in the Millionaire Business in America" concluded:

> The growth of mighty fortunes has merely kept pace with the growth of the whole nation's wealth. . . . The rich man to-day is richer than his predecessors; but the poor man has more comfort, more opportunity, and a better chance to rise than had the poor man in the past.[60]

Other magazines in these years were particularly distressed at the possibility that the new plutocracy might become a closed caste, what W. J. Ghent termed "our benevolent feudalism" or A. H. Lewis called a "nobility of gold." Even Andrew Carnegie had feared the effects upon American society of inherited wealth and position. *Munsey's Magazine,* however, during its second decade seemed to note with pleasure the ways in which children of the rich were beginning to take over key posts in finance and industry. "As a matter of fact," commented a lead article on "Successful Sons of Rich Men," "an important part of the rising generation of financiers is recruited from among the sons and grandsons of the money-kings of yesterday and today." It emphasized that "The sons of the rough-hewn and the self-made are often spendthrifts, while on the other hand, those who form part of a long, glittering, plutocratic chain frequently rival their forebears in their genius for money-making." The conclusion was that "such achievement holds out a healthy hope for our future." Another lead article followed out this tendency on Wall Street by hailing the "Crown Princes of Capital." A parallel development in industry was commended by noting that college graduates who were "the sons of United States senators, of multi-millionaires, of distinguished jurists, of clergymen, of railway presidents, and of foreign dignitaries" received special preference, special training, and "assured" advancement.[61] Now that Frank Munsey had made his millions he could look with some complacency upon signs that the ranks might be closing about him.

Munsey's Magazine also expressed no fears that the growth of trusts would handicap small business or limit individual opportunities. Munsey himself found continued fascination in these huge organizations:

> Personally I can think of nothing more interesting and more vital to people who think, and who stand for something in the country, than a knowledge of these great inter-State properties. They are so big, so vast, so dazzling in the magnitude of their figures, that they furnish a theme for intensely dramatic writing, viewed in no other sense.[62]

He commissioned H. N. Casson to write a series in this vein upon the largest of all the trusts: "The Romance of Steel and Iron in America—The Story of a Thousand Millionaires, and a Graphic History of the Billion-Dollar Steel Trust." To combat the current outcry against these industrial concentrations Casson further contributed an article called "Quebec—A Land Without Trusts":

> It is a land without a Carnegie, a Rockefeller, a Morgan, or a Harriman. It is the idyllic home of the small farm and the small factory. The railway octopus has practically no grip on this northern Eden.
>
> Yet . . . this land of freedom and equality is one of the least developed regions in the world. The mass of its people are poor.
>
> Now that the drums of an antitrust campaign are being beaten in almost every section of the United States, and that railroads and corporations are being pilloried as the enemies of progress

and prosperity, it is a striking fact that up in the strange land of Quebec the whole swing of public opinion is in the opposite direction.[63]

Clearly *Munsey's Magazine* demonstrated little of the characteristic Progressive tension about the new America, little of that anxiety which even the *Saturday Evening Post* displayed about the impact of cities, of millionaires, and of trusts upon older ways of life. Munsey himself described muckraking as "character slaughter and the destruction of institutions." He boasted that *Munsey's* had maintained a "constructive" attitude.[64] The magazine made little criticism of existing institutions even in general terms.*

Yet *Munsey's* also carried numerous articles and editorials in support of Theodore Roosevelt throughout the decade, culminating with monthly boosts for Roosevelt and the Progressive Party during the 1912 campaign. Other reform leaders appeared in its pages with increasing frequency and respect as the decade wore on. In 1905 La Follette had been dismissed as in fact "reactionary rather than progressive" because he was "hostile to the modern structure of industry and finance." [65] By 1907 *Munsey's* was picturing the Wisconsin Senator as a "man of destiny" and giving to him its highest encomium: "His attitude, in general, is rather that of a business man than of a politician or social reformer." [66] In succeeding years readers were introduced to "The Home Life of William Jennings Bryan" and assured that "If Bryan Is Elected to the Presidency," he would carry on the Roose-

* One author, Judson C. Welliver, did contribute a number of articles which approached some of the standard Progressive criticism. See "Washington, Our Beautiful Capital—Its Seamy Side," *Munsey's*, XL (November, 1908), 158; "The Passing of the Reactionary in American Politics," *Munsey's*, XL (January, 1909), 433; "The People's Rule Movement," *Munsey's*, XLIV (April, 1911), 19; "A Vitally Illuminating Article on a Criminally Corrupt Condition in the Republican Party," *Munsey's*, XLVI (January, 1912), 619. Welliver always struck a note in the magazine which was markedly different from the surrounding material.

velt policies and the Roosevelt "picturesqueness." [67] Progressive champions like Beveridge, Hughes, Dolliver, and Wilson were accorded favorable articles while Bryan and Beveridge themselves wrote political pieces for the magazine. To reconcile this attention to Progressive politicians and Munsey's own contributions to the Roosevelt campaign with the general context of thought and feeling which pervaded *Munsey's Magazine* obviously requires further explanation.

The usual answer of historians for Munsey's actions in the 1912 campaign is that Roosevelt seemed less threatening to big business than Wilson and more likely to win than Taft. That answer is certainly correct as far as it goes. Munsey's own appeals to businessmen to support the Progressive Party followed exactly that line of argument:

> Mr. Roosevelt will loom so big as the fighting force against radicalism and dangerous economic theories, that the men who wish to see the policies maintained that have built up industrial America will, before the middle of October, realize that the only way to save these policies is to get behind the man who can win —Theodore Roosevelt.[68]

This reasoning, however, still leaves some questions. Why did Munsey have such strong personal admiration for Roosevelt as he displayed throughout the decade? Why did Roosevelt's radical demand for the recall of judicial decisions not alienate the publisher as it did many conservative businessmen? Why did Munsey throw all his resources into this campaign when he had never before used his magazine for campaign purposes? Why did he leave his fascinating world of business and finance to engage in politics at all, particularly in such a risky enterprise as the Progressive Party? Some sense of Munsey's rather simple view of the world can help to explain his actions in 1912. An understanding of the hero-image revealed in *Munsey's Magazine* can illuminate his feelings for Roosevelt and his venture into politics.

All of Munsey's own writing reveals him as a man of moods and of impulses, not of ideas. His editorials were more expressions of feeling than of policy. At the heart of all his printed utterances was his reverence for wealth, for power, and for the men who possessed them. His world was simply divided between those who had "riches, position, power" and those who did not. He paid little attention to the latter class, and he made no significant distinctions among the former. *Munsey's Magazine* alone among the best-selling American periodicals of this decade devoted page after page to European aristocrats, to "The English Duchesses," to "The Value of Titles," to "The Remarkable Prominence and Popularity of Russian Aristocrats, Millionaires, and Diplomats in Cosmopolitan Society." These were reported with the same fascination as the lives of self-made American millionaires. *Munsey's* alone could describe with pride the success and "assured" positions being enjoyed by the sons of the rich without feeling any challenge to the traditional mythology of success. *Munsey's* alone could describe "The Great Labor Unions and Their Leaders" with no more serious social observation than that "The task of federating the thousand and one labor orders in the United States, Canada, and Mexico was as great an achievement, in its way, as the work of J. Pierpont Morgan and his associates in the building of giant corporations."[69] Frank Munsey's view, as revealed in the magazine whose contents he controlled closely, actually remained that of the poor boy who saw all people of power, prominence, or privilege as a single group. The great difference was that Munsey now could see himself as a member of that group.

A strong tendency toward paternalism stemmed from this vision and characterized Munsey's outlook. One of his editors said after his death, "Nothing would have pleased him so much as to have had his employees look upon him as a patriarch." He was an employer who "wanted to tell us all where to live, how to live, what to do with our money, how to bring up our children, and what to do with our time."[70] In a letter to Roosevelt early in

1912 Munsey extended his paternalism to the whole American people. Asking for a more "parental guardianship to the people," he wrote, "It is the work of the state to think for the people and plan for the people—to teach them how to do, what to do, and to sustain them in the doing." [71] Nothing could have been further from the general Progressive spirit or rhetoric; but with Munsey's simple vision of society and his urge to dominate, the "New Nationalism" may have seemed to the publisher a way to consolidate the nation under the guidance of leaders like Roosevelt and himself. The notion was not too far from his dream of uniting all newspapers into three great chains, one for each of the major parties and one for the independents. Munsey had little understanding and no personal sympathy for the democratic ideals which had been nourished in small towns. The power, privilege, and paternalism of strong men and vast organizations roused his admiration not his suspicions. For him the undiscriminating mood which had made Napoleon a national hero in the 1890's continued unabated. As much as any rational calculations about the best policies for business, this fascination with power drew Munsey toward Theodore Roosevelt and led him into politics.

Munsey recognized certain supermen in his contemporary world, men who were "great, rugged types of overpowering and compelling genius." Their number was limited:

> In literature we have Kipling. . . . In banking we have Morgan, the plumed knight of finance. . . . In business even, that vast arena in which tens of thousands measure their strength, we have less than half a dozen men of towering ability. Among these are John D. Rockefeller, Andrew Carnegie, and J. J. Hill. . . .
>
> Among rulers the old world has but one genius, one man who as both ruler and statesman stands conspicuously above all others of the present time—William of Germany. . . . The only other ruler in his class to-day in all the world is on this side of the Atlantic—our own President, Theodore Roosevelt.[72]

In Munsey's eyes Roosevelt was a "ruler," one of those few supermen who radiated the authentic aura of power. One did not question closely the policies of such a figure. It was a privilege to become his ally, to be admitted to his councils, to correspond regularly with him about ways "to think for the people and plan for the people."

The only significant change which the Progressive decade brought in the outlook of *Munsey's Magazine* and of its publisher can be put very simply. During these years Munsey came to see American politics as a dramatic area of power and to see Theodore Roosevelt as one of those Napoleonic leaders who captured the imagination. *Munsey's* lost none of its admiration for the great business organizations; it simply came to see the United States government as the biggest of them all. *Munsey's* lost none of its reverence for Morgan and Rockefeller; it simply found in Roosevelt a new superman. The magazine spelled this out clearly:

> The biggest business organization under God's blue sky is the United States government. Beside it . . . every other corporation in America is but a pebble to a mountain. . . .
>
> I repeat, therefore, that we need a leader at the head of such an organization, the best man, the biggest man of all the men of the nation. It is not a question of what his politics is, but of what he is—what he can do.[73]

The path of *Munsey's* to Progressivism was a simple extension of its course in the previous decade. No repudiation of past idols was expressed. No sense of crisis for the middle class or for individualism was involved. The course of events and particularly the dramatic personality of Roosevelt seemed to awaken the magazine to a new consciousness of politics as a further arena for the testing of strength. As early as 1904 *Munsey's* indicated this new interest with an article slanted in its own characteristic fashion: "Does Politics Pay?" The conclusion was that ". . . public life is by no means a barren or unattractive field to the youth of high ambition." * By the end of 1912 the magazine demonstrated a more sophisticated sense of the field in Beveridge's article on "The Sacrifices and Rewards of Politics." These two articles at the beginning and close of the decade together with the uncritical admiration for Roosevelt and the unremitting lust for power of Frank Munsey give the essential clues for understanding how *Munsey's Magazine* became involved in the Progressive Party's campaign.

In this kind of response to the ferment of this decade *Munsey's* was unique among the magazines. *Munsey's* alone seemed to feel no essential break between the attitudes of the 1890's and those of the Progressive years, to sense no need for repudiating the older heroes. *Munsey's* alone exposed no villains in its biographical articles. Only in *Munsey's* did there still appear an article on "Napoleon, the Greatest Man in the History of the World" and another defending John D. Rockefeller. Among biographies from the four best-selling magazines *Munsey's* contributed about two-thirds of those on artists, actors, and actresses along with an equally high proportion of those on foreign rulers and aristocrats. Unlike its new rivals, *Munsey's* continued to present many of the same kinds of heroes whom it had honored in the previous decade. But there was one striking difference. It now printed half again as many biographies of political figures as it had previously done. They were Progressive politicians on both the national and local level. To these were added in several biographies an entirely new type of hero, the government bureaucrat. The new focus of attention for *Munsey's* emerged particularly after 1909. Foreign rulers together with actors, actresses, and artists virtually disappeared from the magazine which turned to honor governmental leaders in half the biographies of these closing four years.

* Francis B. Gessner, "Does Politics Pay?" *Munsey's*, XXXI (September, 1904), 801. Interestingly enough none of the men cited at this time as proof of the rewards of a political career were elected officials. They included only cabinet members and bureaucrats, most of whom were noted for their subsequent profitable careers in private industry or finance.

Munsey's was slow to respond to Progressive changes in popular attitudes. When it did change, that response did not spring from the usual Progressive anxieties or idealism. The shift in *Munsey's* seemed to be primarily a recognition that government in America had become a newly important and dramatic center of power. The significant contribution of *Munsey's* in a chronicle of changing American heroes was to demonstrate that the new political heroes of the Progressive decade could be viewed by some as logical extensions and additions to the forceful, Napoleonic types revered a decade earlier. More than any other popular magazine *Munsey's* cast the new heroes in the old mold.

III
Everybody's

We beheld the wonderful vision of owning a great magazine property without the long, hard preparatory struggle of a 'Munsey' or a 'McClure.'

John Adams Thayer, Astir

In 1905 John Adams Thayer, one of the publishers of *Everybody's,* gave a dinner to celebrate the amazing success of the magazine. Only two years had passed since Thayer and his two partners had bought control of the publication for a modest $75,000. Now the whole nation seemed conscious of *Everybody's.* Its circulation was leaping by 50,000 every month as Americans flocked to read the latest revelations in "Frenzied Finance," Thomas W. Lawson's inside story exposing the machinations of Wall Street. *Everybody's* was proving that muckraking could pay sensationally well. It was on its way to being one of the two most popular magazines of the decade, surpassed only by Lorimer's *Post.*

According to the publishers themselves, this success was built largely upon the magazine's exposure of the madness in money-making. They noted with satisfaction that clergymen were using as texts for sermons some articles from *Everybody's* on "The Madness of Much Money" and "Successful Men Who Are Not Rich." In his autobiography Thayer would quote proudly from a contemporary newspaper comment about their new enterprise: "Now it has found itself entered on its own mission, headed out on its particular crusade. . . . [*Everybody's*] shows a purpose to depart from the baleful worship of Mammon and its possessors, which characterizes so much of the writing in current periodicals." [74]

One can understand, then, why a certain note of irony pervaded the newspaper account of Thayer's dinner in 1905. This festive occasion was held at the St. Regis. The meal was served on gold plates. The menus were bound in leather. "It was," wrote the reporter, "a feast fit to celebrate a six-month's hunt for the money devil." Beside the place of each guest appeared a special telephone. At 10:00 P.M. Tom Lawson himself called from Boston and spoke for twenty minutes to the assembled celebrants. "Lawson," the report said, "complimented Thayer on his prosperity in battling with the armies of greed and their vulgar display of ill-gotten wealth." [75]

The same sort of irony ran through many aspects of this enterprise. Lawson has always been noted as an odd figure among the muckrakers.[76] A multi-millionaire stock promoter who had fallen out with the Standard Oil group of financiers, he seemed to be moved to his dramatic exposures as much by desires for revenge and personal fame as for reform. Since he continued speculating in stocks during the publication of his articles and since he had previously reaped most of his profits as a "bear," it was even suggested that "Frenzied Finance" was part of a scheme to depress stock prices for personal gain. The publishers, in turn, added another ironic footnote to the story. In a brief history of *Everybody's* which appeared in the magazine two years after its sensational attack upon the Standard Oil financiers, they recalled how they had been trying to secure Rockefeller's autobiography for the magazine when suddenly the chance came to get Lawson's series instead.[77]

The fact was that *Everybody's* represented a strictly professional magazine enterprise. No single man dominated the magazine or used it to express his personal views. The owners and staff were professional magazine men with long experience in the business. Though they occasionally printed a column of commentary entitled simply "With *Everybody's* Publishers," they ran no regular editorial page. What they desired to publish, as one partner stated, was "something worth telling, something people would be eager to read, something which would boom our circulation." Their vision, as another one put it, was "the wonderful vision of owning a great magazine property without the long hard preparatory struggle of a 'Munsey' or a 'McClure.'" In achieving this vision they succeeded beyond all expectations. By 1910 they were able to sell *Everybody's* to the Butterick Publishing Company for $3,000,000—a sum forty times that which they had paid to acquire the magazine in 1903.[78]

If his own account can be believed, John Adams Thayer was the moving spirit in organizing the venture. In many ways Thayer represented the entrepreneur type of a Munsey or a Curtis. His autobiography testifies to his fascination with his own successful career. He had, however, gained much more experience in the magazine business than either of these predecessors before becoming a publisher himself. Beginning as a printer, Thayer had for six years been advertising manager of the *Ladies' Home Journal*, for one month business manager of *Munsey's*, and for four years advertising director of *Delineator*. His horizons also were not so limited and parochial as those of Munsey and Curtis. His parents had been abolitionists; his mother had written for "The Lowell Offering"; he took great pride in cleaning the patent-medicine advertising out of the *Ladies' Home Journal*; at the peak of prosperity for *Everybody's* he retired and went to live for five years in Paris where he wrote the story of his own success in French, *Les Étapes du Success*; he returned to become owner and publisher of the magazine *Smart Set*.[79]

The other active partner in the Ridgway-Thayer Publishing Company had also had extensive experience in the magazine world. Erman J. Ridgway had been general manager for *Munsey's* from 1894 to 1903. His responsibilities had lain in the manufacture of the magazine rather than in its editorial direction; but on *Everybody's* it was Ridgway who selected the editor and maintained an interest in the contents. If *Everybody's* did show some "purpose to depart from the baleful worship of Mammon and its possessors," perhaps one may read this in part as the natural response of a one-time honors graduate from Yale who had escaped from ten years of service under Frank A. Munsey.[80]

John O'Hara Cosgrave was the man hired as editor for *Everybody's*. He could boast a more cosmopolitan background than most American magazine men. Born in Australia, educated in New Zealand, Cosgrave had served fourteen years as a reporter and editor in San Francisco before coming to New York to be editor of *Everybody's* under its previous ownership. Ridgway and Thayer agreed to keep him on in this post, and Cosgrave responded by showing a great capacity to gather striking features for the magazine.

These men produced a best-selling periodical which seems more difficult to characterize than any of its rivals. It did not have the strong middle-class consciousness of the *Post*, the ardent admiration for power and wealth of *Munsey's*, or the balanced discrimination of *Collier's*. Its varied contents leave an impression of openness, of optimism, and even of innocence. These also seem to be important aspects of Progressive America, and in this sense *Everybody's* reveals further dimensions of the Progressive terrain.

The magazine's openness to many aspects of contemporary life was evident in the publisher's description of their "average reader":

> One of the traits which seem to be peculiar to you is your marvelous desire to learn about almost every conceivable subject. . . . Doubtless this is partly due to curiosity, but in the main it is a real passion to know things and their why.[81]

This wide-ranging curiosity led *Everybody's* to run exposures of stock-market manipulation, the meat-packing trust, "West Coast Land Grafters," business corruption of the judiciary, labor conditions in the coal mines and in the steel industry, occupational disease, and the unpreparedness of the army. It explored such relatively complex topics as banking reform and "The Single Taxers: Who They Are and What They Are Doing." It carried Progressivism abroad by muckraking "A King in Business: Leopold II of Belgium, Autocrat of the Congo and International Broker," as well as by running Charles Edward Russell's series on "Soldiers of the Common Good," a survey of the more progressive men, movements, and measures in various foreign countries. In actual fact, however, *Everybody's* did not seem to wish to learn "about almost every conceivable subject." Its interests were largely restricted to economic and political topics, though it ranged widely within these fields. Here again the magazine seemed symptomatic of its age. In spite of all the contemporary talk about "a spiritual awakening," the Progressive definition of reality was almost exclusively economic and political.

Most relevant for the purpose of this study was a second attitude which the publishers projected upon their "average reader":

> Another trait which no other people has in such marked degree is your hero-worship. You dearly love a man who 'makes good.' You throw yourself before your heroes in a perfect abandon of devotion and admiration. You are almost capable of admiring John D. Rockefeller, because he is unquestionably the best in his line.

Everybody's included a relatively high proportion of biographies for this period. Though it did not finally secure John D. Rockefeller's autobiography, it did run more eulogies of businessmen than any of our other magazines. Yet *Everybody's* also, more consciously and more explicitly than any of its rivals, discussed the tension between an older model of success and the new conditions of American life.

Since *Munsey's* had embodied the older success image in its crudest form, it is tempting to see the tension evident in *Everybody's* as the effort of Erman Ridgway to expose the limitations of his former employer. Read in this light, a short story by O. Henry takes on a more specific significance within the pages of Ridgway's magazine. The story was called "A Ruler of Men," and it satirized the Napoleonic personality. Its hero eventually finds happiness in pushing people around as a subway guard. An even more frequent target for *Everybody's* was the uncritical reverence for wealth which a Frank Munsey felt. The magazine printed Charles E. Russell's series exposing the origins of various contemporary fortunes ("Where Did You Get It, Gentlemen?"). It criticized Marshall Field at length because he had devoted himself exclusively to "money-getting" and "never took the least public interest in any movement to secure better conditions." It deplored the pressures for notoriety and commercialism in the literary world. Though its pronouncements on these matters often seem the most platitudinous posturing, they expressed an idealism which *Munsey's* could never even perceive and an innocence which the *Saturday Evening Post* would scorn.[82]

The real novelty in the attitude of *Everybody's* toward the successful life, however, lay in its readiness to dramatize heroism in previously unheralded vocations. Ridgway and Cosgrave published a relatively low proportion of biographical articles on Progressive politicians—low at least for this period.* But one-third of their biographies described lives which had seldom attracted the attention of general magazines. One might dismiss "Mike Martin, Fire-Truck Driver," as a standard adolescent's hero. The article on "A Mother of Americans: The Story of an Immigrant Woman's Life of Wise Sacrifice for a New Generation," however, revealed a more open view both of Americanism and of heroism than was usual. The special distinction of *Everybody's* lay in its attention to bureaucrats working for the public

* Politicians were featured in 20 per cent of the biographies in *Everybody's* while they filled 34 per cent of the biographies in our sample for all four magazines from 1904 through 1913.

good. This concern ranged over such figures as "A Golden Rule Chief of Police," a government surveyor in Alaska who sought no gold for himself but whose efforts had opened up opportunities for others, to a labor leader who had fought to liberate his fellow men.

Everybody's consciously sought to redefine the meaning of success amid "conditions in our common life unlike any that men have ever faced before." It solicited responses from an international group of leaders on the question, "What Is a Good Man?" [83] Yet *Everybody's* also sought to rehabilitate business and financial success in a way which might stand the test of the new skepticism:

> Success! The time is passing when the mere sordid accumulation of vast wealth may be acclaimed Success. We are learning to make distinctions. The financial brigand, trickster, grafter, however richly he may have reaped is being classed with his brother crooks. But all the world wants to know about Real Success, about men whose personal triumphs have meant benefits multiplied a hundredfold for the nation; men who, in blazing their own trails, have opened wide, safe, clean paths for their countrymen. A series of stories about such men—veritable 'Romances of Success'—begins below with an intimate story of James J. Hill.[84]

These biographies—studies "in individual contributions to our civilization"—argued that men like Hill, George Westinghouse, and Cyrus McCormick proved "clean success" still possible and "that honest men have not died out among our captains of industry." [85]

Everybody's offered its readers a more varied and more sensational assortment of inside stories on corruption and chicanery than any of its best-selling rivals. It more explicitly condemned "money-getting" and more consciously sought to define new standards for success. It found models for that success not merely among Progressive politicians but also among more obscure areas of public service and private heroism. At the same time, this magazine was published by professional magazine men who avoided much direct editorial comment and who made a striking personal financial success from the venture. They greatly enjoyed and celebrated that success, and they printed biographies to laud the enduring worth of "clean success."

From the perspective of a more cynical era one may see only the ironies in this enterprise. To do so, however, would be to lose sight of some particular attitudes which contributed to this Progressive decade. There was little hint of cynicism in the pages of *Everybody's*. The tone of the magazine was openness not defensiveness, optimism not anxiety. The final impression left upon a modern reader is one of refreshing innocence, an innocence based upon the assumption that all the moral tensions of a changing life could be resolved by exposing them—and that it was possible to make a neat, clean profit in the process.

IV
Collier's Weekly

It did not take long for us to jump to the first place,
as far as public influence was concerned,
among the publications of the country.

Norman Hapgood, The Changing Years

It became, and for years remained, the most
influential periodical in the country, in many respects
the most distinguished America has ever had.

Mark Sullivan, The Education of an American

When the men who had edited *Collier's Weekly* during the Progressive decade came to write their autobiographies, they looked back upon this magazine as the most distinguished and the most influential periodical of its time. They would have dismissed the *Saturday Evening Post* as philistine, *Munsey's* as vulgar, and *Everybody's* as sensational. Whatever the objective truth about its editors' claim to paramount influence, the claim itself is a good clue to the distinctive mood of *Collier's* in these years. For this short period of its long career the popular weekly was in the hands of young men who felt themselves in the forefront of the movement to purify and invigorate national life. They made it very much a magazine of the new Progressive generation. Perhaps only in the Progressive decade could special personal and historical circumstances have combined to produce a best-selling periodical like the *Collier's* of 1904 to 1913.

The remarkably fortunate position enjoyed by *Collier's* had its origins a generation earlier in the enterprise of a young Irish immigrant. Peter F. Collier had begun selling Catholic Bibles early in the 1870's and soon developed effective techniques for the mass sale of popular and classical works to families of modest means. He built up a national organization which through agents and through the mails sold books on the installment plan. By the time of his death in 1909, P. F. Collier had distributed fifty-two million books and had earned eighty million dollars.[86] As a premium to encourage book sales he started a weekly magazine in 1888. After ten years of changing policies under a variety of editors, *Collier's Weekly* was turned over to the youthful direction of its founder's only son.

Robert J. Collier possessed all the advantages which his father's wealth could provide. He came to his new editorial post fresh from an education at Georgetown, followed by a year's residence at Oxford. The highest circles of New York society were opened to him by his marriage to a granddaughter of Mrs. William Astor, the reigning queen of the Four Hundred. At his country estate in New Jersey he entertained lavishly, went fox-hunting, played polo, flew in airplanes (as early as 1911), and gathered a wide circle of friends. Handsome, elegantly dressed, with great personal charm, a flair for the dramatic gesture, and a buoyant Irish humor, Rob Collier displayed a grace, an assurance, and an easy democracy which a self-made millionaire like Frank Munsey found unattainable. In *Collier's Weekly* the young man saw the opportunity to prove himself in his own right by making the magazine something more than a tender to his father's book business.

His first impulse was to give the magazine "a little true literary flavor in the style of the *Yellow Book* and the more esoteric *fin de siecle* literary circles." On the cover he placed the picture of a Greek goddess and a cryptic Greek motto. Inside he ran as a serial Henry James's *The Turn of the Screw,* adorned with illustrations by John La Farge. The impact of the Spanish American War, however, abruptly reversed this initial direction and, as in the case of other magazines, showed Collier the dramatic possibilities of public affairs when covered by the new breed of correspondents and photographers like Richard Harding Davis and James Hare:

> It was at that time, when I had been fitting myself to become the editor of the *Athenaeum* or the *Yellow Book,* that the *Maine* blew up and Jimmy Hare blew in. Sending Hare to Havana that morning involved me in more troubles and wars and libel suits than any one act in my life. It turned me from the quiet paths of a literary career into association with war correspondents, politicians, muckrakers and advertising men.[87]

No longer did the young editor seek to establish his own identity by association with the more sophisticated aesthetes. He saw the chance to gain a wide reputation for his magazine by making it "in national journalism what a good citizen is to his community." [88] He spent his money freely for the best illustrators and cartoonists. He paid top prices for fiction and articles. He gave unexcelled coverage to dramatic events like the Russo-Japanese War and the San Francisco earthquake. But to gain stature and influence he felt the need for editorial pages which would be read by the nation and respected by the intelligent. For this purpose he hired Norman Hapgood in 1902.

Hapgood represented an element of society which had not been tapped by Peter Collier's book agents and which was not yet much aware of Robert Collier's weekly; "nobody of my acquaintance," Hapgood remembered, "read the magazine, or even knew its name." [89] If true, this meant that *Collier's* had made little impact among the former Mugwumps or the young generation of intellectuals stemming from them. Hapgood came from old Puritan stock. His father had been a well-to-do independent manufacturer in the Middle West, but the family had many connections in the worlds of politics, literature, and the theatre. Norman Hapgood had been a top student at Harvard, editor of the *Harvard Monthly,* and friendly with William Vaughn Moody, Santayana, and Robert Herrick. He had graduated with honors from Harvard Law School and taken a post with a firm in Chicago which did little but estate and corporation business. Thoroughly bored by this kind of practice, Hapgood abandoned the law and followed the course then being taken by others of his background and tastes who disliked business. He entered the newly attractive field of journalism. A job with Godkin's *Evening Post,* the most respectable of Mugwump newspapers, gave him thorough training as a reporter. A stint as drama critic on the *Commercial Advertiser* nourished his critical faculties and won him some reputation with what he called "the thinking minority." Finley Peter Dunne, the creator of "Mr. Dooley," who served in many ways at this time as the link between the world of the second-generation Irish immigrants and that of the young intellectuals from Mugwump antecedents, suggested Norman Hapgood's name to Robert Collier for the new editorial post.

As custodian of the two editorial pages dramatically displayed in the front of *Collier's Weekly,* Hapgood was no radical campaigner for social reform. At Harvard he and some kindred spirits had formed the Laodicean Club, "based on the idea that Paul was too hard on the church that was in Laodicea, when he attacked it for being neither hot nor cold, and that there was much to say for the balanced attitude of that seldom-praised institution." [90] The characteristic notes of the new editorial comments in *Collier's,* therefore, were a gentle irony and a balanced discrimination. These served to give the magazine that tone of slight intellectual distinction which Rob Collier had been seeking. But they also proved remarkably effective at involving the magazine upon occasion in forms of muckraking for Progressive causes. A sly editorial thrust at William Jennings Bryan, for example, plunged *Collier's* into its first campaign of exposure against patent medicines. Hapgood had noted briefly the ironic fact that Bryan's *Commoner,* while berating the trusts, ran an advertisement for a medicine which promised to cure everything from cancer to dandruff, surely a monopoly in healing if the claims were true. The protests from Bryan and the patent-medicine manufacturer led *Collier's* to print a distinguished series of articles exposing "The Poison Trust" and the control which the patent-medicine industry had established over newspapers and magazines. This campaign also brought to the magazine Mark Sullivan, the last of that triumvirate of editors who made *Collier's* a leader in the Progressive decade.

Mark Sullivan's career had curiously overlapped at points both those of Collier and of Hapgood. Sullivan's parents had been Irish immigrants who lived out their lives thriftily and modestly on a small Pennsylvania farm. Though he always looked back upon the farm and the small town as the seat of all essential American virtues, the son had early abandoned farming for the management of a country newspaper. The returns from this venture enabled him to graduate from Harvard, and he then put himself through Harvard Law School by writing feature articles for a Boston newspaper. Although he lacked Hapgood's strong literary and artistic interests, Sullivan also found the practice of law a pale attraction beside the journalistic coverage of American life. S. S. McClure had identified him as a promising writer; Edward Bok commissioned him to investigate the relations between patent medicines and the press. When the subsequent article proved too lengthy for Bok, *Collier's* bought it for its own campaign against the patent medicines and hired the author for a regular position on the staff in 1906. Admiring both his superiors for their very different abilities, Sullivan soon came to share in the editorial decisions and personal relations of Collier and Hapgood. His particular field became political reporting, and he threw himself and the magazine wholeheartedly behind the Progressive effort to gain control of Congress during the Taft administration. Sullivan brought to the magazine a trained capacity for digging out facts, a clear, simple style, and most importantly a familiarity with small towns and with the more unsophisticated American attitudes which neither of his colleagues could equal.[91]

Despite the diversity in their backgrounds, these three men shared certain attributes which gave a distinctive character to the Progressivism of *Collier's*. In the first place they were all remarkably young. When Sullivan joined them in 1906, he was thirty-one, Collier was thirty-three, and Hapgood thirty-seven. Each of them, in addition, had strong personal reasons for being conscious of his place in a new generation.* Their magazine reflected a youthful zest, an optimism, a sense of adventure and of new possibilities. If Progressivism was to some extent a younger generation's revolt against the standards of its fathers, the editors of *Collier's* were appropriate leaders for a Progressive journal.

As editors of a best-seller they also had a remarkably high level of education. To this they added a circle of friends which reached up to include Mark Twain, Louis Brandeis, William

* Collier and Sullivan were the American-born sons of immigrant parents. Collier had the problem of a wealthy son who must establish a personal identity apart from his self-made father. Sullivan had made an obvious break with his parent's rural life. Hapgood gave the title "Revolt" to that chapter of his autobiography which recounted his decisions to eschew his father's plow-manufacturing business and to quit the practice of law.

James, and President Eliot of Harvard—men who were beyond the range of Lorimer, Munsey, and Cosgrave. Ideas consequently did not frighten them. Intelligent social criticism seemed natural to them. They could engage in it with ease, confidence, and discrimination. Legal training, moreover, gave Hapgood and Sullivan a respect for factual evidence and an assurance of safety in libel suits. If Progressivism was a movement in which the educated took an unusual role in popular leadership, *Collier's* again was the key Progressive journal.

The most significant characteristic which they shared, however, was a certain distaste for the life of business. They were not actively hostile toward business so much as they were bored by it and attracted by other pursuits. Robert Collier found life too full of social, sporting, and journalistic excitements to pay much attention to business affairs, as he proved to the detriment of the magazine after his father's death. Hapgood, of course, had foregone both his father's business and corporation law in favor of journalism, literature, and the theatre. Sullivan, even in law school, had always found his greatest satisfactions in journalism. The one alternative about which he spoke with some nostalgia was the simple, frugal, independent life on his parents' farm. None of them seems to have thought much about *Collier's* as a business enterprise. So long as P. F. Collier's wealth stood behind it, they had no need for great concern. Even the circulation figures were comfortably boosted by the father's book agents.[92] The sense of freedom which this arrangement gave to Rob Collier was expressed in his sole comment on the magazine's economic status in a long review of its origin and its goals: "My father . . . gave me a paper to edit over which no political or financial interest has been permitted to acquire a shadow of control." [93] No other magazine with the circulation of *Collier's* could afford to be as cavalier about its position. No other editors of a popular periodical could be as free to look with gentle amusement upon business idols and business values. If Progressivism in one of its aspects was a challenge by intellectuals to the dominance of business in America, *Collier's* alone among the best-selling magazines could join in that challenge with few reservations.

The result of its editors' predilections and its own fortunate position made *Collier's* noticeably different from its weekly rival, the *Saturday Evening Post.* The *Post's* aura of glamour and compulsion about business success was lacking. When *Collier's* ran a column of advice on investments, it was simply headed: "The Average Man's Money, News and Comment for Investors." Though *Collier's* also believed that the average man was actually in a position to invest, it did not dramatize that pursuit as the struggle for a fortune. The *Post's* intense anxiety about the squeeze upon middle-class business opportunities appeared rarely and with changed emphasis in *Collier's.* Though W. J. Ghent did clearly demonstrate in "The Changing Order" how the plutocracy was threatening the middle class, Ghent was himself a socialist and *Collier's* seemed to treat the article as an interesting social essay rather than a reason to man the middle-class barricades. When *Collier's* printed business fiction, it was more likely to be a somewhat playful social critique or a sheer fantasy than a realistic portrayal of the "great game" of business. A short story called "The Middle Ground," for example, presented an industrialist who knew "no law but prudence, no honor but expediency." "Anarchists, Socialists, and all who preached the survival of the unfit, and who screeched for the equality of the unequal, cited him as their strongest argument." But his son, the hero of the story, went to live with the workers and discovered that the union was the middle ground between ruthless capitalism and irresponsible anarchism.[94] Such a conclusion, however, did not prove the editors' allegiance to unionism. They also published "The Adventures of a Scab" which was a light-hearted account of how a college boy spent his summer vacation helping to defeat a union strike. In the approach of *Collier's* to the world of business there remained a certain detachment. The height of frivolity and Irish fantasy was reached in a story about a German invasion of

England in which the English Army was led by an American, "The Eminent Financier." He allowed the struggle to continue long enough to kill off all the unemployed and to bring stock prices to the bottom. Then a squadron of nearly invisible sky-blue planes manned by Yale alumni from the class of 1900 defeated the invaders, and the financier sold for a huge profit the stocks which he had picked up at rock-bottom prices.[95] Clearly *Collier's* could display a kind of exuberant freedom from the piety and seriousness with which other magazines usually clothed stories of business success.

If *Collier's* felt free to indulge occasionally in fantasy, it was also free to make serious attacks upon a good number of vested interests. The history of the magazine's various muckraking campaigns has been told often and at length. What is relevant here is to note the particular kinds of abuses which roused its wrath. *Collier's* did not seem to care much about the ways in which trusts and plutocrats were taking unfair advantage of middle-class business and small investors. It ran nothing like Tarbell's exposure of Standard Oil. It paid little attention to the general business handicaps which disturbed the *Post.* It had nothing but scorn for Lawson's whole series on "Frenzied Finance." *Collier's* reserved its indignation for the ways in which American citizens were being wronged in their capacities as consumers, as readers, and as voters. The great campaigns which Collier, Hapgood, and Sullivan sponsored were against the patent medicines which made millions by doping and poisoning their customers, against the newspapers which slanted and suppressed news for financial gain, against the opening of the public domain in Alaska and the West to private exploitation, and against the control of Congress by men acting in behalf of great financial interests. What most distressed these young men who had little personal liking for business was the widespread commercialization of American life. There was something of the Tory Democrat about the outlook of Collier and Hapgood at least. They looked with a certain condescension and amusement upon trickery within the marketplace, but they rose in anger when the values of the marketplace threatened to demean American society.

This attitude was apparent in *Collier's* at many points. The magazine first gained national attention by its successful attack upon the editor of *Town Topics,* a metropolitan gossip sheet which preyed upon high society by accepting "loans" for the suppression of unfavorable comments. The direct beneficiaries of this attack were such men as W. K. Vanderbilt, J. P. Morgan, the speculator James R. Keene, and the steel-trust executive, Charles M. Schwab, all of whom had "lent" large sums to the scandal-sheet publisher.[96] But what brought Hapgood and Collier into the fight was a brief item about Alice Roosevelt, the President's daughter, which greatly offended their sense of honor and decency. Their attitude was evident also in the magazine's treatment of John D. Rockefeller. It poked fun at him for his narrow pecuniary interests in "Sunday School Stories; Tales of How John D. Rockefeller Accumulated Some of His Money," which told among other things how as a boy the industrialist had bargained shrewdly over a Bible cover. Yet while other muckraking magazines were thoroughly berating Rockefeller's business tactics, *Collier's* printed "One Kind Word for John D." which pointed out that he had at least been a "creative" millionaire and had never tried to fool the people into liking him. What *Collier's* advocated was to give commercialism its due place but not to glorify it, in short, to keep it within proper bounds. The main task, Hapgood suggested in an editorial, was to enforce the laws "with subordination of the dollar to the sense of human right." [97]

A somewhat greater concern for social justice was a natural part of this viewpoint. *Collier's* supported a wider range of Progressive reforms than any of its best-selling rivals. Its interest in railroad rate regulation and the direct election of senators was shared by most of the others. But *Collier's* went beyond this in its advocacy of measures with social or humanitarian implications like the income tax, child labor laws, settlement houses, slum clearance, and woman suffrage. At one time, to be sure, Mark

Sullivan proposed a wholly reactionary solution for the problems of the urban lower classes:

> As we hinted the other day, most of the city dwellers, whom the reformers seek to mark as objects of pity and governmental solicitude, could cure many of their own ills by a thirty-mile walk into the country. . . . Any sweatshop worker can give his children much more than Lincoln's start by a two days' walk in the country and a self-abnegation sufficient to deny himself Coney Island and the corner saloon.[98]

Yet this too was merely a former farm boy's way of protesting the commercialization of city life. *Collier's* remained consistent in trying to subordinate the dollar to "the sense of human right."

When *Collier's* turned to biographies, therefore, its aim was to celebrate what it called "uncommercialized achievement." Rob Collier explained what he meant by this term:

> Wherever men are applying ideas to life, and lifting the community by battling disease, delving into the unguessed reactions of chemical compounds—wherever they are lighting up darkened minds by making knowledge democratic and vital—there it is imperative that the story shall be told so that the faithful country doctor and the village schoolm'am and loyal workers everywhere may catch the hint and pour that betterment into their own community.[99]

In practice this goal meant that the biographies in *Collier's* presented a wider range of American society than had been customary in other magazines. Within a one third sample of its biographical articles appeared a relatively high proportion of clergymen, medical scientists, bureaucrats, and "soldiers of fortune." At the beginning of the decade the emphasis on "uncommercial" heroes was carried out in a series by Richard Harding Davis on colorful, contemporary "soldiers of fortune" like the young Englishman Winston Churchill. By the end of the decade this emphasis had turned more exclusively to the American scene and to social questions with a series on "Man-to-Man Preachers," clergymen who had taken active parts in civic reforms. A belief in "The Uplifting Influence of Outdoor Life" produced not only a regular section on "Outdoor America" but also unusual biographical articles on "outdoor" figures like a mountain climber or a champion walker. A great variety of new types of heroes and heroines appeared in a series of "Interviews with the Undistinguished" and another on "Everyday Americans." Here were the life stories of a farmer, a farmer's wife, a household servant, a sweat-shop girl, a schoolteacher, a policeman, an editor, a poet, and other Americans outside the business class. When *Collier's* did turn to notice businessmen, it adopted a condescending attitude toward John D. Rockefeller, blasted the ethics of C. W. Post, manufacturer of Grape-Nuts, or praised an advertising leader for his civic activities. The major field for "uncommercial achievement," however, remained the area of politics. The particular concern of *Collier's* led it to join its rivals in concentrating over one-third of its biographies on contemporary American politicians.

The youth, the education, the freedom from business idolatry, and the diverse backgrounds of its editors which cut outside the customary limits of the Anglo-Saxon, middle-class, Protestant core of Progressivism—all these gave *Collier's* a wider sense of American life and a greater range for its biographical attention. The editors' success in libel suits, their assured social position, their distaste for commercialism, and the magazine's freedom from financial concern also gave *Collier's* a greater boldness in biographical criticism. About one-fifth of all its biographies treated contemporary "villains" with a humorous, ironic, factual, devastating critique. Businessmen and especially stand-pat politicians allied with business interests were the favorite targets for attack.

In the creation of a composite magazine hero for the Progressive decade, *Collier's* emphasized more than any of its rivals those elements which made for a new model of success in America.

American historians ordinarily pay little attention to the role of popular magazines. In general histories of the United States only the magazines of the Progressive period have been deemed worthy of consideration, and among those only the muckrakers have received serious scholarly inquiry.

Certainly historians have been right in sensing that magazines achieved a peak of national influence and importance during this decade. Scholars may have been less judicious in focusing their interest almost entirely upon the articles of exposure. The fundamental historical question is not why muckraking arose and then declined. The real question is how Americans responded to changing historical conditions in the early years of the twentieth century. Seldom have American popular magazines shown such a clear consciousness of change and such an extended exploration of its meaning. Muckraking formed only one part of the exploration and the response. A broader investigation of the decade's best-selling magazines reveals that many diverse streams fed into the main current of Progressivism.

Historians have debated how radical the Progressive movement actually was. While this broader look at popular magazines discloses much of the diversity and wide extent of Progressivism, it also confirms much of the basic conservatism of the movement. A closer look at the Progressive model of success will provide a more precise sense of this conservatism. To what extent did Americans in this decade repudiate the Napoleonic model of forceful individualism?

Chapter 6

The Hero as Politician

That decade which climaxed in 1912 was a time of
tremendous change in our national life, particularly
as it affected our national attitudes. The American people
were melting down old heroes
and recasting the mold in which heroes were made.
William Allen White, Autobiography

A SENSE of change was clearly in the air. It began moderately enough. "The centre of attention has to some degree shifted from commerce to politics, and the protagonist is now rather President Roosevelt than J. P. Morgan," concluded *Collier's* in its New Year editorial for January, 1904.[1]

Within a few years, however, change sounded like revolution. "Financial Idols Overthrown," proclaimed the New Year editorial in 1906: "A few years ago the public was hungry for stories of the methods by which our 'captains of industry' had won their 'success.' The year 1905 has been one long battue of the reputations then reverently worshipped." [2] To the new editors of the *American Magazine* the nation seemed suddenly to have been converted from the worship of false gods:

> The old standards are passing. The old gods are dying in the world of greedy finance. We are finding that they were only half-gods, and you know the gods come when the half-gods go.

> The searchings of Colby and Folk and Hughes and Hadley and Glasgow have shown that the success which has been preached so earnestly to our youth for a decade or more is a false light. The list is long of those who, only a few years ago used as types of achievement, are now spit upon in the market place. We see by multifarious examples that great riches do not bring content or happiness or honesty; that they are more often the corrupter of personal and social and political life. We see that business success, the profitable issue of financial adventure, has been put above anything as a sacred obligation which must not be thwarted or prevented by honor or even by the law of the land. . . .
>
> On the other hand, there are almost daily additions to the list of those who are examples of the new standard of success, success of righteousness and honesty and justice . . . [with] rewards that money cannot buy.
>
> Could George Gould's money buy the affection and respect which the people of Missouri have for Joseph Folk? [3]

Napoleon was abruptly sent into exile from the magazines. References to him became conspicuous only by their scarcity and their changed character. Reaction against the idols of finance involved reaction against the hero with whom they had been identified. A leading Progressive spokesman placed the former identification in its new context: "The wholesale fleecer of trusting workaday people is a 'Napoleon,' a 'superman.'" [4] The one article on Napoleon in these Progressive magazines attempted to redeem the Emperor by stressing his social contribution and repudiating all those forceful, individualistic elements for which he had recently been revered:

> It is not the external achievements of Napoleon and the record of them that explain the fascination of the man. . . . [We] must not be content with saying that it is the highly romantic story of his rise and fall. . . . It is the idealism and the human touch discernible in Napoleon's nature which in reality explain his hold upon the minds of his contemporaries and upon our

> own. . . . We now see clearly that all the thousands who died because of him were really martyrs, dying for a future in which at last all privilege and caste and arbitrary rule should be no more.[5]

No attempt at rewriting the Napoleonic image could entirely submerge the old connotations and transform him into the Progressive paragon. No other historical figure emerged to fill his role as prototype for the new decade. Lincoln Steffens did on one occasion try to substitute Moses for Napoleon. In a biography of the Oregon legislator W. S. U'Ren, Steffens claimed that this Progressive hero had never desired like other boys to be a Napoleon. Instead U'Ren had taken Moses for his model, the lawgiver who had delivered his people from bondage.[6] The comparison was significant of the changing perspective, but Moses failed to stir the imagination of other biographers.

If anyone seemed to personify the ideal life to Americans in this decade, it was, of course, the contemporary figure of Theodore Roosevelt. The magazines printed more articles on Roosevelt than on any other individual.* Both the *Post* and *Collier's* published special "Roosevelt" issues at the time of his inauguration in 1905. He was certainly the most conspicuous individual of the decade. He seemed to meet many of its needs and to embody most of its aspirations in a way which Napoleon could no longer fulfill. Like George Washington and Andrew Jackson before him, Theodore Roosevelt's importance as a personal symbol seemed to transcend his actual executive or legislative accomplishments. Washington had filled the Presidency of a new and insecure nation with a perfect model of its most cherished contemporary conception of neo-classic duty and deportment. Jackson had come to the Presidency just at that time when the classic gentlemanly tradition was giving way to a romantic, demo-

* In a sample list of all biographical articles appearing in every third issue of the four best-selling magazines the total came to 176 different biographies. Ten of these or nearly 6 per cent of the total were about Roosevelt.

cratic individualism. Theodore Roosevelt, in turn, emerged with a personal flamboyance and a new social consciousness in precisely those years when the possibility and the adequacy of heroic individualism were coming under question. To Americans anxious over the rise of economic consolidation and of collective ideologies he exemplified a new vitality for the individual. To Americans concerned by the social injustice of a narrow individualism he offered a personal protest against many of the dogmas of economic individualism. In his person even more than in his policies Roosevelt provided the nation with a bridge between the nineteenth century and the twentieth. For William Allen White the appearance of Roosevelt seemed almost an act of Divine Providence:

> It was one of those utterly unthinkable coincidences, coincidences so rare, so unbelievable that they almost force one to believe in the minute Divine direction of human affairs, that a man of Roosevelt's enormous energy should come to the Presidency of exactly that country which at exactly that time was going through a transitional period—critical, dangerous, and but for him terrible—between an old rural, individual order and a new highly socialized industrial order.[7]

It seems puzzling at first to discover that very few biographies in the Progressive decade dwelt upon Roosevelt as an example for youth to follow. In 1901 and 1902 this had been the major theme for the early articles on the new President. Further investigation reveals that this omission after 1903 was part of a general change in the function assumed for biographical articles in the Progressive magazines. The biographies were no longer simple illustrations of how to achieve a universally accepted goal of individual success. Writers assumed a different concern and a different role for their readers. They implied that the underlying question in readers' minds was no longer the simple one, "How can I succeed like Rockefeller?" Now it was the more critical one, "What kind of individual success is worth having?"

—or at least, "How has Rockefeller's or Roosevelt's success affected our society and my own chances for success?" Readers were not to be future copies of the heroes so much as present judges, supporting or condemning them in the immediate crucial struggle over the direction and the tone of American life.

For the first time "villains" appeared in significant numbers among the magazine biographies. At least 12 per cent of the sample articles were highly critical of their subjects. The reasons for this change become evident in any perusal of Progressive writings. "Today," claimed Edward Ross, "the distinction between righteous and sinners is *the main thing*, for upon a lively consciousness of that distinction rests the hope of transmitting our institutions undecayed, of preserving our democratic ideals, of avoiding stratification and class rancor." [8] Progressive biographies aimed to make the necessary distinction. They would enable readers to pass judgment upon the contemporary leaders of society. By doing so, it was felt, they would contribute a major force to the purification and preservation of the whole society.

The nature of Progressive biographies cannot be understood apart from the extraordinary Progressive faith in the power of public opinion. In part this faith sprang from desperation. Amidst a world of organized special "interests," of graft, and of Big Business "influence," there seemed no one left to trust but "all of us," the public as a whole.[9] Public opinion was "a jury that can not be fixed." [10]

In part this faith rested upon a confidence in the intelligence and competence of ordinary middle-class citizens. Progressives insisted, as Roosevelt stated "all healthy-minded patriots should insist, that public opinion, if only sufficiently enlightened and aroused, is equal to the necessary regenerative tasks and can yet dominate the future." [11] Believing with Edward Ross that, "When the praises or blames of many men run together, they become a torrent no one can withstand," [12] Progressives could see active regenerative force in a biographical article damning the reactionary Aldrich or in one praising La Follette. For them the new characteristics of biographies in this decade were more than a simple reflection of social change. For them the new biographies were significant agents in spurring change. It often seems, in fact, that the kind of change about which they cared most was a change in the symbols rather than the structure of American society.

All the assertions about "old gods" dying and about "recasting the mold" for heroes in this decade intimated a sudden, radical shift in the American model of success. The abrupt repudiation or revision of the romantic Napoleonic image suggested a wholesale reaction against the individualism which it had represented. The new role of readers as judges rather than emulators of the biographical subjects implied a widespread distrust of many "successful" figures in contemporary society. Had Americans actually thrown overboard their assumptions about aggressive individualism as the necessary and desirable pattern for life? Had they, within the space of a few years, experienced a revolution comparable to the one by which individualists had displaced the socially oriented gentlemen of 1800? Had individualism, in its turn, died almost overnight?

Some Progressives were prepared to discard individualism. They spoke of it as a dangerous and restricting framework for the new conditions of American democracy. Walter Weyl preferred to put his faith in a "socialized democracy." The individualistic point of view," he complained, "halts social development at every point." [13] Among the academic analysts, however, Edward Ross remained closer to the popular heart of Progressivism. Ross's protests against many of the same evils which Weyl deplored were made *in behalf of* individualism:

> Those who put their faith in a transfigured individualism should make haste to clean the hull of the old ship for the coming great battle with the opponents of private capital and individual initiative. Certainly many of the villainies and oppres-

> sions that befoul it are no more a part of individualism than are the barnacles and trailing weed a part of the vessel.[14]

All the commotion was not a revolution. It was merely a cleaning-up, a patching-up operation. "Th' noise ye hear," commented Mr. Dooley, "is not th' first gun iv a rivolution. It's on'y th' people iv the United States batin' a carpet." The new heroes and the new elements in the Progressive model of success were designed to save individualism not to displace it.

The major tension of the decade appeared most explicitly in an article by Ray Stannard Baker about a coal miner. Baker traced the life of his hero, a man named Gorinsky, through his arrival from Poland, his joining the union, his advance in wages, in jobs, and in consciousness of his rights. "And the chief influence of all in his development was this very union," explained Baker. "It gave him, curiously, a hitherto unexperienced sense of his individuality—a new consciousness, though in itself, and paradoxically, a method of unification and a suppression of individuality." But in the great strike Gorinsky's sick wife and impending starvation had forced him to become a "scab." He was beaten up by a union man, deprived forever of the right to work as a miner, and defeated by union lawyers in court. The article sympathized strongly with Gorinsky, but Baker's chief concern was to dramatize the problem faced by a generation trained to value individualism above all else yet beginning to realize necessities for collective action:

> As a result of the struggle the union is more powerful than ever before, guards more zealously and with greater certainty the rights of its people, is able to grapple more securely with the real—oh the very real—greed of the operators. And who shall stand as judge upon these men? Shall we stamp out the democracy of the union—its aspirations, its ideals, its educative influence, along with its cruelty, its violence—and let Gorinsky live? Or shall we watch Gorinsky and his sick wife starve there in the tenements, or be beaten down for working, that the union may win its victory? This, indeed, is the problem of the century:

> Where shall we set limit upon the individual, and where admit the power of collective action? And can we in any sphere of life possess to ourselves the good of either without the evil? [15]

The impulse to preserve "the good" of individualism influenced all the magazine biographies of the Progressive years. Biographers looked for heroes who in various spheres of life exemplified "the good" of individualism without its evil. They praised especially the men who were highly individualistic leaders in such collective actions as did not threaten "those conditions which call out initiative and hard work." [16] The old pattern of aggressive individualism was not repudiated as unsuitable for the new conditions of society. The hope was to salvage it, to supplement it with a new social consciousness, and to discover new areas of opportunity for this "transfigured individualism."

The new heroes were not independent entrepreneurs. They were deeply engaged in fields of collective social action as politicians, reforming clergymen, or even government bureaucrats. Always, however, the emphasis remained on the individual, on his forceful personality, his initiative, his personal leadership. The new fields of endeavor were pictured as fresh opportunities for the exercise of a vigorous individualism. An editorial in the *American Magazine* set the tone by portraying the new pursuits in the imagery of the American frontier:

> The lands may be filled, the continents explored and surveyed, but the pioneer work is not over. The daring spirits of the time have new domains in which to adventure, new moral and political continents which must be developed, new ideals to be established and new standards of success raised, clearing made and seeds planted, that our sons and daughters may have moral and social and political comforts which we, perhaps, may not enjoy. [17]

In this mood Alfred Henry Lewis's series of biographies in the *Post* focused on social reformers, but its purpose was not so much to demonstrate the possibilities of collective action as to prove that "this is the harvest time, not of capital but of the individual." [18] Peter Clark Macfarlane did a series on reform-minded clergymen for *Collier's*. "The purpose behind the idea" was again to present "a visualization of men who dominate their congregations, and whose achievements argue personalities of unique force and character." [19] Brand Whitlock's account of Tom Johnson, the reform mayor of Cleveland, talked of "the new politics" with its new "consciousness of collective effort," but primarily the article stressed Johnson's "tremendous, dynamic, magnetic personality." "His career," concluded Whitlock, "is but another example of the power of personality." [20] The total effect of the new biographies was to reinforce William Allen White's contention that "the modern movement in American politics is bristling with rampant, militant, unhampered men crowding out of the mass for individual elbow-room." [21]

The Progressive model of success like that of the previous decade was fundamentally designed to preserve American notions of individualism in a rapidly consolidating society. A close examination of the Progressive biographies reveals many significant changes in the direction of a greater social consciousness and responsibility. To readers and to editorial writers at the time these changes may have seemed a revolution. From the perspective of the mid-twentieth century, however, the Progressive hero seems to have been engaged in a rear-guard action before the advancing hosts of "organization men." At least until 1914 the Progressive hero managed to hold the ground for individualism through strategic shifts and the abandonment of indefensible points.

I

The Progressive Villains

The sense of radical change in heroic standards during the Progressive years probably stemmed more from the smashing of some older idols than from the adulation for new ones. The very presence of villains in magazine biographies was largely a novel phenomenon. When one out of every eight biographical articles assailed its subject for sins against the public, obviously a dramatic shift in the popular mood had occurred.

All of the Progressive villains came from the two fields of business and politics. The biographers' barbs were aimed at industrialists like J. D. Rockefeller who climbed to power on railroad rebates, at manufacturers like C. W. Post who fraudulently advertised his Grape-Nuts, or at financiers like J. P. Morgan and Jay Gould who employed monopolistic methods and secret "collusion." In politics the villains were of two kinds, reactionary national figures like Cannon, Aldrich, and Vice President Fairbanks together with local bosses like Cox of Cincinnati, Barnes of New York, and Sullivan of Illinois. In a separate category of political villain stood William Randolph Hearst, the plutocratic publisher whose bid for New York's governorship on a somewhat radical platform seemed to pose a different kind of threat from that of the stand-patters and the party bosses.

The critical exposures of particular business leaders and successful politicians dramatically captured national attention, but these protests did not necessarily imply a loss of faith in aggressive individualism. The attacks more often accused the villains of betraying individualism than of demonstrating its weakness. "The essence of the wrongs that infest our articulated society is betrayal rather than aggression," protested Ross.[22] Many of the former idols, it appeared, had not acted as true, honest individualists at all. Americans were distressed to find that many captains of industry and finance were not as the people had pictured them, but the fault presumably lay with the villains more than with the picture. The monopolists, the rebate-seekers, and the trust-controlled politicians had themselves committed sins against the individualistic order.

What were the sins of the Progressive villain as the magazines painted him? It was revelatory of Progressive faith in the free market and in the rationality of public opinion that the chief fault emphasized by biographers was duplicity, stealth, or the secret betrayal of public interests. Certainly in the seven critical biographies analyzed in detail it was the element of duplicity which received most attention.[23] At least twenty-four times it was referred to as characteristic of these seven figures. "Gumshoe Bill" Stone, political rival of Joseph Folk in Missouri, had a "bent for indirection," and "the dominant note" of his character was "craft and cunning covered over with frenzied assertions of frankness." Biographers described how Aldrich "works in the dark," how Hearst "wears gumshoes when he goes in search of delegates," how "Mr. Fairbanks does most things under cover." Vice President Fairbanks was derided for characteristically concealing his bald spot with wisps of hair. His personally subsidized campaign biography with its account of "a Lincolnesque career" from log-cabin and self-supported education to self-made man answering the people's call to public office was contrasted at length with the facts:

> In school he was a mollycoddle; in early manhood the favored of rich relatives; as a lawyer, he advanced himself by guile and subtlety. . . . It was chiefly by his inside knowledge of manipulations, by the powers of 'high finance,' that he amassed his fortune. . . . Railroad influence coupled with a liberal use of money sent him to the Senate.

In portrayals of every one of the "villains" this element of deceit appeared. The facts of "Uncle Joe" Cannon's life were also contrasted with his official biographies. While Cannon had presented himself to the nation "as the greatest living exemplar of what may be called the railsplitting tradition," investigation revealed that he was actually a millionaire in his home town.

> This seems no mean achievement—to spend practically forty-five years in the public service . . . consistently to maintain on the national field an attitude of pioneer simplicity; yet the while

> to grow exceedingly rich at home without scandal. It amounts really to a considerable feat in politics. Personally, I think the many official and authorized biographies of the Speaker make a capital mistake in not saying a word about it.

The area in which this sin of duplicity, of betrayal of the public confidence, appeared most dangerous and most frequently (in six out of seven articles) was in secret collusion between business and politics. Fairbanks was "partly the tool and partly the subtle leader of moneyed influences which seek to over-reach the people." Cannon's fortune had come from "a highly efficient partnership" with his banker brother which gained high returns from "its dual interests of business and politics." Boss Sullivan and his associates had "usually been found going into action on the corporation side." In Missouri Stone had made a fine art of betrayal to business interests:

> A night of perfect happiness for Stone would consist of an old-time trust-busting, money-bedeviling, emotional speech to a backwoods Missouri audience . . . this followed by an hour in a locked hotel bedroom with a corporation president. The question of money involved would be a minor incident; Stone in his crude way has an artist's soul, and perfection in the double role is the satisfying thing.

The businessman Gould had corrupted courts and politicians, thus betraying democracy. In business ventures he had also betrayed the free market as "an expert at creating coordinate boards of directors over adverse interests. He packed financial juries, and they brought in verdicts of much profit to him." These were the classic forms of the great sin of betrayal in the Progressive period, betrayal of democracy and of the free market for special advantages to large corporate interests.

But betrayal of the people through still another means was condemned in two of the articles. Hearst had gained his power "purely by advertising himself and his propaganda in his own editions." "It amounts," protested his biographer, "to a trust of publicity." Fairbanks, too, not only paid for his own campaign biography and the "spontaneous" brass bands which greeted him but also controlled the major part of the Indiana press. For the Progressive faith in the power of enlightened public opinion a "publicity trust" posed a major threat and became a major sin.

Another major threat to the Progressive conception of government was stressed in the condemnation of Hearst's appeals to class interest:

> Hanna preceded Hearst as a moneyed campaigner, but Hearst is the first man—in the name of Democracy it is insidiously done—to put Americans by the patronage of the aristocracy of wealth into classes. He goes to bakers as bakers, farmers as farmers, engineers as engineers on questions where we are all involved regardless of occupation.

Hearst had laid his political foundation "on trades unionism," had built up "a class following." To middle-class Americans who feared any organization of classes above them or below them, who preferred to think only of individuals or of society as a whole, these tactics of Hearst's were an undisputable characteristic of villainy.

It was also a central feature of these critical articles that all but one of the men involved were millionaires or multi-millionaires. Varying significance was given to this fact. Fairbanks owed his political influence largely to his wealth. Sullivan's wealth proved his ability to make politics profitable. In Cannon's case his wealth simply showed that he was not as people thought him to be. Aldrich's wealth influenced his outlook on public affairs. "Aldrich's viewpoint is largely that of the Captain of Finance, the big manipulator, the great money power." For Gould the consuming drive for money had "destroyed his capacity for happiness." The Hearst millions made possible their owner's one-man political party. In no case was wealth the measure of a man's success. On the other hand, in no case was the possession of wealth in itself a mark of villainy. Only the uses to which wealth was put or the abuses by which it was acquired were condemned. The total impression, however, bore out the *American Magazine*'s editorial that "great riches do not bring content or happiness or honesty; that they are more often the corrupter of personal and social and political life."

One final "sin" was apparent in these critical Progressive biographies. Politicians could be forgiven many past sins if they showed an awareness of the current social unrest and a disposition to step into line with it. Aldrich's trouble was his failure to comprehend the strength of popular disapproval for the standpatter. "And his difficulty, his great weakness, is that he has continued to maintain that viewpoint instead of growing with the country." Boss Sullivan, however, might escape from the disapproved ranks despite his past career because he was "a sort of political barometer." His biographer concluded: "the most hopeful thing you can say about Sullivan today—he is politically wise. He reads the drift—and follows it." Many Progressives from Wilson down had awakened late to the new currents, and they were willing to forgive sinners who saw the light.

These then were the main sins for Progressives as revealed in a limited number of articles: duplicity, collusion between business and politics, monopoly of the press, appeal to class interest, abuse of wealth, and disregard for the Progressive ferment. But what of the sinners themselves? These sins and these articles implied no wholesale repudiation of all elements of the previous decade's hero-image. Most frequently the villains had betrayed or fallen short of the old pattern rather than demonstrated its weakness. Duplicity and collusion were as much a betrayal of the life-pattern of forceful individualism as they were of democracy and the free market. Except possibly for Hearst and Gould these men were not so much bad examples of forceful individualism as they were departures from it.

Leaving out Hearst and Gould the category of Description included only one possible statement denoting personal force. Others emphasized such adjectives as "adroit," "adaptable," "quiet," "plodding," "bland" and such phrases as a "cunning and needless avoidance of straightforwardness." The Road to Success for all the villains included qualifications on straightforward individualism like inherited wealth (Hearst), influential aid from relatives (Fairbanks, Cannon), and underhanded tactics of collusion (all articles). Aldrich could control most Republicans in the Senate "not because he is a man of tremendous intellectual force, not because he is a man of impelling personality," but because "He is politic and a politician . . . knows every trick of trading." "Mr. Fairbanks owes all he has to the timely help of two rich uncles." In these respects the Progressive villains had failed the previous hero-image of forceful men who carved individual careers through sheer personal ability. Thus far biographers had not used new standards for judging their subjects but had condemned them by the old standards.

In some ways, however, these critical articles gave evidence that biographers were emphasizing new elements for the successful life. While not abandoning a faith in forceful individualism, they gave indication that individualism now was to be pursued only with due regard to one's associates and to society in general. This revision can be seen in the changed character of the entries describing the Relation to Others and applying Success Standards. It was characteristic of these villains that little or no spontaneous friendship or cooperation existed between them and their associates. While this might have been true of the earlier heroes, it had not been mentioned as a matter of regret. Now it was pointed out how Gould had betrayed his first employer and his subsequent partners, how he had made a marriage and cultivated a friendship primarily to increase his capital. Lengthy entries emphasized that Hearst "wants no partnership in his journalism or his politics," that the attitude of the men around him

> . . . is not that of the average man of politics toward his leader; it is not that of the men who were around Lincoln yesterday or around Roosevelt or Folk or Taft to-day, which has the quality of fellowship, spontaneous admiration, and friendship. It is not that of the men around big, bluff Jim Hill. Like Rockefeller, the first of the business trust makers, Hearst, the first of the trust makers of publicity, has no intimates. Many men are employed by him. No man is his friend.

Only Sullivan had been on good terms with his associates, but "Leaders of the uplift will tell you that if Roger had but served his commonwealth with half the zeal with which he has served his political associates, that commonwealth would be more certain to support him in the hour of his aspiration to be a Senator of the United States." It was thus required to be loyal to the people as a whole as well as friendly to one's associates. In this respect Aldrich as "the center of special interests" had failed. Others had failed through their duplicity. Gould had been most outspoken about his hostility to all men: "If I did not hate every man as cordially as every man hates me, I should be unhappy—and yet I suppose I am the most miserable devil in the world."

Paralleling this increased concern with an individual's relation to others and to society were the explicit Success Standards which emphasized social contribution more than individual advance, material rewards, personal fame, or personal happiness. Every article could be said to have judged its subject by the standard of social contribution, some more explicitly than others. Aldrich was not "a great constructive statesman." Fairbanks had put "no law on the statute books which bears his name . . . any more than there is any policy, appealing to the people in any way as good or important to the nation, with which the Fairbanks personality . . . can be connected as a cause." Personal happiness, to be sure, was what proved Gould's ultimate failure, but here too the personal misery came from the failure "to learn how to live happily with humanity," and the answer was to be found in the life motto of Sarah Bradford: "If, therefore, there be any kindness I can show, or any good I can do to my fellow human beings, let me do it now."

Here then lay the new emphases in Progressive requirements for the successful life. While most of the villains had fallen short of the old patterns of forceful individualism, it was now also possible to pursue individualism too far in the wrong direction. Hearst and Gould, though partially damned for inherited wealth or collusive tactics, were endowed by their biographers with many of the forceful traits of the old heroes. Their fault lay primarily in blindness to the rights of their fellows and the requirements of society. Hearst had "a striking dignity and force about him—the force of the proprietor, of the man who is of and for himself, the leader by command, the head of a vast owned enterprise," but "of restraint he has no sense, nor of the ordinary obligations of the individual to society."

That these were the basic elements of the period's "villain-image" can be corroborated by analysis of an interesting article which was a partial defense of John D. Rockefeller.[24] Here the author granted that Rockefeller deserved condemnation because his individual success had gone too far: "That he has too much money and too much power is as unquestioned as that slavery was wrong or that scores of our rich who escape criticism altogether have no sense of patriotism or decent responsibility." He had also employed unfair tactics in his Road to Success: "John D. founded his fortune in rebates . . . by wickedly crushing out small producers." And finally in his Relations to Others Rockefeller could count only on the ties of blood and money:

> No one bade him Godspeed except his own blood kin. . . . In the place of fighting men the modern baron has the law and lawyers. This is progress. It obviates the necessity of any sentiment whatsoever; it requires nothing but mercenary service.

Nevertheless Rockefeller was defended as not wholly deserving the public's abuse for several reasons. He had made a definite social contribution even if for selfish motives:

> He is a creative millionaire. . . . If John D. has made countless millions for himself, he has also made countless millions for the United States. . . . He has been a creator of markets. In hard, matter-of-fact efficiency of organization the Standard Oil Co. has had no equal.

So far as American individualism contributed to general social advantages it was admirable and even at that date was presented as far superior to the state-sponsored industrialism of Russia:

> Whether it is a Cassatt, a Hill, or even a Rockefeller, the masterful organizer represents the energy that has made the rapid development of our country the wonder of this age. . . . In Russia . . . they have undertaken to accomplish development in another way. Witte was the Government hothouse Rockefeller. . . . His rise to the command of industrial expansion . . . was through the intrigues of St. Petersburg politics instead of in the hard school of experience on the plains.

If millionaires did become a threat to the general welfare, "let us remember that millionaires who are hardened to abuse will be sensitive to regulations which are honestly enforced." Above all, Rockefeller had not engaged in duplicity:

> He has never jollied us into thinking that he is a good fellow. You know what he is standing for and why, and on which side to line up in the battle.

This article on Rockefeller contained most of the assumptions evident in Progressive biographies. It placed the reader in the position of judge upon its subject. It assumed that the basic question was "on which side to line up in the battle." It strove to draw with care "the distinction between righteous and sinners" which Ross had claimed as the main hope for preserving American ideals and institutions. In making that distinction it still prized the masterful individual who made a creative impress upon his environment. Yet it now insisted that individual success must be measured by its social contribution. It looked for some touch of humanity in relations with other people, rejecting alike domination by force of wealth and the impersonality of corporate, institutionalized relations. It demanded openness, honesty, and no unfair advantages in the climb to success. Finally it recognized a threat (which could be associated vaguely with slavery) if some individuals were permitted to accumulate too much money and irresponsible power. That regulations "honestly enforced" would be sufficient to meet this threat remained a central tenet in most Progressive magazines.

II
The Standards of Success

The denunciation of sinners and the definition of sins have usually formed but a prelude in the process of regeneration. Some vision of the new, transformed life has been at the heart of any efforts toward individual or social awakening. As with many preachers before them, however, Progressive biographers found it easier to be specific about sins than to be entirely clear about the requirements of the new life. The outlines of the Progressive villain-image were sharper than the outlines of its contemporary hero-image. Quite understandably the attempt to create a "transfigured individualism" appropriate to the new conditions of society did not achieve a unity nor a clarity equivalent to the old-style heroic individualism of the 1890's. The Progressive model of success emerges from the magazine biographies as a mixture of old and new elements.

In 1894 writers had taken for granted what "success" meant. After 1904 they seemed to feel the need for some redefinition. Albert Shaw urged that, "New meanings must be written into such terms as 'success' and 'getting on in the world.'"[25] *Everybody's* observed that Americans were experiencing "conditions in our common life unlike any that men have ever faced before." The situation seemed to call for some fresh consideration of the question "What Is a Good Man?" A panel of distinguished contributors were asked:

> Do we need a new Decalogue because of the complexity of our lives? Is goodness still a man's private attitude to his God and to the small group bound to him by ties of blood, or does he owe a debt outside his home and his business? How much of time and thought must he pay to his community if he would be a good man? [26]

In response to this heavily loaded question only the Reverend Ireland failed to conform to the editorial implications. He portrayed the good life in terms very similar to Carnegie's Gospel of Wealth and stated that "the service of society is a misty dream." Contradicting and outnumbering him, however, were H. G. Wells, T. W. Lawson, E. A. Ross, and the Japanese Katsura, all of whom gave varying requirements for a life devoted to social service.

The chief new element in the Progressive model of success was the insistence upon Social Contribution as a standard for the esteemed life. Three-fourths of the Progressive biographies explicitly applied this standard to their heroes—twice as many as spoke about the achievement of Personal Fame. In all fields of endeavor the new emphasis was upon some form of social service.

The most enthusiastic praise for any active business leader was reserved for the President of the Advertising Clubs of America. It was not his eminence in the newly important field of advertising, however, which won him attention. The biography concentrated upon his community spirit in organizing Ford Hall, an educational, philanthropic institution in Boston. This, claimed the article, "comes near to being the most conspicuous single contribution so far in this new century toward social salvation in America." Politicians too were no longer measured by their personal achievement of high office. Despite three defeats in Presi-

Table XI

Standards of Success, 1904–1913

The frequency of appearance of five categories of terms used to describe the nature of the hero's success in a one-ninth sample of biographical articles from four best-selling magazines.

Category	No. of Articles in Which It Appeared	Per Cent of Total Articles*
Social Contribution	45	75
Personal Fame	23	38
Achievement in Field	11	18
Monetary Standard		
Anti	10	16
Pro	9	15
Personal Happiness	7	12
Total	105	174

* The total adds up to more than 100 per cent since various standards were often applied to the same hero.

dential elections Bryan's "has been a successful life," concluded William Allen White. "For he has been one of the instruments used by Providence in bringing the people out of the wilderness of crass materialism into a wider, fairer view of life." Among the arts this new concern turned attention to heroes like Maxim Gorky whose writings were remarkable "not so much because of what are known as literary qualities . . . as because of their social significance." Bureaucrats became important as examples of "self-sacrificing" public service or because they were "at the very center of those forces . . . for industrial and economic reforms." Even members of foreign royalty were now singled out for "a natural inclination toward liberal and democratic ideas." While there was no rigid formula for the way in which heroes should serve society, they must now generally be pictured as fulfilling some function beyond personal advancement and personal power.[27]

The new definition of success placed the need for Social Contribution first. It did not repudiate the older concern for Personal Fame, for "making one's mark" as an individual. Quite to the contrary, the service of society now emerged as a more feasible avenue for individual renown than the clogged channels of business and moneymaking. Albert Shaw tried to reassure the ambitious young man who found the world of free competition vanishing:

> Least of all should he fear lest there be somehow a diminished opportunity for him to play some fitting part in the world's activity, and to reap some fitting reward. The margin of individual risk is destined to diminish. I think it true, also, that the margin of opportunity for obtaining every exceptional advantage over one's fellows in some particular direction is also to be diminished. But there will be corresponding increase in the opportunity to earn honorable renown by the full devotion of one's talents to the social good in any chosen field.[28]

The rise of journalism and the advent of popular national magazines emphasizing "timely" topics had made the new social avenues to personal fame more rapidly negotiable. The *Saturday Evening Post* noted: "Ever since Mr. Bryan, in 1896, sprang over night from comparative obscurity to national fame, the power of the individual nowadays to impress himself speedily upon our whole eighty millions, upon the whole of mankind, has been coming more and more in evidence." [29]

The situation had simply been reversed. In the previous decade some form of social benefits had been assumed as the necessary by-product of the individual heroic quest for fame. To Progressives the achievement of personal renown emerged as the consequence of individual devotion to "the social good."

No such easy reconciliation of old and new attitudes proved possible over the question of wealth as a measure of success. Was the Monetary Standard a proper measure of the hero's success or not? The number of bographies which applied it with approval (15 per cent) was almost equal to the number which explicitly repudiated it (16 per cent). Obviously money and material success raised certain tensions in Progressivism.

Contemporary writings indicated a wide spectrum of attitudes toward pecuniary success. Even those which united in deploring the idealization of wealth were divided in the grounds for their disapproval.

Socialists like W. J. Ghent protested that "The pursuit of material success has been transformed into a sort of religion, and a horde of priests and oracles interpret its dogmas and disseminate its practical precepts." For Ghent the pecuniary success stories blinded Americans to real conditions, diverted them from the ideals of Jesus and Karl Marx, and formed the primary barrier to popular acceptance of socialism.[30]

Walter E. Weyl complained that the identification of material success with the old American qualities of initiative and self-reliance was a major prop in the power of "the plutocracy":

> In this interested attachment to old ideals, as in the very humbleness of its merely pecuniary ambitions, lies the strength of the plutocracy's appeal to public opinion and the menace that it may corrode our national morals, or at least tend to maintain them on a low level. What is so transcendently perilous in our present conditions of industrial success and failure is not our inequality of wealth with its evil effect upon the consumption of the nation's goods, nor even the subtle corruption of our politics—although both are evil—but rather the echo of the rich spoiler's ambition in the soul of the average men. . . . Today in America just as the standard of democracy is borne aloft by some men of fortune, so on the other hand, wealthy plutocrats are backed up by millions of like-minded poor men, *penniless plutocrats, dream-millionaires.*[31]

In this atmosphere Weyl found it difficult to win support for his positive program of "social democracy."

Most Progressives, however, did not have as clear a vision for the future as Ghent and Weyl. For most of them the worship of material success did not loom primarily as a barrier to an ideal future society. Rather it seemed one way in which an ideal past was being obscured by a sordid present. James O. Fagan reported an interview with President Roosevelt in which this became apparent. After inquiring into Fagan's pay as a railroad clerk, Roosevelt had replied:

> Well, your wealth bears about the same proportion to mine that mine does to the multi-millionaire. Not so long ago we heard that Mr. So and So was coming to live at Oyster Bay. The news caused a mild sensation, even among the well-to-do residents. If there is anything that one enjoys at these small places in the country, or the seashore, it is the simplicity of our everyday life and of our surroundings. Yet one and all of us at Oyster Bay understood only too well that if So and So with his unlimited wealth and love of display, settled down in our midst, it meant good-bye to everything that made Oyster Bay such a delightful retreat. We knew our single and efficient servant-maids would be displaced, sooner or later, by butlers, in all the pomp of livery and buttons. . . . In a word, the money-god would soon become supreme instead of the simple deities, whose worship endears to us the woods, the fields, and the home. The nation at large has to guard against the same danger that threatened our community at Oyster Bay.*

A still more conservative response to a threatening idealization of wealth emerged in Ross's *Sin and Society*. Ross, who had put his faith in "a transfigured individualism," saw pecuniary standards of success as a major inducement to socialism among the middle classes:

> In the sphere of opinion nothing so favors the root-and-branch men [socialists] as the ascendancy of commercial standards of success. Certainly you may rate the business man by the money

* James O. Fagan, *The Autobiography of an Individualist* (Boston, 1912), 212–13. This is obviously a classic account of the kind of status revolution described by Hofstadter in *The Age of Reform.*

> he has been able to make under the rules of the game. But the sages of all time agree that the writer, thinker, scholar, clergyman, jurist, officer, administrator, and statesman must not be mere profit seekers, nor may their social standing depend on their financial rating. The intrusion of Mammon's standards into such callings makes socialists of thousands who do not really believe that the exchange of money for labor is 'exploitation.' [32]

The magazine biographies which repudiated the Monetary Standard of success were much closer in outlook to Roosevelt and Ross than they were to the more utopian current writers. Biographical derogations of wealth almost always amounted to affirmations of the value of some non-commercial middle-class career. The Progressive hero might be a government surveyor who had braved the hardships of Alaska "not for the purpose of making strikes, but with the intention of compiling a report that would enable other fellows to make strikes." He felt that "a man who would allow considerations of money to interfere with his scientific work was beneath contempt." [33] Such a scientific hero might be a medical researcher who was not tempted by "the allure of earning an income of $50,000 or $100,000 a year from his skill as a surgeon" and found it "hard to understand why one should wish to be a typical money-grubbing American." [34] The Progressive hero might be a clergyman who turned down a large salary if it threatened to interfere with his independence. He might even be a businessman who "deliberately refused to become rich" in order to devote his time and talents to social service.[35] The Progressive biographer, in short, explicitly repudiated a Monetary Standard only when it seemed necessary to defend the prestige and independence of a non-business career or of the individual's responsible performance of his role as public-spirited citizen.

Despite these significant qualifications, Progressive biographers still strove to find acceptable ways to preserve some monetary measures of success. William Jennings Bryan was commended for earning "as much as $1,500" for a speech at the big Chautauquas. He was "well-to-do" with a living "as secure as that of any millionaire in the land." [36] In business Americans were gratified to find that wealth could be "clean," could still be evidence of real accomplishment as in the case of George Westinghouse:

> It is a comfort to turn to him and to his work in these days when so much reeking, filthy money is being exhumed in the dark corners of our industrial and financial world. America owes a great debt to George Westinghouse for many things, but especially for the proof he furnishes that wealth and success, after all, do not always depend with us upon chicanery and corruption; that our industrial greatness is founded upon solid work and achievement; that we are sound at the core; that honest men have not died out among our captains of industry.[37]

To commend professional earnings in non-business fields, to honor material success gained in honest, independent business activities—these remained possible, even necessary, measures of achievement for the Progressive decade.

Frank Munsey never really came to doubt that virtue could and should be measured by dollars. The Progressive tensions on this matter, however, forced even Munsey into an interesting and tortuous assessment of the question. The wealthy publisher's views appeared in a personal article on John D. Rockefeller which presumably did not involve "either approval or disapproval of his career." The significant fact was asserted to be that John D. had risen from "a poor farm-boy" to become "the richest man in the world." "And this," claimed Munsey, "means more, vastly more, when you come to analyze it, than it would mean to be the greatest painter, or greatest statesman, or greatest lawyer, or greatest physician in the world." Realizing the heresy of such an assertion in Progressive eyes, Munsey hastened to explain himself: "I don't mean to say, and no one must fancy that I do say, that to be the richest man in the world is greater than to be a great statesman, a great lawyer, or a great physician." His point was that "The professional man, at most, competes only with a single generation." Both he and his competitors inherit only brains or talent. "In contrast with this, the rich man must measure his possessions with the accumulated possessions of centuries—the savings of generations." Rockefeller had to compete with the Astor and Vanderbilt fortunes.[38]

Munsey's reassertion of his fundamental belief that the meaning of life lay in financial competition is obvious. The interesting feature of his article is his semi-conscious sense of the real question, the basic challenge, which Progressives were raising to the adulation of material success. Munsey clearly felt it necessary to defend the prestige of moneymaking against the rival claims of non-business middle-class pursuits. It was a final proof of the fact that derogation of the Monetary Standard by most Progressives came from their desire to affirm the values of diverse middle-class careers and of accustomed middle-class styles of life. When those were not threatened, they had nothing against pecuniary achievement. They were, in fact, glad to admire it in cases where they could do so with a clear conscience.

III
Description of the Hero

If the old gods were dying, the new gods looked very much like them. Descriptions of the Progressive heroes were more remarkable for continuity than for change. One is led to suspect that there were important reasons for endowing the new idols with the Napoleonic characteristics of physical force, mental shrewdness, and a masterful character. Theodore Roosevelt embodied these elements of the transitional model to perfection. He had also consciously laid down the prescription for it. Men working for "decent politics," Roosevelt had asserted, must not only be "disinterested, unselfish, and generous but also possess the essential manly virtues of energy, of resolution, and of indomitable personal courage." [39] Progressive biographers correspondingly portrayed in their descriptive phrases the familiar forceful figure of the previous decade while adding an overlay of increased social virtues.

Physically the Progressive heroes in all occupations were models of the strenuous life. A clergyman had "the squared shoulders of an athlete, the firm face of a fighter." A labor leader "was able-bodied in every sense—stalwart, square-shouldered, powerful." A bureaucrat was noted for his "good fighting weight." Only the reactionary villains appeared with flabby physiques in these articles: "When one thinks of aged Aldrich, of old Uncle Joe, of Ballinger, of Knox, of men of ordinary physique who have lost vigor in the political game . . . one appreciates what a tremendous advantage rests with Roosevelt should he pitch into any or all of them." [40]

A successive decline of interest in mental characteristics could be traced from the biographies of the early republic to those of the Progressive period. The writers of 1800 had been less interested in the physical appearance than in the minds of their subjects. By the 1890's this relative proportion had been reversed, and in the Progressive decade mental traits were still further subordinated to physical attributes and qualities of character. Biographers now remarked upon the mind of their heroes about half as often as they commented upon their physique or their character.

Even where mental references did appear, nearly one-fifth of the comments were negative in tone. Several heroes, it was noted, had not been good students. Bryan was "not wise." Another hero was guided by "instinct not reason." The positive references were, in turn, extremely diverse, yielding no clear mental pattern for the hero. The two most frequently cited qualities remained "intellectual strength" (7 times) and "shrewdness" or "astuteness" (6 times).

This relative derogation of intellect at a time when the more intellectual professions were reasserting themselves and an intellectual revolution was occurring seems somewhat surprising. Perhaps the answer lay precisely in certain middle-class, moderate fears of the more drastic intellectual remedies being proposed for social evils. Perhaps intellect was associated for too many with socialism. Moral qualities like courage, honesty, and unselfishness may have seemed more relevant to the moderate program of Progressivism than intellectual penetration and planned reconstruction.

Tenuous as it may be, such an explanation is supported by an interesting article on Theodore Roosevelt in the *American Magazine*. Its anonymous author found "the psychological key" to Roosevelt in his power of "energizing to the extent of his capacities." Those capacities were described as limited to "the plain ordinary virtues." Roosevelt was able to accomplish "so much" by acting on instinct not reason, "by being exactly like us," by trusting the multitude, by articulating the people's desires. As an example of "the supreme development of human will" he provided the "very pattern, *in a new sense*, of the self-made man." As such he had been "an instrument in letting off Revolution as evolution" where the need was for "unimaginative commonness, energy, and fearlessness." Smoothing over the evils would have brought an explosion. But an explosion would also have been produced by a "visionary radical" through "the violence of his remedies." [41]

Whatever the reasons, Progressive heroes were no more intellectual than their Napoleonic predecessor. They retained his qualities of "intellectual strength" and of shrewdness. Conspicuously lacking, however, was his emphasis on "foresightedness," "vision," and "imagination." These qualities had seemed essential when the focus was upon carving out an individual career. Now that the concern was for the regeneration of society, perhaps too much vision seemed potentially dangerous.

With one significant exception the Progressive model of character also resembled the Napoleonic type. Biographers still endowed the hero most frequently with those qualities of character appropriate to the mastery of others or of his environment (see Table XII). The Forceful Traits together with the traditional Business Traits remained the essential base of the approved character.* A wide diversity of Personal Traits and of explicitly Individualistic Traits appeared as frequently in this decade (27 per cent of all traits) as they had in the previous one (26 per cent of all traits).† The very low proportion of attention devoted to Religious or Idealistic Traits rose no higher (4 per cent of all traits) than it had in the supposedly more materialistic years of the 1890's.‡

The one noticeable difference was a rise in the proportion of Social Traits attributed to the Progressive heroes. Such qualities as geniality, kindliness, unselfishness, humanitarianism, fairness, and patriotism appeared more frequently in Progressive biographies than in those of the preceding decade (27 per cent of all Progressive character traits versus 20 per cent of all traits from 1894 to 1903). The new Progressive hero had gained considerably in his consideration for others while his forceful, aggressive characteristics, though still prominent, had been markedly toned down (from 36 per cent of all traits to 23 per cent). Here lay the only major distinction in the description of the new gods compared with the old ones.

The distinctive Progressive character lay in the combination of

* Typical Forceful Traits (and the number of times they appeared) were: Forcefulness (17), Fight (8), Tenacity (6), Aggressiveness (4). Typical Business Traits (and the number of times they appeared) were: Businesslike Behavior (5), Hard Work (5), Honesty (5), Practicality (3).

† Typical Personal Traits in the Progressive decade (and the number of times they appeared) were: Simplicity (9), Modesty (5), Wholesomeness (4), Straightforwardness (4), Purity (2). Typical Individualistic Traits in the Progressive decade (and the number of times they appeared) were: Self-confidence (6), Self-reliance (3).

‡ Typical Religious or Idealistic Traits in the Progressive decade (and the number of times they appeared) were: High Ideals (6), Moral Purpose (1), Religiousness (1).

Table XII

Character Description, 1904–1913

The relative frequency of appearance of four categories of qualities of character ascribed to the hero in a one-ninth sample of biographical articles from four best-selling magazines.

Category	No. of Traits	Per Cent of All Traits	No. of Qualities	Per Cent of All Qualities
I Qualities Directed Toward Mastery of Others or of the Environment:			89	42
Forceful Traits	49	23		
Business Traits	40	19		
II Qualities Directed Toward Consideration of Others:			58	27
Social Traits	58	27		
III Qualities Directed Toward Cultivation of Self:			57	27
Personal Traits	44	21		
Individualistic Traits	13	6		
IV Qualities Directed Toward God or Ultimate Values:			9	4
Religious or Idealistic Traits	9	4		
Total	213	100	213	100

forcefulness and social concern. The Progressive hero was the man who fought valiantly for the people. He was "a man of rare force whose sympathies are with the people." He displayed at times "the underlying quality of intense, passionate sadness that is inherent in the character of men who fight, as he has fought, to liberate their fellow men." [42]

Clearly descriptions of the Progressive hero preserved all the essential features of forceful individualism. The new model, however, adapted traditional individualism to new conditions by endowing the hero with a social consciousness.

IV

The Hero's Personal Habits

Continuity seems more apparent than change also in accounts of the Progressive hero's Personal Habits. Though writers were now more likely than in the previous decade to describe his Personal Habits (in 85 per cent of the Progressive articles versus 82 per cent), this whole area of life was still made definitely subordinate to the heroic career. Comments were brief and often tended to stress the insignificance of such things as clothes, food, or recreation in the life of the hero.

Varieties of recreation were noted in almost one-third of the biographies. Many of these references, however, still dismissed any interest in such activities for their own sake. From Cyrus McCormick's outright rejection of any recreation since "his business was his life" to President Taft's "exercise for a purpose" the central importance of the sphere of work was made clear.[43] At other times recreational references seemed but another means to stress the vigor and vitality of the hero. Outdoor activities comprised the predominant form of recreation attributed to the Progressive hero. More passive pursuits were pointed up as incongruous for these forceful figures. Mayor Francis, it was noted, "claims a love for art, literature, and music, but it is as if a twelve-inch gun claimed a similar love."[44]

Almost half the references to home life, clothing, eating, or drinking were made to emphasize the hero's simplicity or carelessness for minor matters. District Attorney Jerome wore ready-made suits. District Attorney Moran was "careless in his dress." It was a "surprise" to find that in Europe Roosevelt's clothes were well pressed.[45]

Philanthropy became a less frequent characteristic of these heroes who were finding other avenues for social concern. A majority of the cases where it was mentioned, in fact, explained that the hero was "profoundly interested in the problems of private and public charity" but gave to them "his time and ability not millions." [46]

Religious beliefs and activities played an insignificant part in the image of heroes who were not clergymen. References were rare and perfunctory, noting only that Hughes went to church regularly while he was in college or that Gorinsky, the coal-miner, went to mass twice a year. Cyrus McCormick's religious beliefs were largely incidental to his work. "'Providence has seemed to assist me in all our business,'" was the sentiment recorded by his biographer who went on to observe: "Not that he left to Providence any detail to which he could personally attend. He was a Puritan of the 'Trust-in-God-and-keep-your-powder-dry' species." [47]

While contemporary prophets were predicting that "the average man" would soon find his chief outlet for individuality in leisure activities,* the average magazine reader was still presented with heroes who found their work to be the only meaningful aspect of their lives.

V

The Hero's Relation to Others

The new gods were clearly new in some respects. The Progressive heroes were placed in a world where many other people existed, where it was important to recognize their existence, to "like" them, to fight for them, and to be "loved" by them as well as to continue to dominate and lead them. The Progressive

* "The world is steadily moving toward the position in which the individual is to contribute faithfully and duly his quota of productive or protective social effort, and to receive in return a modest, certain, not greatly variable stipend. He will adjust his needs and his expenses to his income, guard the future by insurance or some analogous method, and find margin of leisure and opportunity sufficient to give large play to individual tastes and preferences." Albert Shaw, *The Outlook for the Average Man,* 32, 33.

style of individualism required a warm, reciprocating form of human relationship which the more inner-directed model of the previous decade had ignored or even scorned.

In Progressive eyes the most significant relationship was that between the individual on the one hand and "the people" on the other. References to "the public," "the people," "his fellow citizens," or "voters" appeared almost twice as often as in the Napoleonic biographies (in 54 per cent of all Progressive articles versus 29 per cent). The new hero displayed an open democracy of manner and a dedication to the public benefit.* He was a man who "likes people and likes to have people like him." As a reformer he might be "the best hated, most feared man in Seattle. But also," continued his biographer, "he is the best loved."[48] No longer was the public an adverse force standing in the way of heroic achievement. Nor was it merely a jury to register the hero's fame. Progressives looked for some positive, human engagement between the hero and tho public.

The desired quality of warm, spontaneous association with others could best be demonstrated in specific terms by endowing the hero more frequently with wife and friends. Just as dominating colleagues and besting competitors had been the essential pattern of relations for the Napoleonic hero, so regard for the public and a talent for friendship became distinctive merits in the Progressive hero. George W. Coleman was "the idol of his world. He does not make money, but friends."[49]

Progressive biographies did not so often present human beings as part of that material environment which the hero had been expected to conquer. Relations tended to be more reciprocal, emphasizing others' attitudes to the hero as well as his treatment

* ". . . the door of his office is wide open, so that all who would might enter, and no one was denied." Isaac Marcosson, "Woodrow Wilson, Presidential Possibility," *Munsey's*, XLVI (October, 1911), 3.

"He went on with his mapping so that the public, whose servant he is, might be generally benefited." Theodore Waters, "Plain Heroes of Science," *Everybody's*, X (March, 1904), 367.

of them. His actions could not be separated from their impact on the feelings and welfare of others. The hero now acted for the benefit of others more than for his own gain. When he forced his will on the world, he had to make the world like it. These were the new elements in the Progressive model of success.

Yet much of the old remained. It was important for the hero still to be a forceful, dominating personality. Where biographers made explicit the nature of his Relation to Others the leading

Table XIII

The Hero's Relation to Others, 1904–1913

Others Mentioned in Articles

The frequency of appearance of ten categories of people other than the hero in a one-ninth sample of biographical articles in four best-selling magazines.

Category	No. of Articles	Per cent of All Articles
The Public	32	54
Spouse	20	34
Friends	18	30
Colleagues (or Rivals)	16	27
Parents	13	22
Children	10	17
Inferiors	9	15
Siblings	5	9
Teachers	3	5
Superiors	3	5
Nature of the Relations		
The frequency of appearance of five categories describing the nature of the hero's relation to others in the same sample.		
Dominate Others	14	24
Loved by Others	11	18
Cooperate with Others	9	15
Aid Others	7	12
Aided by Others	7	12

pattern was clearly dominance rather than cooperation. Even though dominance appeared only half as often as in the previous decade (in 24 per cent of the articles instead of 50 per cent) and cooperation appeared twice as often (15 per cent instead of 8 per cent), the Progressive idol remained a vigorous, assertive leader. George Coleman was portrayed as the friendliest, most loved hero of them all. Yet his biographer put the emphasis upon his dominating personal leadership:

> Men gather about him like flies round a sirup jar. They hum and buzz and slap him on the shoulders, and laugh and chuckle and admire—and follow! Let us write that particular attribute in italics—*they follow!*—black-face it, capitalize it, frame it in fireworks, touch off the fuse, blaze the letters against the sky —*men follow Coleman.*[50]

Particularly in their feeling for the hero's Relation to Others writers seemed to be groping for some new formula which would be more satisfactory than the simple inner-directed dominance of the Napoleonic hero. They looked for the "good" of individualism without its previous tendency to treat other people as objects. They feared also the impersonal qualities of collectivism. The result was a dynamic, personal leader of "the people." He was a man who made friends, who cared for the welfare of others. But he was definitely a man who exerted dominance not through formal position or power in an organization so much as through his personal qualities.

VI
The Road to Success

In 1906 a writer for *Munsey's* attempted to describe the typical American. His summation began with all the familiar clichés of the 1890's. It ended, however, by stressing a new Progressive requirement:

> In general, the typical American is said to be the man who is self-made and who has learned worldly wisdom by hard knocks. He must be shrewd and forceful, fond of big enterprises, a good talker, and many-sided. There must have been more or less of romance and adventure in his life. He must have loved and hated and taken risks. Above all, he must respect public opinion and keep in close touch with the rank and file of his fellow countrymen.[51]

Progressive accounts of the heroic Road to Success generally followed this same formula. Most of the traditional individualistic route remained. To it were added new guideposts designed to point the successful individual in directions leading to a wider democracy and justice for all. Both the continuities and the changes in the Progressive Road to Success demonstrated again the fundamental concern to preserve individualism by endowing it with a sense of social responsibility.

Any faithful magazine reader of the previous decade would have recognized the Childhood Environment of the Progressive heroes. Again modest origins were stressed out of proportion to the apparent class origins of all the heroes.* Again a rural upbringing was emphasized wherever possible.† Again youthful hardships were enumerated in about one-third of the biographies.

The one traditional element conspicuously lacking from the childhood inculcation of the inner-directed character was any

* Biographies which paid explicit attention to the class origins of their subjects implied that 10 came from the lower class, 9 from the middle, and 8 from the upper class. Again upper-class origins had to be explained away or qualified. See for example: *S.E.P.* (February 23, 1907), 5; *S.E.P.* (March 11, 1905), 13.

† Of the 10 "lower-class" heroes 7 came from farms. The *Post* did, however, remind its readers: "While we are reckoning the farm boys who have become philanthropists, let us not forget that the greed which created Standard Oil was nourished in a barnyard." Editorial, "Country Boy and City Boy," *S.E.P.* (February 11, 1905), 12.

intimation that the hero had charted the course of his future life while still a child. No longer did biographers mention fathers who had counseled the young hero, "Exert yourself, improve your opportunities." No longer did they find it certain "that many a great life-plan has been formed before ten, and carried through with an unbending rigor to the end." Perhaps Progressives felt too keenly a break with the simpler individualistic standards of their fathers. Certainly many Progressive heroes had experienced a turning-point in their own lives when they had become aware of a new social dimension to success. Tom Johnson "had been a mere rich man" before he read Henry George and felt "a spiritual awakening." [52] The decade was full of a sense of change. Biographers looked for those men who had proved able to change with the times, not for those who had clung inflexibly to the standards of the previous generation.

Formal Education became a more significant element in the Progressive career than it had been for the Napoleonic hero. By 1907 a book on *The Outlook for the Average Man* pointed to a new basis for power:

> The thing in general to be attained is power. The thing in particular is the special training of some kind that enables a man to make expert application of his developed force and ability. If trained capacity has been a valuable asset in the past, it becomes the one indispensable asset under the new conditions.*

Politicians, clergymen, and bureaucrats were naturally more likely to have advanced education than the nineteenth-century captains of industry. Sixty per cent of those whose education was mentioned at all had been to college, and half of these in turn had gone on to graduate school, mostly to law school. Still

* Albert Shaw, *The Outlook for the Average Man,* 4. It should be noted that this book was a compilation of lectures to college audiences. Hence "the average man" was probably understood to mean a young man in college.

Table XIV

Road to Success, 1904–1913

Formal Education

The formal education of the hero as it was mentioned in a one-ninth sample of biographical articles from four best-selling magazines.

Nature of Education	No. of Articles	Per Cent of All Articles
Graduate School	8	13
(Law School)	(6)	(10)
College	7	12
High School	3	5
Country School	2	3
Tutor	1	2
Technical Training	1	2
Musical Training	1	2
Total	23	39

biographers reported on these facts in generally objective terms. No effort was made to stress the value or dramatize the significance of formal education in the heroic career.

The real drama and the significant value-laden phrases still centered around the hero's Means to Success. Writers now seemed more interested in judging the legitimacy of certain paths to power than in spelling out the standard steps to success for emulation by ambitious readers. This shift in emphasis, however, did not diminish the attention devoted to this whole area. Two impressions emerge with striking clarity from Progressive treatments of the hero's tactics.

The first impression is one of radical change. Biographers dwelt upon a whole range of Democratic Tactics which had played little part in the Napoleonic hero's climb to fame. They raised these social activities to a level equal with the traditional Individualistic Tactics (see Table XV). The Progressive hero might achieve success by winning the trust of others as often as by his independent, "self-made" behavior. Pushing through new legislation or enforcing the existing laws became an accepted means to heroic status. These did appear to be new gods acting in newly fashionable ways.

The second impression, however, is one of basic continuity. Even in his social activities the Progressive hero was essentially an individualist. Again and again biographers took pains to point

Table XV

Road to Success, 1904–1913

Means to Success

The frequency of appearance of certain types of activity displayed by the hero in his career as described in a one-ninth sample of biographical articles from four best-selling magazines.

Activity	No. of Articles	Per Cent of All Articles*
I Individualistic Tactics		
Independence	13	22
Hard Work	11	18
Fighting His Way	9	15
Executive Ability	6	10
Oratorical Ability	6	10
Total	45	75
II Democratic Tactics		
Winning Trust of Others	20	33
Keeping the Social Balance	8	13
Pushing New Legislation	5	9
Enforcing the Laws	4	7
Acting Openly	3	5
A Social Awakening	4	7
Total	44	74

* Total adds up to more than 100 per cent because various activities were displayed by the same hero.

out the independence of their heroes. His success had to be gained without relying upon assistance from any entrenched political or economic group. He did not rise through the ranks of any existing organization. He shunned collusion or "what is popularly known as 'inflooence.'"[53] Now that Americans had discovered the taint of collusion between business and politics in much previous success, writers were more insistent than ever in stressing the pure individualism of their hero's career.

The acceptable business success of James J. Hill was entirely "a one-man affair." It "was won, not only in face of the apathy and positive hostility of American capital, but in face of Government and Congressional hostility as well." Cyrus McCormick had been a "consistent individualist of an outgrown school":

> From first to last the stout-hearted Reaper King received no favors from Congress or the Patent Office. He built up his stupendous business without a land grant or a protective tariff. . . . He was not at all a modern 'community of interest' financier.

The few remaining models of success in business were precisely those men who had not betrayed the canons of individualism.[54]

A scrupulous independence was no less necessary for the Progressive model of a politician. Theodore Roosevelt was

> . . . a man whose position is due to himself, not to party influence. In studying his career from the time when he first came into public view until the present day, it is what he has done as an individual which stands out. He is a living proof of the fact that the record of a man's life may—at least in this country—give him popularity independent of any particular class or party.

On the state as well as the national level the Progressive politician was one who had "always been independent," who "had no reverence for bosses, no fear of machines." The "needs of the national hour" were for this type: "Both State and Nation need the services of independent men—independent alike of a coarse lobby influence and the more subtle, yet no less dangerous, social and political influence of strong corporations and our high financial magnates." In the midst of its most urgent social and political activities Progressivism clung to a vision of the independent individual as the redeemer of society.[55]

Particular middle-class fears contributed to Progressive insistence upon the independent individual. A present threat of rule by the plutocracy raised the specter of a future rule by class-conscious workers in retaliation.* This sense of the situation clearly called for heroes who would themselves be free from any special class interests. Only such leaders could avert danger by "keeping the balance" and giving all "a square deal":

> Our civilization will survive only as it is just. And he who errs on the side of the weak errs just as fatally to the final settlement of this contest as he who errs for the strong.

Hence the Progressive hero was "related to no interest. He has no class feeling." He was the one who "dared to be impartial." Like President Taft he might, when necessary, have "the courage to decide against labor." Like the labor leader Andrew Furuseth

* "Suffering the big player to violate the rules of the game is doubly dangerous at the present stage. In twenty years two developments—the disappearance of free land in the rain belt and the triumph of the big concern over the little—have narrowed the circle of opportunity for workingmen to achieve independence, and therefore tend powerfully to consolidate wage-earners into a conscious class. It does not yet appear whether this will make impossible that government by public opinion which has contributed so much to the good temper and steadiness of the American people. . . .

"So long, indeed, as civic feeling is deep, the great majority of citizens shrink from using the state for the furtherance of their special group interests, and will not unite on such lines save to ward off the aggressions of some less scrupulous group."

E. A. Ross, *Sin and Society*, 139, 143.

he must achieve independence of his group in order to attain heroic stature:

> Furuseth had acquired philosophy and balance. He looked upon the rich and the poor with impartial eyes and found the same frailties in both. He became almost class-unconscious, if the term be permitted.

Biographers strove to maintain an image of the world where the only legitimate entities were the independent individual on the one hand and the people as a whole on the other.[56]

The Progressive Road to Success was not a lonely road. It was not, as in the previous decade, a narrow ladder up whose rungs the hero struggled to win the plaudits of the crowd below. It was a route to greener pastures for all the people. The hero's role was to clear the obstacles, to point out the perils, and to inspire others to follow. His own success depended upon the degree to which his efforts opened the way for others.

Though the hero was no longer to travel alone, he must clearly travel on his own. This was not a route for marching columns arrayed in organized ranks. The hero must maintain his independence. He must show no favoritism. He must allow no disciplined group to usurp his leadership. He must rely upon no authority beyond his own personal qualities. Only such a leader could find a path for individualism through the narrowing confines of the new American countryside.

VII
The Heroic Occupations

The most obvious novelty of the new gods lay in their occupations. No change in the Progressive heroes seemed more dramatic than the suddenness with which politicians replaced businessmen as the objects of public attention and prestige.

The impact of the change could be sensed in statements about "The old gods . . . dying in the world of greedy finance." The extent of the change could be measured in the occupational statistics of Progressive biographies (see Table XVI). Politicians now outnumbered businessmen by four to one. Compared with the preceding decade, magazines nearly tripled the proportion of political heroes (from 12 per cent to 34 per cent), while the proportion of business biographies was cut nearly in half (from 16 per cent to 9 per cent). Clergymen (11 times) and government bureaucrats (10 times) now appeared almost as frequently as business figures (15 times). At least within the world of magazine biographies a status revolution had occurred which made of the businessmen a newly displaced elite.

The revolution was a general one against the previous Idols of Power. Along with business the arts suffered a decline of attention by nearly one-half (from 33 per cent to 18 per cent). New types of heroes emerged from the ranks of labor (from 0 to 3 per cent) and from the field of technical government service (from 0 to 2 per cent) in the persons of government engineers and a government surveyor. Along with physicians who had rendered notable humanitarian service (from 0 to 2 per cent) these now displaced the former scientists and inventors who had been engaged in individual mastery of the material environment (from 5 per cent to 0).

Biographers had apparently adopted the advice which John Brisben Walker once offered to the trust-builders of the 1890's. They had turned their attention from the problems of production to the "broader . . . field of 'distribution.'"[57] The new heroes can best be understood as the Idols of Justice. More than anything else the shift in occupational emphases testified to the recognition of a new context, of new problems for American life. The major productive facilities of the nation had been built. Control over them was consolidating into the hands of a few whose prestige in the previous decade had overshadowed that of all other citizens. Progressive biographers reacted in two ways.

Table XVI

The Heroic Occupations, 1904–1913

The occupations of the heroes in a one-third sample of biographical articles from four best-selling magazines.

Category	No. of Articles	Per Cent of All Articles
Politics	60	34
The Arts	32	18
Foreign Rulers	22	12
Business	15	9
Religious Leaders	11	6
Bureaucrats	10	6
Labor	5	3
Military	5	3
Physicians	4	2
Government Technicians	4	2
Outdoor Sports	3	2
Miscellaneous	5	3
Total	176	100

They held up to public notice those occupations concerned with the just distribution of power, of economic benefits, and of the new scientific and technological advances. They played down and raised questions about the prestige formerly granted to the major Idols of Power in business.

Almost all the changes in the heroic occupations served to identify the Progressive heroes as the Idols of Justice. The numerous politicians were clearly concerned with their traditional function of determining ultimately who got what, when, and how. Biographers specifically charged them with the task of "keeping the balance." But the other ascendant groups in this decade also were involved with the question of who was rightfully to get what. Religious leaders were no longer the creators and founders of a religion or a sect. They were contemporary clergymen of a Social Gospel persuasion (in three-fourths of the cases) deeply engaged in questions of social justice. Not their views of God but their views of society were elaborated. Not their religious experience but their achievements in municipal reform were outlined. They did not differ greatly from the government bureaucrats who were at the heart of "the eternal struggle between the public welfare and private interests." [58] Bureaucrats on local levels, in fact, were transforming jails into secular churches or "moral hospitals, where advice, good will, protection, correction, and, if possible, reformation is the watchword." [59] The new articles on figures from the field of labor, on labor leaders, a household servant, a sweat-shop worker, or a coal miner, were also studies in social justice. How to distribute power and economic rewards so as not to destroy the worker's individuality was the central question they raised.

Even within those occupations which declined in biographical attention a shift could be observed away from the more creative, productive, individual emphasis. During the 1890's four-fifths of the heroes from the arts had been writers, painters, or sculptors, artists producing individual works of their own. Now a majority of biographies in the arts featured actors, actresses, singers, or musicians, people who brought to audiences the roles and music created by others. Foreign rulers were not merely the emperors, czars, and empire-builders. They now included kings noted for their "democratic" inclinations, aristocrats who were socialists, and the leader of the Labor Party in the House of Commons. The projection of domestic Progressive concerns onto a world scale was best illustrated by a series in *Everybody's* on "Soldiers of the Common Good," the result of a world tour by Charles E. Russell searching for democratic leaders in other nations. The whole world seemed to have turned from production and creation to the distribution of justice, of power, and of culture.

Among these Idols of Justice the shift from businessmen to politicians remained the most obvious and significant. Its dimensions extended beyond the simple statistics of change. Politicians clearly emerged as the most vital figures on the contemporary scene. Almost all of the political heroes were living, active participants in the present struggle (96 per cent of the political biographies in this decade versus 52 per cent in the previous one dealt with living politicians). And they were active on all levels of political life from the national arena down to the states and the cities (38 per cent of the political biographies in this decade versus 4 per cent in the previous one dealt with men holding office at state or city levels). Nor was it any longer assumed that business naturally provided the best men for political office even on the local level:

> Commonly a business man does not make a good public executive. In sorrowful truth, your man of business, pure and undefiled . . . has furnished mankind its greatest disasters—and in offices of Mayor and Governor has cost it millions if not billions of dollars.[60]

As an avenue to national prominence, as a field for a new kind of "rags-to-riches" story, politics took on added glamour:

> Less than two years ago Woodrow Wilson was president of Princeton University, where, bulwarked by books, he fitted into an aloof and scholarly atmosphere. Today he is Governor of New Jersey, boss wrecker of corrupt machines, and militant master of his party. To-morrow he may be the Democratic candidate for the Presidency of the United States. Here is a spectacle which any American . . . must view with interest and with a certain satisfaction that he lives in a country which can produce such a development within so brief a period.[61]

"Public life," concluded *Munsey's Magazine*, "is by no means a barren or unattractive field to the youth of high ambition." [62]

Business, however, appeared in the biographies as a rather unpromising field for any youth of high ambition and minimum decency. The downgrading of business prestige was not fully measured by the decline in the proportion of business biographies. Even the remaining ones did little to enhance the status of contemporary businessmen. One-fourth of the business leaders portrayed were dead (as opposed to one-twentieth in the previous decade). Forty per cent of the articles were critical in varying degrees. The few favorable treatments of living, active businessmen took pains to distinguish their heroes from many of the attitudes and practices assumed to be current in business. Far from being the major test and proof of a man's character as it had been in the previous decade, business in the Progressive biographies seemed a field where character was questionable and success was open to suspicion. Never before had Americans found it so difficult to indicate a positive correlation between the business elite and the contemporary model of success.

The dramatic aspects of the Progressive biographies seemed to be the changes. Certainly the changes were both numerous and striking: the appearance of villains, the role of readers as judges, the standard of social contribution, the derogation of wealth as a measure of merit, the close association between the hero and the people, the requirement of social virtues and democratic tactics on the road to success, above all the displacement of businessmen by politicians. All these innovations in the Progressive model of success testified to popular realization of new social needs. A recognition of disturbing developments in the social and economic order as well as in the previous pattern of prestige and values had stirred Americans to redefine their conception of the desirable life. They had been forced to question the adequacy of the Napoleonic model of individualism. Writers had responded by hailing the new Idols of Justice.

The lasting impression, however, remains one of fundamental continuity between the old gods and the new ones. The Progressive villains were convicted more often for betraying individualism than for exposing its limitations. The new social virtues of the Progressive hero were all superimposed upon a strongly individualistic frame of forcefulness, independence, and dominance. The Idols of Justice symbolized the tensions of Americans torn between cherished notions of individualism and the new demands of a consolidating society.

These tensions can be traced not only at popular levels. They appeared in much of the writing of political leaders. They shaped the concerns of advanced intellectual figures. In his *Autobiography* Theodore Roosevelt recalled the "individual morality I was taught by the books I read at home and the books I studied at Harvard." He had no fault to find with this training except that it omitted "the fact that in addition to, not as a substitute for, individual responsibility, there is a collective responsibility":

> I grew into manhood thoroughly imbued with the feeling that a man must be respected for what he made of himself. But I had also, consciously or unconsciously, been taught that socially and industrially pretty much the whole duty of the man lay in thus making the best of himself; that he should be honest in his dealings with others and charitable in the old-fashioned way to the unfortunate; but that it was no part of his business to join with others in trying to make things better for the many by curbing the abnormal and excessive individualism in a few. Now I do not mean that this training was by any means all bad. On the contrary, the insistence upon individual responsibility was, and is, and always will be, a prime necessity. Teaching of the kind I absorbed from both my textbooks and my surroundings is a healthy anti-scorbutic to the sentimentality which by complacently excusing the individual for all his shortcomings would finally hopelessly weaken the spring of moral purpose. It also keeps alive that virile vigor for the lack of which in the average individual no possible perfection of law or of community action can ever atone.[63]

Similarly William James, the psychologist and philosopher, strove to maintain the freedom and power of the individual to shape his world while recognizing the needs of society. A description of James's views sounds like a description of the tensions and the form of reconciling them which ran through Progressive biographies at the same time:

> In order that the wills of individuals . . . shall be realized collectively, it is necessary that each shall assert itself and at the same time make room for others. Both of these strains were prominent in James. The first appeared in his admiration of the individual who exerts himself, endures, and overcomes obstacles, in behalf of his own demands. The second appears in that tenderness and humanity which in James invariably triumphed over self-affirmation. There was thus in James an oscillation of emphasis between the ethics of aggression, militancy, and heroism, and the ethics of conciliation, peace, and social utility. And he was deeply concerned to find a solution of this opposition—in a 'moral equivalent of war,' that is, in an aggressive, militant, and heroic devotion to the cause of conciliation, peace, and social utility.[64]

This was the kind of solution which the Progressive biographers also offered—an aggressive, militant, independent individual devoting himself to the cause of the people. The changes wrought in the Progressive model of success had been introduced at least as much to salvage the traditional model as to meet the new social conditions. "The growth in the complexity of community life," said Roosevelt, "means the partial substitution of collectivism for individualism, not to destroy, but to save, individualism." [65]

With Woodrow Wilson in the White House by 1913, Progressives could look hopefully to a "New Freedom" for social-minded individualism. Even the coming of war might seem to promise fresh opportunities for aggressive, patriotic individual achievement. The nature of modern warfare, however, would call for a collective effort which largely nullified the New Freedom, restored the leaders of big business to heroic status, and effectively submerged the long American fascination with individualism.

The Progressive decade had forestalled any fundamental revolution in the American model of success. But the New Style hero for a corporate society was waiting to emerge in the magazines by 1914. Amid the clamor of war his entry would come without notice.

Part Four

THE IDOLS OF ORGANIZATION

1914-1918

In which our hero becomes
a Manager of Massive Organizations portrayed
in magazines for the masses

Chapter 7

Mass Magazines and the War

Quite apart from the European war, it was already apparent that there were in America the strong beginnings of a swing toward reaction, a fatigue with tumult, a tendency to shut the ears to the din of agitation, a growing distaste for the harsher and noisier leaders of reform, a tolerance, almost a sympathy for their victims.

Collier's, *1914*

THE PROGRESSIVE MOOD of the magazines ended even more abruptly than it had begun. For about a year after the election of Wilson, magazines continued to echo Progressive themes in articles, stories, editorials, and biographies, though the frequency diminished and the note of urgency was muted. By January of 1914 *Collier's* marked the close of an era by observing that "the ten years ending about January 1, 1914, was the period of the greatest ethical advance made by this nation in any decade." The most important economic task of the *next* ten years, concluded the editors, would be the building of good roads.*

Some reaction from the fervent atmosphere of the Progressive years was undoubtedly natural. Even among the most dedicated

* Editorial, "We Take Stock," *Collier's*, LII (January 24, 1914), 11. Note that the anti-climactic plea for good roads obviously catered to the automobile manufacturers whose advertising was becoming increasingly essential for a profitable magazine.

Progressives a sense of exhaustion prevailed. William Allen White, after a meeting of Progressive Party leaders in 1914, reported to Roosevelt:

> First of all, I was struck by the big fact that everyone was spiritually weary. We were sapped dry. . . . For two or three, and in some cases for four years—since 1910—we have been living upon our emotions. . . . We need emotional rest. We need complete change.[1]

Progressivism itself had been spurred by a reaction against the excessive idolatry of business success in the McKinley era, but it had by no means abandoned all the values of that era any more than it had envisioned a radical reconstruction of society. Now the pendulum of the popular mood was swinging back. Magazines seemed very conscious of the cycle in popular attitudes:

> Some twenty years or so ago social thinking in this country was mainly directed to the faults of politics. . . . Many good citizens sighed for able business men to take charge of public affairs and run them as capably as big private enterprises were run.
>
> Then the country woke up to the painful fact that big business was the beneficiary of much of the corruption of politics. . . .
>
> Whereas at one time the word of almost any big business man weighed heavier with the public than the word of almost any politician, at another time almost any politician overtopped almost any leading business men.
>
> The scales are now turning to a truer balance. Politics, on the whole, is much better than it used to be. . . . Big Business is better too. . . . We have boxed the compass, but are by no means where we started from.[2]

The reaction in the magazines, however, was not simply a response to the changing popular temper. More direct pressures operated to bring magazines closer to the outlook of big business. In some cases militant muckraking journals had been bought out by business interests. In other cases creditors and advertisers forced changes in editorial policy.[3] Less obvious but more fundamental were the forces which increasingly made magazine publishing itself a big business. In the five years which closed with the end of World War I the "mass magazine" came to fruition as the product of an organization which offered to advertisers the momentary attention of a national market numbered in the millions. To reach this market and to maintain its interest the best-selling periodicals turned increasingly to the role of entertainers. And as large organizations competing shrewdly for the advertising of ever larger and more sophisticated businesses they presented an image of the business world which paralleled fairly closely the "corporate images" with which public-relations counselors began to fill the advertisements.

An enhanced prestige for business leaders and for business values, a hostility toward government "interference" and toward "agitators" were apparent in the magazines even before the war made a serious impact upon American life. As early as October, 1914, however, *Collier's* noted that "The tendency toward conservatism will be accentuated by the European War."[4] In succeeding years, as war hysteria mounted, the glorification of business leadership and the drive for conformity reached startling proportions in the magazines. Under these conditions it was not surprising that business men rose again to heroic stature. The most significant development was the recasting of business leaders, of government bureaucrats, and of the military commanders alike into a new character-type, that of the manager. In these years American magazines marked the emergence of "The Organization Man" as a model for the successful life.

I

Magazines for the Millions

In the evolution through which all popular periodicals were passing, to meet the need for greater circulation required by the great advertisers, entertainment became increasingly important, discussion of public affairs less so.

Mark Sullivan, The Education of an American

On the surface the magazine world from 1914 through 1918 seems to show no significant changes to compare with the revolution of the 1890's or the urgent spirit of the Progressive decade. No new magazines rose to prominence during World War I. The four leading best-sellers were (in order of circulation) *The Saturday Evening Post, Cosmopolitan, Collier's,* and *McClure's*—all magazines which had begun their careers before 1900. No new forms of magazine writing emerged like the muckraking exposures of the previous decade. No enterprising publishers like Munsey, McClure, and Walker broke through existing patterns to make their personal marks. No new young writers made an impact on the popular mind equal to that of Hapgood, Sullivan, Steffens and the other Progressive journalists. Yet the wartime period did see a most far-reaching and fundamental development in the nature of American magazines. During these years magazine publishing definitely entered the organization society of the twentieth century. What had been popular magazines now became "mass media."

The change was evident in many ways. Circulations continued to rise. By 1918 *Cosmopolitan* and *Collier's* had passed the million mark while the *Post* hovered near two million. Though *McClure's* maintained fourth rank in these years, it reached its peak with 563,000 in 1918, and its financial difficulties thereafter seemed to prove that economic conditions had raised the circulation threshold for survival of a popular magazine to the level of at least a million. The trouble was that publishing costs had also risen rapidly. Advertising provided a greater and ever greater share of the revenue, and advertisers were becoming more sophisticated and more demanding.* Guided by market research and other increasingly rationalized procedures the great national advertisers tended to concentrate their expenditures upon a few outstandingly successful periodicals.

The key to the changing character of the magazines could thus be found within the developing field of advertising. The rise of the new popular magazines had already benefitted greatly from manufacturers' efforts after 1890 to reach a national market and to appeal directly to consumers. Advertising expenditures in newspapers and magazines during the twenty-five years from 1890 through 1914 had risen from about $71,000,000 to about $256,000,000—an increase per capita of the American population from $1.13 to $2.61. This expansion within a relatively new and disorganized field had opened the way for new careers, had been accompanied by many abuses, and had sanctioned many rather intuitive, hit-or-miss procedures.[5] These conditions had made possible the profitable existence of a relatively large number of general magazines which ranged in circulation from 200,000 to 600,000. Within this group had been all the muckraking magazines.

The war, however, both coincided with and helped to stimulate a great acceleration in advertising. Where total expenditures had been $256,000,000 in 1914, they leaped to about $528,000,000 in

* I have not been able to discover any exact figures for the relative amounts in 1918 of magazine income from subscribers as compared with advertisers. The direction in which magazine finances were moving, however, is clearly indicated by Frank Presbrey's estimate that in 1928 the *Saturday Evening Post* was receiving about $80,000 a week from sales of the magazine while its weekly income from advertising was about $1,000,000. By that time, he continues, it cost *Liberty* 13½ cents to deliver to the dealer a copy for which it received from him 3½ cents. Frank Presbrey, *The History and Development of Advertising* (New York, 1929), 597.

1919, and the advertising expenditure per capita of the population rose in this short time from $2.61 to $5.03.*

Of greater consequence for the fate and the character of general magazines was the development of more systematic, more rationalized procedures within the field of advertising. Around 1910 some advertising agencies had begun to establish departments for market research. In the same year some of the larger advertisers founded the Association of National Advertisers with the declared purpose "To make every dollar spent in advertising bring back greater returns." By 1914 the Audit Bureau of Circulations was organized to provide accurate, objective figures on magazine circulations. Repeated efforts to standardize the practices of advertising agencies culminated in 1917 with formation of the American Association of Advertising Agencies.[6] Careful planning and "scientific" calculation of advertising campaigns displaced the more random, intuitional, and opportunistic practices prevalent during the 1890's and the first decade of the twentieth century.

As a result of these movements advertisers became more selective in their choice of magazines. They spent more on advertising. They bought larger space for individual advertisements. But they concentrated their expenditures in periodicals with the largest proven circulations and in those which could offer evidence of real returns upon the investments. Under these circumstances the general magazines of moderate circulations and limited staffs were hard pressed to compete or even to survive. The leading magazines benefitted disproportionately, and the pressure for

* Figures from Borden, *Economic Effects of Advertising*, 48. The increase was apparently gradual through 1918 and then rose most sharply in the first postwar year as advertisers faced increased competition, tried to avoid excess profits taxes through advertising expenditures, and strove to tap the war-swollen incomes of American consumers. No total figures are available for the years between 1914 and 1919, but see the comments and partial figures in: Hower, *History of an Advertising Agency*, 107–109, 536; and Gaw, *Trends in Development of Magazines in an Advertising Medium*, 211.

higher and higher circulation grew intense. In the best position of all were the publishing companies which operated a chain of magazines with circulation leaders in the general field, in the women's field, and in the farm field. Such an organization could offer advertisers not only its vast circulations but also the services of an extensive staff for market research and special promotions. This pattern of organization became the dominant one in the magazine world. The Curtis Publishing Company with its *Saturday Evening Post*, its *Ladies' Home Journal*, and its *Country Gentlemen* emerged as the most successful of all. In 1918 the Curtis publications garnered 43 per cent of all the advertising dollars spent in general, women's, and farm magazines. Two other best-selling general magazines also fell into this pattern. *Cosmopolitan* had become part of a Hearst chain which included *Hearst's Magazine*, *Good Housekeeping*, and others. After Robert Collier's death in 1918, *Collier's* became a part of the Crowell chain which challenged the Curtis publications with *Collier's*, the *American*, *Woman's Home Companion*, and *Farm and Fireside*, a group which attracted 12 per cent of the total magazine advertising in 1920.[7] Large-scale organization was taking over the magazine world, and the day of the independent editor-publisher like McClure, Walker, and Collier was passing.

The history of each of the best-selling general magazines after 1913 demonstrated how the pressures for business organization, for advertising, and for circulation became dominant. The *Saturday Evening Post* showed the least change because the pattern of organization developed by the Curtis Publishing Company proved its clear advantage in these years and became the model for other publications. The *Post's* circulation actually grew very little and even declined at times between 1914 and 1918. Yet the *Post* retained the leadership it had built up during the Progressive period with a circulation nearly double that of any of its rivals. The great difference now became the vast increase of advertising revenue which this leadership secured for Lorimer's magazine. Though circulation dropped by about 37,000 from 1912 to 1917, the *Post*'s advertising revenue rose from $7,114,581 to $16,076,562 in the same years.[8] Such a development could only encourage publishers to view their readers more as a great market of consumers than as patrons of literature or citizens of the republic. The primary advances and innovations which the *Post* demonstrated after 1912 were in its services to advertisers rather than in its editorial policies or features.

While the *Post* continued to sell more copies every week than any other magazine, *Cosmopolitan* had emerged by 1914 as the best seller among the monthlies. Its recent and rapid climb to leadership offered proof that a new kind of editorial emphasis in the monthly magazine could be immensely successful. When Hearst first took over the *Cosmopolitan* from John Brisben Walker in 1905, the magazine had embarked upon an extensive campaign of muckraking. The very word "muckraking" had been coined by Theodore Roosevelt as a derogatory term for the sensational character of *Cosmopolitan*'s attack upon the Senate. "Sensationalism" was the common charge hurled at *Cosmopolitan*'s brand of exposures which focused from 1905 to 1911 upon the Senate, child labor, "The Owners of America," the Mormon Church, graft in the states, and the ways in which university professors were challenging traditional religion. Despite the striking and often extravagant nature of these exposures, they had not brought *Cosmopolitan* to the top rank of the best sellers. Like *McClure's* the magazine during its muckraking phase attracted a respectable but secondary level of circulation somewhat over 400,000.

In 1912, however, Hearst's editors not only dropped their critical articles, but they virtually dropped any serious discussion of public affairs and cut down radically the proportion of all articles. The new emphasis was to be on fiction, and preferably on fiction of a particular kind. Taking their cue from the circulation boost provided in 1911 by Robert W. Chambers's slightly risqué serial story, "The Common Law," they proceeded to spice the magazine with the titillating effusions of such authors as Elinor Glyn and Fannie Hurst. These changes more than doubled the circulation which rose to over a million during World War I. *Cosmopolitan,* benefitting from the business resources of the extensive Hearst organization, edited by a shifting staff of professional "magazinists," providing escape, entertainment, and titillation for millions of readers, helped to establish a new pattern for "mass media." A *Cosmopolitan* editor capped the achievement by articulating the "successful formula" which would be repeated endlessly in succeeding decades: "Find out what your readers want and give it to them. And give it to them regularly!" [9] Here was the ultimate view of the reader as consumer and of the magazine as business organization.

Collier's maintained its distinct Progressive character through 1913, but already developments had eroded much of that special position which for a decade had sustained the magazine's detached and disenchanted attitude toward business values. After his father's death in 1909, Robert Collier assumed control of the Collier book business as well as the magazine. The very temperament which made him an effective critic of a business civilization also made him an ineffective manager of the family business. *Collier's* soon fell into debts which could no longer be defrayed from the dwindling profits of the book sales. He was forced by 1912 to turn for a substantial loan to his friend, Harry Payne Whitney. Though Whitney imposed no conditions, Whitney's bankers, the conservative house of Lee, Higginson & Company, soon moved in to assure the security of the loan by supervising the operation of the magazine. Their auditors checked on its financial activities, and one of the bankers became an advisory manager with increasing influence in all areas of the magazine's policy.

The financial crisis was in turn aggravated by a personal crisis which broke up the Progressive trio of editors. In 1912 Norman

Hapgood had become increasingly distressed by Robert Collier's profligacy and by the consequent threat to the magazine's independence. Hapgood also found himself both by conviction and by temperament as much attracted to the program and personality of Woodrow Wilson as he was distrustful of the flamboyant Theodore Roosevelt and of the trust plank in the Progressive Party's platform. Collier, on the other hand, felt a strong personal attachment to Roosevelt, a distaste for the "professorial" Wilson, and a defiant sensitivity about the magazine's financial situation. Relations between the two finally reached a dramatic clash at the height of the presidential campaign. Hapgood resigned and for weeks traded charges and countercharges with Collier in the newspapers.[10] Collier himself took over editorial management of the magazine and for a year longer maintained much of its particular flair and Progressive outlook. By 1914, however, his personal difficulties forced him to hand the editorship over to Mark Sullivan.

Even if he had been strongly inclined to try it, Sullivan was in no position to continue the Progressive character of *Collier's*. Hapgood was gone. Robert Collier was beginning to fail mentally and physically. The old camaraderie which had provided a mutual stimulation, a buoyant confidence, and a useful division of labor was no longer possible. Theodore Roosevelt, to whom both Collier and Sullivan felt close, was out of power, and the magazine was committed to opposing Wilson. The popular mood had shifted. Above all, Sullivan had to reckon with the advisory manager imposed by the bankers, a man who thought that a magazine should give to the public "the kind of instruction . . . which comported with the well-being of business." The very burden of Sullivan's role as chief editor meant that he simply did not have the time to sustain his previous familiarity with public affairs. With all the pressures "to meet the need for greater circulation required by the great advertisers, entertainment became increasingly important, discussion of public affairs less so."

Sullivan found himself giving "more and more of my time to contacts with writers of fiction, less to politics."[11]

In the struggle for circulation *Collier's* was remarkably successful during the war. It rose from 562,000 in 1913 to 1,055,000 in 1918, and its advertising, particularly from the automobile industry, grew apace. Unlike many of the former muckraking magazines, *Collier's* adjusted to the new requirements of the marketplace. It moved closer to the model of the *Saturday Evening Post* by dropping its price to five cents, reducing its news pictures, and diminishing its emphasis on art work and striking cartoons. As the organizational revolution in mass publishing overtook *Collier's*, Sullivan became more and more unhappy in his editorial post. In 1917 he resigned. In 1918 Robert Collier died. And in 1919 the logical climax was reached when *Collier's* was absorbed into the publishing empire of Joseph Palmer Knapp, a shrewd manufacturer of mass magazines who had built up the Crowell Publishing Company.

The fate of *McClure's* has been pictured as the result of a conspiracy by "special interests" against muckraking. The charge is that S. S. McClure lost control of his magazine "because muckraking was 'on the spot.'"[12] This kind of explanation stems from that viewpoint, common among historians, which considers muckraking as the only significant element in the magazine history of the early twentieth century. It tends to misjudge somewhat the actual popular mood of the Progressive period, dismisses too easily the change in that mood, and ignores almost entirely the fundamental lines of development of the mass magazines. McClure himself protested that his troubles came from "bad business methods,"[13] an explanation which, if not very revealing, at least suggests more was involved than a simple conspiracy against muckraking.

The essential story of *McClure's* after 1911 is the effort to prosper or even to survive by transforming the magazine and its organization along the lines being established by the Curtis, the Hearst, and the Crowell publishing chains. S. S. McClure had always been more remarkable for his editorial genius than for his business acumen. John S. Phillips, until his departure in 1906, had been the man who brought profitable order out of McClure's chaotic and creative enthusiasms. By 1911 McClure's son-in-law, Cameron Mackenzie, was filling the functions of general manager. He had to face the facts that the magazine's business was declining and that McClure's health was bad. Mackenzie consequently secured a partner, and under the name of McClure Publications these two men purchased control of the magazine while retaining Sam McClure as titular editor. The new direction in which Mackenzie was looking appeared evident from the man whom he chose as partner. Frederick Lewis Collins had been editor of the *Woman's Home Companion* and secretary for the chain of the Crowell Publishing Company. In accordance with the pattern of the Crowell, Curtis, and Hearst organizations, the partners immediately added a woman's magazine, *Ladies' World,* to their enterprise.

Sam McClure himself dropped his editorial post entirely by 1913, and Mackenzie did likewise by 1915. Collins continued his effort to mold *McClure's* into the new requirements for mass magazines by greater emphasis on entertainment, by adopting the quarto size which advertisers favored, and by combining text and advertising in the back pages.[14] His efforts did secure a moderate gain in circulation which brought *McClure's* to its all-time peak of 563,000 in 1918. Though higher than any point reached in its muckraking phase, that figure no longer was sufficient to enable *McClure's* to compete adequately for the all-important advertising. Collins recognized the new facts of magazine life and sold out in 1919. For ten years more *McClure's* dragged out an increasingly precarious life. At one stage S. S. McClure returned for a fruitless attempt to revive it. Finally the famous magazine met a merciful end after it had been retitled the *New McClure's—A Man's Magazine!* under the direction of the publisher of *Photoplay*. The revolutionary popular periodical which had helped to dethrone the *Century* and *Harper's* could not itself survive the advent of the mass magazine and of the movies.

II
The Rehabilitation of Business in the Magazines

The hands that have molded industry
now shape the destinies of nations.

Saturday Evening Post, 1918

As magazine publishing became a bigger business which was increasingly dependent on advertising revenue, the editorial comments on business and business leaders came to resemble the advertisements themselves. This process appeared most strikingly in *Collier's*, the magazine which had previously called for emphasis on the "uncommercial" aspects of American life. The new emphasis was to be on the ways in which commercialism was pervaded with humane and democratic values.

Institutional advertising was largely a new technique of the war years. It could be extremely profitable for magazines since this type of advertisement required considerable space to create its "corporate image" with maximum effectiveness. It also encroached most closely upon the editorial function of a magazine so that its very nature helped to blur distinctions and cut into the independent integrity of a periodical's editorial viewpoint. A very clear example of these tendencies was a full four-page advertisement in Collier's by the Reo Motor Company:

> The Reo plan has made good . . . in its demonstration of the fact that it is possible to combine business with friendship, efficiency with good feeling, commercialism with comradery. And to these Old Fashioned business men it is a source of the

> keenest pleasure . . . that those from whom they buy and those to whom they sell, refer to them not as manufacturers, or as a mere Corporate Something, but familiarly, affectionately, as 'the Reo Folk.'"[15]

In another full two-page advertisement the Union Pacific Railroad attempted to endow itself with virtual governmental status: "The Union Pacific is one of the great industrial triumphs of republican government, the result of individual initiative combined with wise government interest and cooperation."[16]

The editors moved to blur still further any distinctions between advertisements and editorials by writing themselves an "Advertising Bulletin." This novel form of commentary struck the new emphasis in a heading: "Idealism and Commercialism." It then proceeded to congratulate the United Cigar Stores on their public approval of the Federal Reserve Act and to point up the lesson:

> It emphasizes the New Spirit in Commercialism as admirably expressed by Lehn and Fink, manufacturers of Pebeco Tooth Paste, in the introductory pages of their Dentist's Diary of 1914, 'the book that breathes the New Spirit in Dentistry.' The paragraph reads:
>
> 'There are many who still believe that idealism suffers considerably through too intimate association with commercialism, but progressive thinkers are agreed that the process is all in the other direction. Commercialism is inspired and ennobled through its intimacy with idealism.'[17]

Meanwhile, in those best-selling magazines which still paid much attention to public affairs,* editorials and articles evinced a renewed confidence in the nation's business leadership. Any past abuses, it was assumed, had been remedied by a combina-

* *Cosmopolitan* took little notice of public affairs, *McClure's* somewhat more, but the two leading weeklies, *Collier's* and the *Post,* far outdistanced either of the monthlies in commenting upon political, economic and war matters despite their general increased emphasis on entertainment.

tion of government regulations together with the "New Spirit" in business. The danger now was that Wilson and "the politicians" might go too far in "reckless experiments with business." [18] The *Post* summed up the new mood in October, 1914:

> Admit that the business leadership of fifteen years ago was quite too free and easy; that various supervisions and restriction have been placed on it for the general good—the fact remains that leadership is tremendously important. . . . For some years business leadership has been a more or less unpopular and uncomfortable occupation. . . . Our new captains of industry, it is said, must hold new ideals; but they cannot hold the idea that conspicuous success in business is ground for suspicion and be captains of industry.
>
> More than all, they cannot be able business men and approve merely vexatious and experimental restrictions on business. . . . The political atmosphere just now is not favorable to the development of business leadership.[19]

This rehabilitation of editorial confidence in business leadership reached new heights when the United States entered the war. In the mass magazines the contributions of industry and finance to the war effort seemed to endow business men with a new aura of altruism:

> The first vigorous and effectual response to the call to arms came precisely from Wall Street. . . .
>
> Only a blockhead could fail to see that the condition which preceded a declaration of war was more profitable for High Finance and Big Business than the condition which followed a declaration of war would be.
>
> War, with its demand for a common purpose and a common sacrifice, makes this a good time to discard popular prejudices against Wall Street as merely stupid and demagogic.[20]

The war years enabled magazines to clothe business not only in a new garb of altruism but also with the older raiments of efficiency and productivity which now took on a new importance for the nation. *Collier's* noted:

> Many leading business men are now engaged in constructive work for the nation, and are having the time of their lives at it. They are inventing, organizing, lowering costs and prices, bringing the whole industrial and financial strength of the country to bear on this greatest problem of applied skill and power, the problem of war.[21]

It seemed a time when "results" alone counted. The Supreme Court was praised for dismissing anti-trust action against the United Shoe Machinery Company since "the country could not afford to deprive itself of the results obtained by doing an important sort of work in what appears the most effective way yet discovered." [22] The *Post* contended that England's wartime experience had proved the superior ability of businessmen to manage all national affairs:

> When you strip away the glamour from the great war and analyze the larger results, you find that nothing achieved so far is of more permanent value than the infusion of business methods into the conduct of governments. . . . The hands that have molded industry now shape the destinies of nations.

"The Supreme Lesson for America," concluded the *Post*, was that here "as in England, the business man will eventually do everything but stake out the strategy of battle." [23]

Business leaders could scarcely ask for more deference from the magazines unless they wished to write the articles themselves and to be loved as well as respected. Even these things were added unto them. *Collier's* ran a series which presented the views of George Perkins, Judge Gary, and Thomas Lamont on America's postwar prospects.[24] When Charles M. Schwab wrote on "Doing the Impossible," an editor's note commented, "Anybody who hears Mr. Schwab talk will feel that he is not only a man who gets things done, but also a kindly, unaffected, appreciative person."[25] Through advertisements, advertising bulletins, editorials, articles, and editor's notes the rehabilitation of business leadership in the magazines was complete.

III
Magazine Reactions to the War

A revolution must first be worked in the mind of each citizen in his conception of his relationship to the state. We must achieve the will to think nationally.

Collier's, *1918*

The magazines' reactions to the war itself also played a part in creating the context for the new managerial heroes. Direct responses to the war varied somewhat from magazine to magazine. *Cosmopolitan,* influenced by its new focus on entertainment and by William Randolph Hearst's opposition to the war, virtually ignored the conflict. It paid far more attention to developments and personalities on the Broadway stage or in the young motion picture industry than to any events or leaders in any theater of war. *McClure's,* the other best-selling monthly, was also rather slow at first to modify its concern for entertainment with any serious discussion of the war. During the period of American neutrality its chief contributions were two lengthy serials which imaginatively portrayed "The Conquest of America in 1921" by the German Army and how all political factions united in "Saving the Nation." * After the United States entered

* Cleveland Moffett, "The Conquest of America in 1921," *McClure's,* XLV (May–August, 1915) and "Saving the Nation," *McClure's,* XLVI (December, 1915–February, 1916). Meanwhile S. S. McClure, no longer editor, followed one of his characteristic hasty enthusiasms in December of 1915 by embarking on Henry Ford's Peace Ship to end the war in Europe.

the struggle, "*McClure's* Win-the-War Magazine" filled its pages with articles and stories oriented almost exclusively to support of the war effort.

The two leading weeklies maintained a more continuous interest in the war from the moment of its outbreak in 1914. *Collier's* generally followed a line close to the views of Theodore Roosevelt, who was vehemently denouncing Wilson's conduct of our neutrality policy. In the *Saturday Evening Post,* on the other hand, the President found a welcome and consistent support for every stage of his diplomacy up to but not including the final Treaty of Versailles.* The most notable feature of magazine response to the war was not so much the minor divergences during neutrality as the almost hysterical tone of conformity which emerged in *McClure's, Collier's,* and the *Post* once we had entered the fighting. This surge of "Americanism" and of savage suspicion for all dissent or difference seems an important element in the acceptance of the new heroes of organization.

As reflected in the magazines, the fundamental process at work in these five years was a transference in the fears of middle-class Americans. By 1914 Progressive anxiety about the trusts, the plutocracy, and the cities had been largely dissipated. Magazine writers no longer showed concern for an individualism threatened by business consolidation, for a democracy endangered by political machines and special interests, or for an older morality imperiled by pervasive and impersonal commercialism. The Progressive sense of potential threats from above and from within had faded out of the magazines before any shots were fired in Europe. As the war dragged on, however, and as Americans were drawn more closely into the maelstrom, the magazines reflected a new and more desperate kind of fears. The threats seemed to come from areas clearly outside the old American middle-class world, the threat to democracy from "Prussian Absolutism," the

* Wilson wrote Lorimer a letter of thanks in 1918 for the *Post*'s "admirable" interpretation of the Administration's diplomatic purposes. Tebbel, *Lorimer,* 179.

threat to private property, Anglo-Saxon supremacy, and Protestant moralism from "alien" groups and ideologies which had infiltrated American society. The old Progressive fear of threats from within the nation and from above the middle class gave way to an "Americanism" which saw perils from abroad and from below.* The result was to drive middle-class magazines into an identification with the state and the dominant business community. The actual merging of governmental and business leaders in the common war effort helped to remove any sense of cross purposes between them. Efficient, cooperative, unquestioning exertion for victory in war became the prime standard of judgment. In this process the long American preoccupation with individualism became submerged. The war provided a tremendous and dramatic acceleration in the transition to the new managerial models of success.

Collier's and the *Saturday Evening Post* followed somewhat different paths to this wartime conformity of fears and standards. In August of 1914 *Collier's* felt the major threat to be the war itself and expressed no choice between the combatants. "Civilization itself stands in jeopardy," proclaimed an editorial which went on to explain more precisely by speaking of "the spiritual penalty we shall pay as members of the white race for this white man's suicidal war." [26] Within a month, however, *Collier's* had chosen sides. It pointed to the Kaiser and his military absolutism as the great menace. The editorial formula was to profess neutrality while castigating Germany:

> We shall obey President Wilson's neutrality order faithfully. All the same, we know the man who, stripped of monarchical prerogatives, in any American court, under American law, could be indicted and convicted for incitement to murder.[27]

* For an analysis of the psychology of 100 per cent Americanism during World War I see John Higham, *Strangers in the Land* (New Brunswick, 1955), 204–12.

> We shall observe President Wilson's neutrality order rigidly. And yet suppose Germany should win? . . . With a triumph of the military spirit and absolutism in Europe, we would have to step unwillingly into France's shoes.[28]

Succeeding months found *Collier's* urging that neutrality involved no embargo on shipments to the Allies and no hesitation in granting them loans. "The American people feel powerfully about this war," concluded the editors. "They believe that right and justice are on the side of Belgium and her allies." [29] By the summer of 1916 the magazine was going all out for American preparedness and beginning to make hysterical comments about those who opposed it. A dramatic article, "The Last Message of Richard Harding Davis," attacked pacifists and labor leaders. Shells and bombs were blind, said Davis. "Occasionally they will knock holes in the homes of the labor agitator and the pacifist. At least, let us hope so." [30] As the Germans began unrestricted submarine warfare, *Collier's* announced "The Real Issue" to be "World Democracy or World Absolutism" and insisted "the administration must infallibly realize that metaphysics have no place in the present entanglement. No half measure will do!" [31]

America's entry into the battle against Germany came as a necessary and logical step in the course which *Collier's* had followed, and the magazine accepted the "horror of war" with considerable zest: "Many men and women are finding that a cause greater than themselves, a cause in which self can be sunk utterly, affords a joy which life had not seemed able to yield." [32] It seemed rather stimulating to abandon individualism for the duration: "We are giving up individual property—in order to make, until the war is over, a national unit, a compact fighting machine." [33]

After a year of conflict *Collier's* was willing to entertain the idea that individualism might be something of a handicap for the nation's security even after the war. A rather mystical, fear-ridden article on "The New America" identified the continuing future threats to our society as coming from (1) German nationalism, (2) alien groups in America, (3) international socialism, and (4) agnosticism. "What shall we oppose to this disciplined anarchy?" it asked. "The same disorganization of the forces of order, the same loose ideal of Americanism—opportunism, individualism, drift, and confusion?" Against the persisting strength of German nationalism it saw only an ineffective Anglo-Saxon "centrifugal movement toward individualism." Somehow Americans must "achieve the will to think *nationally*." The New America must create "a fraternity of discipline to meet the challenge of rival civilizations and to breathe into the spirit of Americanism everywhere a dedication to all things American."[34] By now a writer for a mass magazine could see individualism itself as potentially un-American.

The *Saturday Evening Post* first responded to the war by recoiling from the follies of Europe. It felt that an alliance of France and Germany against Austria and Russia would be a "more natural alliance" and concluded that the actual situation showed "how completely detached from real human interests this whole statecraft stuff of diplomacy and war is."[35] As Americans fled from Europe to safety at home, the *Post* rejoiced that the war had cured them of the strange "disease of Europitis."[36] Until late in the spring of 1915, Lorimer opened his pages impartially to articles which reflected the views of all the major combatants. Irwin Cobb testified as an eyewitness that there was no reliable evidence of any German atrocities in Belgium. "An American Private in the German Army" reported that the German soldier was "just a man, a plain man like you and me . . . fighting as best he knows how to save his country and his dear ones." This article had been printed just before the *Lusitania* went down. It represented the last favorable reference to Germany in the *Post*.[37]

The sinking of the *Lusitania* appeared to be "the act of barbarians," yet the *Post* insisted that America's "deep reaction from the bloody and heathen barbarism of war is the finest prize of our culture and our highest justification. We should be trebly careful not to lose it." From this point on the *Post* supported increasing involvement with the Allied cause. It opposed any embargo on war shipments since this would be "tantamount to a declaration of opinion that the Allies ought to be beaten." It favored loans to the Allies. It discovered "the hollowness of the notion that the United States stands apart, sufficient to itself, largely indifferent to the rest of the world." It categorized German "contempt for a scrap of paper" as "simply contempt for civilization" and pointed to the great difference between Allied and German violations of our neutral rights.[38]

Unlike *Collier's,* however, the *Post* maintained a continual insistence on peace and looked to Wilson as the best hope for keeping the nation out of war. Even while protesting German actions it ran an editorial on "Our Needless Wars" which would never have been fought "if they could only have been postponed a few years." Wilson's proposal for a League of Nations elicited warm approval from a usually isolationist *Post*: "To declare that we want lasting peace, and then to sit back and merely advise Europe how it may secure lasting peace, without being willing to take our share in securing it, would be a contemptible role." As late as March of 1917, one month before we declared war, Lorimer felt Wilson deserved "the implicit confidence of that great majority of the people of the United States who earnestly desire peace." Up to the moment of our entry, the threat of war itself seemed more disturbing than any other evil. To avert war Lorimer had brought himself to support a Democratic President whom he otherwise distrusted and to advocate a League of Nations which he would later repudiate.[39]

The very disappointment which Lorimer felt about American involvement in the war probably contributed to the extraordinarily virulent tone which the *Post* adopted during the war years and for some time thereafter.[40] The whole concept of war had to be identified with the enemy. A lead article elaborated upon "The

Prussian Paranoia" and an editorial explained that, "It is against this bloody, brutish, Prussian cult of war that America is now in arms." [41] Those who seemed to profit undeservedly from the war or those who, worst of all, continued to oppose it after the nation and the *Post* had been dragged into it seemed particular aggravations. Workers with high wartime wages were exposed to ridicule.[42] Conscientious objectors were accused of being "grafters" and of harboring pro-German sympathies.[43] In the spring of 1918, at the time when *Collier's* spawned its vision of a new disciplined "Americanism," the *Post* also reached an unprecedented pitch of fear and hysteria. Alien elements in our midst loomed as the source of all America's troubles. Lorimer blasted editorially at the "Scum of the Melting Pot." He printed a lead article on "Our Imported Troubles and Trouble-Makers," especially "The Half-Baked Reformers." [44] Meanwhile, *McClure's* was advising its readers to "Constitute yourself a secret-service agent, and if at any time you hear a remark against our Government or against our Allies, no matter how trivial or unimportant it may seem to you, either arrest that person or report to your nearest police station his or her name and address." [45]

Throughout the closing months of the war extravagant fears of radicals and aliens erupted in the *Post*.[46] Nor was the coming of peace sufficient to allay the wartime anxieties. The last issue of the magazine in 1918 still pointed to the new source of evil:

> Two-thirds of our troubles in America are imported. . . . From our silly system of smart society, taken from European capitals with their class distinctions and monarchical traditions, down to our bogus Socialism, made in Germany and Russia as a panacea for conditions that were utterly foreign to America until indiscriminate immigration planted them in a few plague spots in our great cities, our worries are due to our carelessness as to who and what comes to America.[47]

Some of the old notes familiar to *Post* readers could still be discerned in this outburst. There was the concern for a middle-class style of life which the glamour of "smart society" threatened to eclipse. There was the old bogey of socialism. There was the partial distrust of cities. Yet the dangerous, corrupting element in each of these was now identified exclusively with foreign sources. Evil came from without. The remedy was to close ranks, to bar the gates, not to countenance change or reform within. This defensive, conformist fearfulness was itself a most significant change in mood. Conspicuous by their absence from the *Post* were the old confidence in American opportunities and the old demands for heroic individualism. It seemed a time for guards to man the walls of existing American institutions, not a time for heroes to open new paths outward.

A combination of forces thus operated to produce in the magazines after 1913 a new attitude toward individual heroes and a changed model for the successful life. Fatigued by a decade of the strenuous moral life, satisfied that the worst abuses had been remedied by governmental action and a new sense of responsibility in business, alarmed perhaps at a downswing of the business cycle in 1913 and 1914, the popular mood had reacted against Progressive fervency even before any trenches were dug in France.

Meanwhile the magazines themselves were being taken over by organization men. They were coalescing into great publishing chains run by editorial managers. Their now inescapable dependence upon advertising revenue forced the development of an editorial formula which could be persuasively purveyed to advertisers as the reason for a large circulation and as an appropriate context for large-scale advertisements. All of the leading general magazines had by now been in existence for two decades or more. Their problem was how to keep a successful organization going, not how to create a new enterprise by challenging the existing leaders of the magazine world. The magazines which solved this problem most convincingly were those which understood the need for organization and rationalization of their procedures. If the war had never come, these mass magazines could scarcely have avoided idolizing managerial heroes. In the field of publishing, as in the other major areas of American life, power was flowing into the hands of a new type of leader. Though businessmen regained most of their former prestige in the magazines, these were a new kind of businessmen. The situation produced changes in the model of the successful life which, if judged by the traditional standard of individualism, were more revolutionary than anything envisioned in Progressive preachments about the dying of "the old gods."

At its outbreak, *Collier's* noted that the World War would accentuate a swing toward conservatism in America. Many historians have since confirmed this judgment. In one sense it is certainly a true judgment. If the magazines give any fair measure of national attitudes, the war did contribute to a renewed confidence in business leadership, to an antipathy toward labor, to a fearful suspicion of "radicals," and to a compulsive defence of those national attributes and institutions which the business classes identified as truly "American."

Yet in another sense the war accentuated revolutionary developments in America. Historians have also noted how the war speeded the process of consolidation in American industry and labor, how it established precedents for extensive government regulation of the economy, and how it proved a training ground for future administrators of the New Deal. From a long-range perspective the most significant contribution of the war seems to have been the way it awakened many Americans to recognition of the facts of life in the twentieth century. In tracing the changing conceptions of success in American magazines, one is struck primarily by the way World War I dramatically confirmed the existence and the value of new Idols of Organization. Perhaps only the war could have led magazines to subordinate as much as they did during these years their previous admiration for individualism.

Chapter 8

The Heroes of World War I

In the present war, more than in any other, dashing leadership has counted for little; organizing ability and scientific military thinking for everything.

Collier's, *1916*

THE MAGAZINE MUSTER of heroic individuals suffered heavy casualties during World War I. The demands of an organization society and of a wartime mobilization seemed to dissolve the previous preoccupation with individualism. Popular magazines in the 1890's had seen the world in terms of powerful individuals making a personal mark. Progressive magazines had tried to preserve a sense of individualism by honoring a new breed of forceful, independent heroes for making contributions to society. But in the mass magazines after 1913 this concern for individualism seemed to be dwindling away to join other outmoded notions like the eighteenth century's concern for the gentleman. Evidence for the diminishing importance of assertive individualism comes from the sharp decline in the number of biographical articles, from scattered comments in the magazines, and from the nature of the remaining biographies themselves.

The frequency of biographies in the best-selling magazines declined steadily after the McKinley era when an average of more than one biographical article had appeared in every issue. During the Progressive decade this ratio dropped to slightly less

Table XVII
Frequency of Biographies

The ratio of biographical articles per issue in a one-third sample of the four best-selling magazines for each period.

Period	Biographies per Issue
1894–1903	1.34
1904–1913	0.42
1914–1918	0.24

than one biography in every second issue. By World War I the ratio was down to one biography in every fourth issue. For some reason the most successful editors of popular magazines were losing interest in the lives of individuals.

In 1914 Edwin Lefevre offered an explanation to readers of the *Post*:

> I am inclined to think the [reason for the] decline in the importance of the character sketch is that we have overthrown so many popular idols that people now are less interested in the leaders than in the cause. Roosevelt is an exception; and if you will think over his case carefully . . . you will see how he has already begun to savor of an anachronism.[1]

Yet in 1914 this explanation for the decline of biographies was itself something of an anachronism. It may have applied to the Progressive years in some degree, but the rest of Lefevre's article hinted at a more fundamental reason for the submergence of individual heroes in the magazines. No longer, he noted, did corporation heads and Wall Street magnates say "theirs is not the public's business." In fact the new policy of business organizations called for a continual "lobbying" with the public. For this reason, "Publicity experts . . . have become part of the office furniture of the big corporations and banking houses." As a result, "The interview of our fathers is out of date," and writers responded with boredom and "Unwritten Interviews." Changing circumstances had taken much of the zest away from the writing of character sketches. A sense of loss was evident in Lefevre's reminiscences of former encounters with authoritarian business leaders. The new atmosphere where cautious business organizations professionally merchandized the personalities of their managers had little appeal to this veteran writer.

Further comments showed how the ideal of forceful individualism was yielding to the pressures of an organization society. *Cosmopolitan* predicted a change in "the main business faculty that is going to count in the next twenty years":

> The smooth-running man, all strength and gentleness, who makes rough places smooth by having some human give-and-take in him, the man who is supplied by nature and by training with air-cushions, the pneumatic-tired employer, is going to be seen displacing the old, hard, rumbly, bumpy, iron-tired employer on every highway in business.[2]

Collier's ran a series of "Business Man's Talks to Young Men." It was in the old tradition of advice on success, but it struck some new notes. For the first time in a popular magazine it passed over the old admonitions for the "inner-directed" character—the recommendations of thrift, honesty, industry, perseverance, and self-assurance. In their place it substituted many of the elements of the "other-directed" character. The whole burden of the series was that young men should govern their conduct by what others might think of them.

The author asserted that tobacco and alcohol should ideally be avoided. Yet since "There is an unreasoning prejudice against the man who is 'too nice,'" young men could not afford to court disapproval. The point was then driven home:

> If I were twenty-one again, I should try to be entirely human, no matter how many and exceptional my virtues or how exemplary my deportment. I should be one of the boys, for the rea-

son that the fellow who hasn't been one of the boys is likely to have trouble in becoming one of the men when he reaches man's estate.

The old focus on opportunities for advancement was shifted to stress the "countless opportunities in every young man's life to demonstrate that he is a regular fellow." A similar consideration would lead the prospective businessman to attend law school. Since law was said to be the crystallization of public opinion, "Nowhere else can you learn better methods of seeking public approval." The salesman must learn to think of his customers as friends and must train himself to "Smile Like a Dog." Self-esteem, it was granted, "is rather important to a young man's success." "However," cautioned the author, "the other man's viewpoint is always important as the best sort of self-esteem results from your consciousness that you are deporting yourself as decent people expect you to act. Any other sort of self-esteem is either bluff or self-delusion." [3]

This focus upon the acceptance and expectations of others was a drastic change from the Napoleonic hero of twenty years earlier who had boasted: "Nothing awed me; I feared no one. I struck one, I scratched another, I was a terror to everybody." [4] The Progressive emphasis upon society's judgment of the individual had now been extended to a point where society was all-important and where individuality itself might be dismissed as a "delusion."

Magazine comments like these indicated the direction of change, but only the biographical articles could give any measure of the extent to which new assumptions about the desirable life were being applied. The biographies, of course, demonstrated no sudden, universal conversion to the standards of the "other-directed" character. Old and new concerns continued to appear in the selection of heroes and in the accounts of their careers and personalities. Amid the confusion, however, it is striking how clearly biographers revealed a sense of a changing society and of new patterns for life. They focused as never before upon the contemporary scene. Within it they portrayed far more heroes of a New Style than of a familiar Old Style.

One obvious fact about the reduced number of biographies after 1913 was their almost exclusive concentration upon living heroes. This preoccupation with the present carried forward a tendency begun in the cheaper popular magazines of the 1890's and accelerated in the Progressive period. But when a full 96 per cent of biographical articles dealt with living figures (even the remaining 4 per cent were about men very recently dead), they indicated a radical change of perspective from the time when Alexander the Great, Cromwell, Napoleon and other historical personages had composed 40 per cent of the magazine heroes. No longer was this a world in which individuals of all ages were measured against one another. In the new world of the wartime biographies historical individuals were apparently irrelevant while even the contemporary heroes were few and far between. The implication was that individualism itself might be irrelevant in the new conditions of society.

Whether in fact the older notions about individualism were now outmoded became the central question behind two biographical articles in 1914. Both of these biographies focused upon

Table XVIII

Historical Versus Contemporary Heroes

The number and per cent of heroes dead and alive in a one-third sample of biographical articles from the four best-selling magazines of three periods.

	Number		Per Cent	
Period	Dead	Alive	Dead	Alive
1894–1903	85	130	40	60
1904–1913	33	143	19	81
1914–1918	2	49	4	96

men who were not at all remarkable in their own right. In both cases the writers were explicitly interested in using their heroes to prove a point about the individual's place in present society. Though the question remained the same, two very different responses to it emerged.

Peter Reard's successful career as a gardener and real-estate investor was offered by *Collier's* as evidence for the continuing viability of an Old Style individualism. His biographer reminded readers of Mark Sullivan's earlier contention that any penniless city-dweller could drop off a freight train in the West and within five years own a farm and make a new life for himself.[5] The case of Peter Reard, it was argued, "actualizes the theory." Certainly Reard seemed a perfect model of all the traditional virtues. He avoided liquor and tobacco with no concern for the views of others. He worked seventeen hours a day. He had risen from a penniless state to the ownership of a large farm, fifty-seven houses, two stores, "and a neat bank balance." He ruled over his family like Kaiser Wilhelm. And he assured young men: "What I have accomplished in the way of amassing a fortune others can do if they work hard, pass up liquor and tobacco, and tie to the garden or the farm." Only a quibbling skeptic would note that Reard had begun his career during the Western boom of 1885, a full generation before the appearance of this biography.[6]

A very different mood pervaded the *Post's* account of "The Floating Laborer; The Case of John Smith." This composite, semi-fictional hero would not have been worth notice "if his case were not typical or were not common." Like all Americans, John Smith had been stirred by ambition. He had "pioneer blood," and his biographer asserted, "Four-fifths of the people for whom the Pilgrims pioneered and the Revolutionary forefathers bled are like John Smith." He possessed "a good, usable body," "a passably clear and active mind," along with "the average quota" of will power. As a youth his pioneer blood had been stimulated by reading "*Farmer Bill; or From the Plow to Wall Street,*" and he had set out for the city to make his fortune. John Smith was portrayed, in short, as a good Alger hero, but the world which he encountered bore little resemblance to an Algerian America.

It was a world in which "Fate and social forces" were "the determining factors." Because of "the disappearance of a frontier" his father had found himself stranded as a tenant farmer in the Middle West. In Chicago young John Smith had sought his opportunity through an employment agency which, together with his employers, took most of the returns from his hard labor in graft and then dismissed him. Drifting to California he tried and lost a succession of jobs, walking out himself from a strike-breaking job since "he had absorbed the ethics of labor." At thirty-four he had gone "from ambition to hopelessness, from the efficient man to the unemployed man to the unemployable man." Yet the fault was not his:

> The whole world had changed. . . . The undeveloped resources were all preempted. The age of specialists had arrived. To get along in any occupation an average man must have some special training.

Readers were faced with the question: "What can we do about John Smith, both for his sake and for our own?"[7] Although no answer was given, the article clearly assumed that a Peter Reard, a Rockefeller, or a Carnegie was no longer a relevant model for the "typical" American in a changed world.

The dichotomy of assumptions evident in these two articles also appeared, in less explicit form, among the other wartime biographies. About one-fourth of these* were devoted to Old

* Nine out of the thirty-four biographies which I examined closely for this period. As in previous periods I listed all biographies which appeared in every third issue of each of the four best-selling magazines (a total of 51 articles from 1914 through 1918). The tables on Frequency of Biographies, Historical versus Contemporary Heroes, and Occupations of Wartime Heroes are based on this one-third sample. From this list I then examined closely two out of every three articles (a total of 34). Upon this two-ninths sample is based the table of Diverse Heroic Styles.

Table XIX

Diverse Heroic Styles, 1914–1918

Four categories into which may be divided the heroes from a two-ninths sample of the biographical articles in four best-selling magazines.

	No. of Articles	Per Cent of Articles
New Style Heroes of Organization	21	62
Old Style Heroes of Individualism	9	26
Outmoded Progressive Heroes	2	6
Miscellaneous	2	6
Total	34	100

Style heroes and employed many terms which would not have seemed out of place in the magazines of the McKinley era. Several others dwelt upon fading Progressive heroes in ways which stressed their present irrelevance.* But nearly two-thirds of the biographies from 1914 through 1918 presented New Style heroes. These were the new models for success in an organization society.

In the small proportion of Old Style biographies, writers seemed to reach back for many of the familiar clichés of the years before Progressivism. A majority of these Old Style heroes were forceful, independent business leaders like Carnegie, Rockefeller, and the English newspaper magnate Lord Northcliffe. Once again they were held up as examples for emulation, and it was felt "logical to assume that most who achieve far above the average have worked on sound, sane lines and merit their recognition." [8] Once again the comparisons with Napoleon abounded, and the hero

* Bryan, though Secretary of State, was treated with gentle humor and condescension as essentially a campaigner and Chautauqua speaker. Theodore Roosevelt was portrayed solely as the father of soldier sons in wartime. Edward G. Lowry, "Troubadour Bryan," *Collier's*, LII (February 28, 1914), 9, 30; Philip Thompson, "Roosevelt—And His Boys," *McClure's*, LI (November, 1918), 10–12, 39.

was "the dynamic force before whom obstacles melt away." [9] Restored to magazine favor was the man of "huge, cosmic energy" who "started with nothing," who "naturally acquires enemies," who "judged by the material standard . . . is the biggest man in the world" since unlike the President, the Czar, or the Kaiser he "owns his power." [10] Gone were the Progressive scorn for mere money-getting, the Progressive suspicion of unfair advantages, the Progressive anxiety about opportunities closed off by the monopolists.

These Old Style heroes appeared in sufficient proportions to indicate a surviving faith in the forceful, competitive, domineering business leader. Yet even in these biographies which struck so many of the old notes there was a changed mood. Rockefeller was described as "a drab, relentless type of genius." Carnegie's rise had "nothing spectacular about it—no jaw-set determination to seize fame and beat the jade to capitulation—merely an eye, shrewd for favorable chances—each successive job intensively cultivated, and promotion by easy stages through meritorious but not strikingly brilliant work." [11] Most of these Old Style business individualists were the same men as before. Biographers gave them most of the same attributes as before and judged them by the same standards of personal fame and power. Yet somehow much of the old glamour was missing. In an organization society even a former classic individualist like Carnegie was transformed almost imperceptibly into a successful bureaucrat.

The reverse was also true. While the Old Style individualists shaded at times into a bureaucratic image, the New Style heroes of organization were in their turn given many of the Old characteristics of individual forcefulness. The new salaried manager of some vast government, business, or military organization might have "a strong, self-reliant character" or have "early developed an instinct for striking out on his own." He too upon occasion "had made powerful enemies." Even as the head of a great humanitarian cause he might have come from "a ruthless, fighting world." He might, in other instances, have "looked on the world with the eyes of men who are born to have power and to hold dominion over lesser men." He might be termed "a benevolent despot," and "absolute lord," a "czar," a "dictator with an empire all his own."[12] Yet in the total context of the new biographies these familiar phrases often seemed the reassuring remnants from an age that was passing. In each of our standard categories the New Style hero emerged with the attributes appropriate for an organization society. He was judged by a new standard and described by new characteristics. He found his relation to others in a new way and pursued a different path to success. His occupations were proportionally different from those of preceding decades, but the greatest change in his occupational role was his new status as a salaried manager within some large organization.

I
The Standards of Success

The new standard of success was most simply summarized as "results." * The New Style hero was the man who "is always there with the goods," the man "who could put things through." A desire for Personal Fame no longer provided his chief motivation. Since he was "of the type interested only in seeing the results of his work, it did not matter to him whether or not he was known to the public." He was concerned more with results than with stamping his personal mark upon events: "What he wants now is to get results regardless of whose first opinion, even if it be his own, is shattered in the getting of them." Efficiency in the attainment of results brought additional praise to the managerial hero for "doing it all at the cheapest cost." His performance was remarkable "particularly as to the methodical system and the

* All the following comments are based upon the twenty-one New Style biographies among the total sample of thirty-four articles which were examined closely for this period. Because the sample is small, no statistical tables are offered within the various general categories.

incredibly low cost." With the success of an organization or the survival of a nation at stake, the hero naturally became the manager who could produce results. His own personality, his own origin and career became secondary to the organizational achievement which he made possible: "If he delivers the goods, we shall not ask about his origin." His heroic status depended not so much upon his own accomplishment as upon the success of the organization which he directed: "If the British army should break the line this summer, the greatest figure in all British military history will be Sir Douglas Haig." [13]

This emphasis upon results, results efficiently achieved through a large-scale organization, displaced not only Personal Fame as a prime measure and motivation for success. It also subordinated Social Contribution and a Monetary Standard as the important criteria for heroism in the new society. As for Personal Happiness, it was not mentioned at all during the war years. The New Style hero won his recognition for Achievement in His Field. He might be, as in the case of Goethals, the man who "is now, by virtue of achievement, the ranking engineer of all the ages." He might be, like Elbert Gary, the "head of the greatest industrial corporation in the world." [14] In any case it was his official position as a leader in some particular, organized field of activity and his achievement in that field which merited his recognition. The New Style hero, more than any of his predecessors, lived in an age of specialization.

The relative neglect of the new hero's Social Contribution probably stemmed as much from the war atmosphere as it did from a decline in the Progressive social consciousness. In wartime no biographer needed to dwell upon the obvious social role of generals, admirals, and war ministers. One writer, however, did elaborate upon the particular Social Contribution of Herbert Hoover as Federal Food Administrator. The passage strongly resembled those observations made one hundred years earlier by Washington Irving about American naval commanders in the War of 1812, and yet the slight differences between the two commentaries help to demonstrate a century of change in the nation's society, its problems, and its heroes.

In 1813 Irving had hailed the naval victories as "a little precious hoard of national glory" which would fill the greatest need of Americans at that time:

> They want something to attract and concentrate their affections; to call them off from brooding over those virulent and petty local feelings which have of late occupied their attention. They want, in short, some great universal bond of union, distinct from any convention whatever, and that bond, we firmly believe is only to be found in National Glory.[15]

The dangers of the young republic had been localism, disunion, anarchy, and a lack of national self-confidence, the natural problems of a new, weak, and disorganized nation.

By 1917 Hoover's biographer found in the person of the new Food Administrator a new kind of symbol to remedy the problems of a new kind of society in wartime:

> A better leader could not have been found. To rouse the will of this nation—a will mysteriously vast, compounded of the purposes, the small desires, selfish plans, the hopes and dreams and great ideals, the firm beliefs and the suspicions of more than a hundred million people—here is one whose very name is a great national asset now. For it has become a symbol of that honesty and generous will, that clean, efficient action, which will sweep out of our Yankee minds the suspicion of graft and slackness here.[16]

In a highly organized nation the great dangers seemed to have become "graft and slackness," those twin evils which could sap the morale of any bureaucracy. The most important Social Contribution which the New Style hero could make was to prove that a vast organization could be made honest, efficient, and humane. Though he himself continued to speak and to write largely in terms of an older American individualism, Herbert Hoover was admirably adapted to be the New Style hero par excellence.*

Although wartime biographies generally made little mention of it, a number of articles did indicate a renewed and unabashed devotion to the Monetary Standard of success. Yet once again there was a significant difference in the application of this standard to the New Style hero. Interest now came to focus upon the high-salaried manager rather than upon the independent owner of great capital. *McClure's* ran a series on "$100,000 a Year men." They were men who earned salaries of at least that amount and who worked for large organizations which they themselves did not own. One was Pope Yeatman, consultant mining engineer for the Guggenheim interests, whose career proved "Mr. Mellen must be wrong when he says that no man is worth more than $25,000 a year." Another was Samuel Insull, "the executive head and creative genius of interests worth, in the aggregate, a billion dollars. He is a rich man in his own right—a millionaire many times over—yet his own personal holdings are trifling beside those of the capitalists whose properties he directs. He is a salaried man in the real sense of the term—the highest salaried man in Chicago." [17] The opportunities in an organization society were felt to be managerial opportunities, and the new Monetary Standard for the hero had become the amount of his annual salary.

II

Description of the Hero

In their description of the hero, writers also began to emphasize new features and new qualities. Physical description received only passing attention. Its changing direction was well illustrated

* Hoover was the only American about whom more than one biographical article appeared within this sample of the best-selling magazines for the period.

in an article on Admiral Sims which found "the face is that of a man who has given over belligerent sword play for the more wearing work of steady planning, steady thinking." Though many heroes still displayed the physical forcefulness of "a big head, a powerful neck, tremendous shoulders," the new hero might bear "a Socratic brow" or a "studious droop to his shoulders." It was no longer felt necessary to portray businessmen, politicians, bureaucrats, or even soldiers with all the bodily attributes of a Hercules.[18]

Intellectual traits continued, however, to receive relatively scanty attention, and the category of Mental Description bulked no larger for the wartime heroes than for their predecessors of the previous two decades. Yet their qualities of mind, when noticed, did vary somewhat from the "foresight," "vision," and "shrewdness" which had been dominant before. Now the hero was more likely to possess "a clear habit of thought," "truly a scientific mind," or "a passion for rationality."[19] The creative vision of the innovator and the practical shrewdness of the independent exploiter were yielding to the rationality of the organizer.

Once again writers devoted most of their descriptive comments to Character Description. The changing nature of the heroic character was suggested by the comparisons which two biographers drew. One quoted from a description which he himself had written about his subject "many years ago." At that time he had described the man as "grim" and possessing "all the features of a strong, fierce, dominant nature." After an interview with this same man in 1914, however, the earlier description seemed "a too harsh impression of his appearance." The writer now found that his hero "has all the stern strength; but . . . looks genial, talks freely . . . is the very reverse of that grim, silent Sphinx." Somehow the heroic style had changed either in the subject himself or in the writer's perception of the man.

The second biographer implied a comparison with a former heroic type by noting what his New Style hero was not:

> Unlike many men below average size, he is not cocky and does not keep a framed picture of Napoleon in his study. He is mild in manner, self-contained, polite, and modest. Moreover he is friendly and likeable.

Ironically the war, instead of heightening the aggressive, belligerent characteristics of the hero, seemed to be accompanied by a new respect for the sociable, civilized virtues.[20]

The New Style hero was, above all, "The Hard-Working Organizer Type." As "a systematic organizer" he was a man whose "main aversion is any form of inefficiency." He was endowed with an "unswerving devotion to his duty and with a modest but complete sense of consecration to his public and private responsibility." He had, in fact, "a passion for responsibilities." These he discharged with an "infinite patience" which was appropriate for "the master with steel hand under velvet glove, taciturn, urbane, tirelessly systematic," who "never allows himself the temperamental vagaries of genius." He was a man of tact, of "finesse as well as force," a man "who prefers a deal to a struggle; and though he can be so stern, has yet a diplomatic tact that gets him and his country out of difficult hours." [21]

In some ways these descriptions of the new wartime hero seemed closer to the gentlemanly, neo-classic models of 1800 than they did to the forceful, domineering individualists of 1900. The merits of disciplined thought again seemed superior to the flashes of creative genius. The claims of duty, of responsibility, and of position again seemed more important than personal ambition and individual assertiveness. The necessity for tact, for a measure of urbane self-control, again seemed preferable to boldness and an indomitable will. Yet a certain similarity between the original Idols of Order and the new Idols of Organization should not obscure the difference between these two heroic types. The earlier respect for reason was not quite the same as the new demand for rationality and system. The old emphasis on moderation was not exactly paralleled by the new appeal for finesse. The former notion of duty as "the spring, the rule, and the measure of his conduct" was not entirely fulfilled by the later hero's "passion for responsibilities." The essential difference was that the one described a way of life, the other described ways to achieve results in an organization. The original character traits had formed the code of conduct for the upper class of the young republic, a code partly inherited from English traditions and long since adapted to relatively static social conditions. The new wartime character descriptions represented fresh recognition of the new requirements for success in a rapidly changing society.

III
The Hero's Personal Habits

The Personal Habits of the New Style hero seemed even more austere than those of his predecessors. Biographers continued to display a work-centered view of life which indicated that the organization society had not yet become the consumption society into which Americans would enter during the 1920's. The hero still lived almost exclusively for his work: "Some men play golf for amusement, some go to baseball games, some ride in airships; but Samuel Insull hunts kilowatts. That is the only hobby he has. It is his business and his pleasure." Even the rationale for those recreations which would keep the hero fit for his work was undermined by wartime necessities: "There was no time to keep 'fit.' It was the nation which must be kept fit." Again the hero's style of life was ostentatiously middle-class. "He is not a 'dashing' officer; he is not afraid to be bourgeois." Hoover was "no society man at all—his manners are not 'finished' and small talk bores him." [22]

As work-centered and bourgeois as his immediate predecessors, the New Style hero's Personal Habits were more clearly those of an organization man. The "routine" in his small house was "exact." "Punctuality . . . was part of the furniture." His personal life was made subservient to the purposes of his occupational organization. He (Haig) "regulated his own life in order that he might get the most out of himself for the service of the army." Only in a general's rigidly scheduled daily horseback ride could a biographer find any trace of a bygone style: "This was the only feature of his systematized life which had any of the histrionic display associated with the authority of the command of twenty times as many men as Wellington ever had on the continent." When an American officer in England violated proper middle-class customs by keeping a man in livery at his door, he was excused on organizational grounds: "It is a part of the ritual over here," and "a ritual indicates organization." [23]

Religion had virtually vanished as a significant element in the life of the wartime hero. For the first time no clergymen were included in the heroic ranks. The closest approach to one was a professional labor relations mediator who was briefly identified also as President of the Illinois Unitarian Association. Here a writer for once ventured to comment on the long-shunned area of personal belief by noting that "he doesn't believe in God—in the traditional way." Only one other reference to a hero's religion appeared at all in these years, and that followed the pattern of describing only a formal, behavioral idiosyncracy of the subject, in this case a British general who "every Sunday morning listened to a long Scotch Presbyterian sermon." Whether he actually heard it or believed in it was beyond the bounds of the biographer's interest.[24] The purpose and meaning of the hero's personal and professional life alike seemed now to come from the secular organization within which he had attained his heroic position.

IV

The Hero's Relation to Others

Nowhere was the New Style more apparent than in the changed nature of the wartime hero's Relation to Others. Although almost every biographer commented upon this aspect of his subject's life, the cast of characters became severely restricted. No longer were the hero's relations with parents, with spouse, with children, or with friends depicted with any frequency. Even his relation to the general public was largely ignored. The new hero's personal dealings were almost exclusively focused upon his superiors, his inferiors, and above all upon his colleagues within an organization. The nature of those dealings marked him preeminently as a good organization man.

The recent reverence for the dominating personality seemed to have been diluted by a new demand for working with a "team." Honus Wagner, the baseball player, could ignore the fans when they "hooted and jeered him," but he was noted for his loyalty to the owner of the Pirates and for his generous help in training the younger players. Whether in baseball, the army, the government, or the corporation a good team man possessed a "loyalty" which "did not allow growling or criticism of superiors." He was also the man who "attracts the best talent and gets the most out of his men because he is just to them." "Considerate to subordinates," he had the ability to choose them well, to give and receive confidence until they worked "for him and with him."[25]

The previous priorities which had made cooperation one of the least of the heroic attributes were now clearly reversed. The New Style hero was the one who did not simply impose his own ideas, his own desires, or his own authority upon others: Hoover "took the Russian ways of work and whenever possible made them his own. He cooperated in every way, and they had soon taken him as their friend." The hero was one who "acts through the agency of other men," one who "invites agreement and creates the atmosphere of unaffected equality." Biographers found much more frequent use for the preposition "with." Colonel House was "not the man behind Wilson. House is *with* Wilson." The admired officer was the general whose "communiques say 'we'."[26]

Although the New Style in Relations to Others departed from the recent pattern of domination, it did not revert entirely to the quality of relations praised in the gentlemanly circles of 1800.

The New Style was one of teamwork rather than of personal friendship. It implied cooperation for the sake of a common objective rather than respect for the rights and individuality of others. Nor was it entirely a pattern of "other-direction" in the sense which David Riesman has given to that term. The emphasis remained on objective tasks, on work to be accomplished through cooperation rather than upon prestige and status to be gained through sensitive perception of the expectations of others.

V

The Road to Success

Biographers of the New Style hero continued to devote a major part of their articles to an account of his Road to Success. They still touched, where possible, on youthful hardships. They still dwelt on the virtues of hard work. They still found creativity a part, though a lesser part, of some heroic careers.

Yet any reader could sense differences from the route to success which had been charted two decades earlier. Although still a major part of the articles, the space devoted to this aspect of the hero's life was proportionately less. More significantly, the tone of fascination with each stage in the heroic development had been largely dissipated. Writers no longer interjected the older notes of awe and excitement ("How he did these things, how he became a great American millionaire, how he developed from a country lad to what he is to-day: that is the fascinating romance."[27]).

Articles might recount the early hardships in the lives of some New Style heroes, but no longer were these hardships offered as an explanation for the later character and success of the hero. No biographer attributed rural origins to his subject. Even more striking was the fact that biographers seemed to feel no strong need for explaining away or qualifying any initial advantages of family background, of comfortable wealth, or of formal education which the hero might have enjoyed. A new tone of objectivity characterized all the comments on these matters. It seemed to mark the end of an era which had found life's ultimate meaning in the self-made career.

Understandably the New Style hero had more Formal Education than his immediate predecessors. It was also a more practical, more specialized education in many cases than the early gentlemen of the young republic had acquired. Vocational schools like West Point, the French Polytechnic, or the Stanford School of Mines were training grounds for numbers of the wartime heroes. Yet biographers made only passing reference to education. The whole question of the relation between success and education was not yet one upon which magazine writers spent much concern.

The most obvious changes lay in the new Means to Success. In order to rise in an organization society the hero had to induce other people, usually his superiors, to select him for posts of increasing responsibility. Hoover won rapid promotion in a British mining firm and established such a reputation that he "was inevitably selected by the President for the gigantic task" which brought him to popular notice. Yeatman "was chosen by the Guggenheims to succeed." Joffre gradually "rose rank after rank." A minister of munitions had found that "life . . . was just one continuous promotion. He seemed to find the magic key and all doors opened to him." [28] A world in which success came through promotion or appointment to high posts in existing organizations was a rather different one from that inhabited by the earlier Idols of Power or even by their Progressive successors. Success in the 1890's had seemed to come to individuals who seized individual opportunities creatively. To this conception the Progressives had added a requirement for a sympathetic relation between the independent individual on the one hand and "the people" on the other. After 1913 the hero seemed to prove his success by some high official position in a particular organization. The "magic key" was the key which opened doors in that organized area of life.

For this new climb to success a new form of tactics was required. Neither the Individualistic Tactics nor the Democratic Tactics which had come to supplement them in the preceding decade proved adequate for the New Style hero. What he required were the Bureaucratic Tactics which in his early career would win him the confidence of colleagues and superiors and which in his later career would make the whole organization most effective.

Consequently, the new heroism was "not so much a matter of genius as of well-reasoned application." In the beginning the new hero demonstrated he was "not of the pushful, intriguing sort, but quiet, strictly subordinate, and always working." He followed "a very simple, straight career. Straight in all meanings of the word, free of the slightest taint of intriguing, of gallery playing, of charlatanism." He impressed people as a man who was "always studying, always working in this systematic fashion." A biographer concluded: "Hard work, patience, and the utilization of every second of time, the eagerness always to learn—these are the chief secrets of [his] enormous success in life." [29]

Once the hero had been selected for leadership in his field, he demonstrated his knowledge that "without organization you never get anywhere on a big job." He knew the necessity for "acceptance of other people's ideas; other people's ways of doing things if such acceptance will bring results." He knew that "the man who works himself is ineffective in great things unless he has the gift to choose the men who can work for him and with him." A just treatment of his men was "the secret of what has been called his knack for 'organization.'" As "a born executive" he did not allow himself to be harassed by details. He remained "a silent man in the background directing vast forces." When a problem arose, he "not only solved it, but in a way that pleased both sides to the controversy." "You might readily think of him as a machine of a man, with no waste words or motion, who was organizing a machine of men." [30]

No wonder the excitement, the glamour, the moral urgency of former years were missing from these accounts of the New Style career. The old Road to Success had been a test of character, of will, of individual force. The new one called instead for system, for patience, and for compromise. The Progressive career had been a drama of high moral tension. It had demanded an individual independence which nevertheless was exerted for the good of "the people." The New Style career encountered no moral tensions. The life of the individual was not distinct from the life of the organization. The prized "results" of organized activity were assumed to serve the common good whether those results were Insull's monopoly of electric power in Chicago or Goethals's construction of the Panama Canal, Kitchener's mobilization to wage war or Hoover's arrangements to feed the victims of war. In such circumstances biographers could find no previous human model for their hero. Instead of comparing him with a Napoleon or a Roosevelt, they ended by comparing him with a machine.

VI
The Heroic Occupations

The occupations of the wartime heroes provided final testimony to their new role as Idols of Organization. For this conclusion the occupational areas omitted after 1913 became as revealing as the fields within which the new heroes concentrated.

All of the more independent, individual professions and pursuits virtually vanished from among the magazine models of success. Clergymen and physicians now fell into the oblivion which had earlier engulfed the professors. No longer did magazine biographies include any of the unusual or eccentric careers which had previously made up a category of miscellaneous occupations.

Most startling of all, perhaps, was the drastic decline in concern for the arts. This creative and distinctly individual field of human endeavor had contributed twice as many heroes as any other to the magazines of the 1890's. It had retained second place among the occupations of Progressive heroes even though the emphasis shifted from the creative artists to the performers of other men's works. But from 1914 through 1918 only two men from the arts received any attention in the magazines. Both biographies appeared in *Cosmopolitan,* and in each case special circumstances seemed to have dictated its inclusion. One was about a painter of society portraits. It was accompanied by a full-page illustration of his portrait of Mrs. William Randolph Hearst, wife of the magazine's publisher. The other spoke in Fannie Hurst's most glowing rhetoric about a writer who regularly contributed his "romantic realism" to *Cosmopolitan*'s own pages.[31] As much as the absence of all other artists the presence of these two emphasized the low rating to which the Arts had fallen in mass magazines.

The few other minor occupations touched on by magazine biographers after 1913 similarly indicated change more than continuity. In sports the representatives of individual activities like mountain climbing and walking were now replaced by a model team player from organized baseball. The one figure from Labor was the semi-fictional John Smith whose dismal fate proved that "the whole world had changed." The one Scientist was the discoverer of a new anesthetic, perhaps a peculiarly appropriate contribution to the Brave New World of an organization society.

More than ever before the magazine heroes clustered in a few fields of activity. Business (23 per cent), Politics (23 per cent), and Government Bureaucracy (22 per cent) shared almost equally in heroic status. Together with the Military (10 per cent) they mustered nearly four-fifths of the wartime heroes. The only other significant area of biographical interest lay in the personalities of Foreign Rulers (12 per cent). Among these alien figures writers seemed to look for the elements of drama, individuality, force, or human sympathy which were comparatively lacking in their

Table XX

The Heroic Occupations, 1914–1918

The occupations of the heroes in a one-third sample of biographical articles from four best-selling magazines.

Category	No. of Articles	Per Cent of All Articles
Business	12	23
Politics	12	23
Government Bureaucracy	11	22
Foreign Rulers	6	12
Military	5	10
The Arts	2	4
Science	1	2
Labor	1	2
Sports	1	2
Total	51	100

accounts of American or Allied leaders. Perhaps for this reason as much as any other they wrote three articles on Pancho Villa, two on Yuan Shi Kai (new Chinese President and "military dictator"), and one on the unfortunate Queen of the Belgians. These dramatic leaders of disorganized nations provided intriguing contrasts to the managers of the tightly mobilized societies in the United States, England, and France. With this one major exception, however, wartime biographies focused almost exclusively upon the contemporary centers of nationally organized economic, political, and military power together with the government bureaucracy which coordinated their energies for common national purposes.

The typical occupation of the new hero was a managerial post in a massive organization. He might be a Cabinet officer or the head of a new federal agency. He might be a Chief of Staff or the President of the United States Steel Corporation. In any case the new Idol of Organization was neither the creator nor the owner of the enterprise which he ran. The new demand was for men who could take over existing organizations and run them with a minimum of human friction and a maximum of practical results.

Despite his unassuming, unspectacular manner, the New Style hero who emerged during World War I was a revolutionary character. He, far more than his Progressive predecessor, bore the stamp of a new mold for the nation's heroes. His new attributes were not simply additions to a basic model of independent, assertive individualism. His function was not to preserve the "good" of individualism by aggressively combatting the "interests" which threatened it. His task was to make an organization society work, to keep it running smoothly at home while he harnessed its energies for effective combat abroad. Under the pressure of these demands, his departure from the former canons of individualism went unnoticed and unlamented. He was suddenly just there—in the important positions of power and in the magazine biographies.

Epilogue

The Ideal Man of the eighteenth century was the
Rationalist; of the seventeenth, the Christian Stoic;
of the Renaissance, the Free Individual; of the Middle Ages,
the Contemplative Spirit. And what is our Ideal Man?
On what grand and luminous mythological figure does
contemporary humanity attempt to model itself?
The question is embarrassing. Nobody knows.

Aldous Huxley, Texts and Pretexts

THE ADVENT of a new bureaucratic hero during World War I gave to Americans their third major model of success. The change seems, in retrospect, fully as momentous as that first long-term transition from the early republic's dutiful, socially minded, neoclassic gentlemen to the forceful, ambitious individualists of the later nineteenth century. In the years from 1914 through 1918 independent individualism in turn had become irrelevant.

The fall of individualism as the essential model for life occurred with surprising ease. Its reign seemed to end finally with neither a bang nor a whimper. Ever since the 1890's this view of the world had been under increasing tension. The consolidation of industry, the concentration of wealth, the impersonalism of urban life, the political "machines," and finally the claims of social justice had threatened it. From 1894 through 1903 magazine biographers had responded by offering frequent examples of the most powerful, most creative, self-made individuals. These Napoleonic heroes had been put forward to expose "the fallacy that the individual does not count." [1] In the succeeding decade Progressive biographers had strained to preserve the "good" of individualism. They had castigated the "villains" who betrayed it. They had praised the independent, socially conscious politicians, prosecutors, and preachers who fought to exemplify a more viable form of individualism under the new conditions. Amid much fanfare about the "old gods" dying and about "recasting the mold in which heroes were made," Progressives had actually tried to preserve their inherited sense of the importance and the moral rightness of the independent individual.

By 1914 the strain of maintaining and recasting the ethics of individualism in a changed world had become too great. The Progressive energies were drained. The popular mood had become one of acquiescence. The best-selling magazines were themselves large organizations inclined to view their readers as consumers and spectators rather than active principals and judges of contemporary society. The war put a premium upon "results." In the wartime atmosphere mass magazines could state with no ideological qualms that "nothing is more wasteful than indiscriminate and unregulated competition." [2] They could see the "greatest menace" of trade unions not in a threat to individualism but in "the tendency to curtail production." [3] They could, in one despairing moment, call individualism a "loose" and "ineffective" ideal for meeting the great threats of the present and of the future.[4] They could make efficiency in organized effort a success standard which overshadowed personal force or social righteousness.

Under these conditions the long-held concern for independent individualism faded. The tension which had sustained magazine biographies for two decades relaxed. The number of biographies declined drastically. The lives of historical personages dropped out of sight. The more independent occupations were ignored. New Style organization men captured the major attention of the remaining biographies. An era had passed—that era when Americans had found the meaning of life exclusively in the fate of the independent, self-made career.

Yet the change was not as complete as it was easy. The new managerial heroes did not entirely displace Old Style biographies from the wartime magazines. More importantly, the new men were not endowed with a new organization mystique to rival the ethos of individualism. Biographers wrote about them with an objectivity which had been lacking in the adulation for Napoleonic or Progressive idols. The virtues of efficiency, loyalty, conciliation and cooperation were essentially undramatic ones. The organization men seemed to represent the facts of life more than a new way of life.

The truth was that World War I had simply made it possible for magazine writers to recognize and to accept the human requirements of their highly industrialized, organized society. If they could not be very excited about the new pattern for life, they could no longer ignore it. If they would not abandon the older vision of individualism, they could no longer make it the sole measure of meaning and success.

Efficiency, rationality, and bureaucracy were not the ingredients for a new vision to capture the American imagination. American magazines in 1919 preached no sweeping revolution to enthrone the organization man. Yet in the trade associations of the 1920's, in the New Deal agencies, in all the organized activities of World War II and of the Cold War, Americans would settle for the new style of life. More and more of them would find their hopes for affluence, for prestige, even for survival, dependent on the great bureaucracies of business, of government, of the military, and of education. New sanctions and new rationales would grow up to surround the organization life with meaning and value.

When this process had gone forward for thirty years, the span of another generation, Americans would awaken with alarm to a fuller recognition of the revolution in their lives. They would devour the writings of sociologists and journalists who spelled out the ramifications of the "other-directed" character and the rationalizations of the organization man. Many would be shocked at the discovery and would embark again upon the old Progressive quest for ways to reconcile individual independence with the structures of a changed society.

A Note on Procedures

THOSE INTERESTED in devising ways to analyze the materials of popular culture may wish to know something about the procedures employed in this study. For materials of this sort some systematic efforts at quantification seem a necessary supplement to the historian's usual method of immersing himself in the relevant documents of the past, selecting those general themes and patterns which strike him as significant, and citing the selected evidence which supports his perceptions.

To determine the four best-selling magazines in each of my periods after 1894 I first compiled the circulation figures from *Ayer's American Newspaper Annual and Directory* for fifteen of the leading general magazines from 1894 through 1919. I then listed the annual circulation rank of each magazine (first, second, fifth, tenth as it might be in any particular year). Within the ten or five years of each period I then listed the ten or five annual rankings held by each magazine during that period. The four magazines selected for analysis in any period were those which maintained the highest total of annual rankings during the period.

In selecting the sample of biographical articles for analysis in any magazine I first examined every third issue of a magazine during any year and listed every biographical article which appeared in that issue. To avoid any bias of periodicity (as might have been produced, for example, by a heavy proportion of political biographies appearing each time in October before November elections), I began with the first issue of each magazine in the first year of a period, the second issue in the second year, the third issue in the third year, the first issue again in the fourth year, and so on.

From this one-third sample of the magazines during any period I compiled statistics about the biographies on the occupations of their subjects, on the sex of their subjects, on the number of subjects who were dead or alive and who were American or foreign. The tables on the heroes who fell into these kinds of categories during any period are thus based on all the biographies appearing in a one-third sample of the magazines during that period.

The closer analysis of other categories and themes in the magazine biographies required intensive analysis of the contents and thus, simply to be manageable, required a smaller sample to be read. For this purpose I took a further sample from my list of those biographies which had appeared in every third issue of a magazine. During the ten-year periods (1894–1903, 1904–1913) that sample consisted of one out of every three biographies already listed. Hence most of my comments on the heroes of these periods, and most of the accompanying tables, are based on a close analysis of about one-ninth of the magazine biographies during the period. For the five-year period from 1914 through 1918 I read and analyzed closely two out of every three articles on my list of biographies from every third issue of a magazine. Hence most of my comments on the war-time heroes and my one table on the New Style versus Old Style heroes during this period are based on about two-ninths of the magazine biographies during World War I.

For the analysis of a biographical article I prepared five separate categories: Description (with sub-categories of Mental, Physical, and Character), Personal Habits, Relation to Others (with sub-categories of Others Mentioned and Nature of the Relation), Road to Success (with sub-categories of Success Standards, Childhood Environment, Formal Education, and Means to Success), and Environment (general statements about the hero's social and historical environment). In reading a magazine biography I wrote down under the appropriate category all adjectives, phrases, sentences, or paragraphs as I came to them. These extensive notes, arranged in these categories, then provided the basis for my conclusions on the distinctive characteristics of the hero during any period and for the remaining tables of statistics giving some quantitative basis for those conclusions where such a basis seemed appropriate and significant (that is, based on a significant number of articles).

For the period from 1787–1820, however, any selection of magazines on the basis of circulation proved impossible and inappropriate. Likewise, the files of the magazines available to me during this period were not fully complete, and the frequency of biographical articles seemed rather irregular. Hence I read and took notes, under the categories mentioned, from all of the biographies appearing in the files of the magazines available to me. Since throughout this early period all of the biographies I encountered seemed to fall clearly within the patterns described, I do not think the relatively unsystematic basis for selection of the early magazine biographies seriously distorted in any way my conclusions about them.

This is a time-consuming process. In particular such a process meant that once one's research had been completed, most of the work still lay ahead in trying to make sense out of the materials accumulated. I am grateful to Professor Lazarsfeld of Columbia University who, in the process of a course with him, put me in the way of many materials on content analysis. My procedures, however, were devised strictly by myself for my own purposes. They will surely seem not rigorous enough for the specialists in content analysis. They may also seem far too pedantic for some of my fellow historians. I can only hope that they have made it possible to explain with some confidence a sequence of interesting changes in pervasive American values and attitudes.

Notes

Prologue

1. David Riesman with Reuel Denney and Nathan Glazer, *The Lonely Crowd: A Study of the Changing American Character* (New Haven, 1950).
2. William H. Whyte, Jr., *The Organization Man* (Garden City, N.Y., 1957).
3. C. Wright Mills, *White Collar* (New York, 1951).
4. See also Orrin E. Klapp, *Heroes, Villains, and Fools: The Changing American Character* (Englewood Cliffs, N.J., 1962).
5. Seymour Martin Lipset, "A Changing American Character?" in Seymour Martin Lipset and Leo Lowenthal, eds., *Culture and Social Character: The Work of David Riesman Reviewed* (Glencoe, Ill., 1961); Carl N. Degler, "The Sociologist as Historian: Riesman's *The Lonely Crowd*," *American Quarterly*, XV (Winter, 1963), 483–97; David M. Potter, "The Quest for the National Character" in John Higham, ed., *The Reconstruction of American History* (New York, 1962), Ch. 11; for a useful bibliography of the debate over a changing American character see Michael McGiffert, ed., *The Character of Americans* (Homewood, Ill., 1964), 368–75.
6. Frank Luther Moot's multi-volume *History of American Magazines* is a mine of information, but its encyclopedic range necessarily sacrifices any really coherent and comparative grasp of the structure and outlook of general magazines in particular periods. Several scholars, on the other hand, have made close studies of certain magazines in the Progressive period. Their attention has been directed exclusively to the muckraking journals and even more narrowly to the articles of exposure within them. See C. C. Regier, *The Era of the Muckrakers* (Chapel Hill, 1932); Louis Filler, *Crusaders for American Liberalism* (New York, 1939); David M. Chalmers, *The Social and Political Ideas of the Muckrakers* (New York, 1964).
7. See the excellent historical analysis of the continuous theme of individ-

ualism, "America and the Individual," in Russel B. Nye, *This Almost Chosen People* (East Lansing, Mich., 1966), Ch. V.

8. In the depths of the Depression A. Whitney Griswold wrote an initial, disenchanted study stressing the continuity of success themes from Cotton Mather to Bruce Barton: "The American Cult of Success," unpublished dissertation, 1933, Yale University.

   In the more properous 1950's Irvin G. Wyllie described more fully and more sympathetically the main characteristics attributed to *The Self-Made Man in America* (New Brunswick, N.J., 1954).

   Only after my own study was completed did I discover John G. Cawelti's *Apostles of the Self-Made Man: Changing Concepts of Success in America* (Chicago, 1965). Cawelti succeeds in his aim "to show that attitudes toward success have not been as unchanging and monolithic as has generally been assumed; on the contrary, the ideal of self-improvement has had a rich and varied history." He examines a wide range of materials, primarily fiction, and many of the changes which he describes seem compatible with those I discovered in magazine biographies. Nevertheless Cawelti still assumes that "the ideal of self-improvement" or the concept of "the self-made man" is the *only* significant tradition of the successful life in America. It is that assumption which I have tried to avoid in an effort to see whether, at several crucial periods in our history, contemporary magazine biographies were in fact dominated by such an ideal or did actually reflect a rather different model of success.

   Sigmund Diamond has traced changes in the *Reputation of the American Businessman* (Cambridge, Mass., 1953) by focusing upon obituaries. The difficulty is that the obituaries upon which he primarily relies were written at the time of death and do not reflect popular attitudes toward these individuals at the time of their chief power in the business world. Necessarily too, of course, his study is limited to businessmen.

   Dixon Wecter, in his charming book on *The Hero in America* (New York, 1941) offers various helpful leads to changes in the selection and in the images of heroes at different times. He arranges his book by individuals, however, traces the writings about each one through our history, and makes no effort to pull together his random observations on how different periods viewed the heroic life.

9. *The United States Magazine and Democratic Review*, XI (September, 1842), 225.

10. See John William Ward, *Andrew Jackson: Symbol for an Age* (New York, 1955).

11. Brooks Atkinson, ed., *The Complete Essays and Other Writings of Ralph Waldo Emerson* (New York, 1940), 63.
12. See Marvin Meyers, *The Jacksonian Persuasion* (Stanford, 1957).
13. For provocative analyses of the anti-institutionalism of these decades, see Stanley Elkins, *Slavery: A Problem of American Institutional and Intellectual Life* (Chicago, 1959) and George M. Frederickson, *The Inner Civil War: Northern Intellectuals and the Crisis of the Union* (New York, 1965).
14. See the works by these authors cited above, note 8.

Chapter 1
Magazines for the Few

1. "Plan of the Undertaking," *American Magazine* (January, 1741), as quoted in Frank Luther Mott, *A History of American Magazines* (New York, 1930), I, 22.
2. Quoted in Algernon Tassin, *The Magazine in America* (New York, 1916), 23.
3. Lyon N. Richardson, *A History of Early American Magazines, 1741–1789* (New York, 1931), 363–69.
4. Twenty-four magazines in forty-five years from 1741 through 1784 compared with seventy-one magazines in fifteen years from 1786 through 1800. Cf. Mott, *History of American Magazines,* I, 788–91.
5. Mott, *History of American Magazines,* I, 17.
6. *Ibid.,* 18, 19.
7. *Ibid.,* 119, 120.
8. *Ibid.,* 33, 34.
9. *Ibid.,* 14, 199, 200.
10. Isaiah Thomas in his *Worcester Magazine,* as quoted in Tassin, *Magazine in America,* 22.
11. Quoted in Tassin, *Magazine in America,* 11.
12. Quoted in Mott, *History of American Magazines,* I, 198.
13. *Ibid.*
14. Mott, *History of American Magazines,* I, 243.
15. Quoted in Mott, *History of American Magazines,* I, 156.
16. *Monthly Anthology,* V, 1.
17. *Ibid.,* I, 2.
18. This account of *The Columbian Magazine* is based upon examination of a microfilm copy of a complete file of the magazine and upon: Mott, *History of American Magazines,* I, 94–99; Richardson, *Early American*

Magazines, 276–93; Albert H. Smyth, *The Philadelphia Magazines and Their Contributors, 1741–1850* (Philadelphia, 1892), 61–67.

19. This account of the *Monthly Anthology* is based upon examination of a file of the magazine and upon Mott, *History of American Magazines,* I, 253–59 and Tassin, *Magazine in America,* 28–32.
20. William Tudor, *Miscellanies,* as quoted in Mott, *History of American Magazines,* I, 254–55.
21. Tudor, *Miscellanies,* as quoted in Mott, *History of American Magazines,* I, 258.
22. Quoted in Mott, *History of American Magazines,* I, 279. This account of the *Analectic* is based upon an examination of its file, upon Mott, 279–83, and upon Smyth, *Philadelphia Magazines,* 178–80.
23. *Analectic Magazine,* II, 186–208.
24. Quoted in Dixon R. Fox, *The Decline of Aristocracy in the Politics of New York* (New York, 1919), 7.

Chapter 2
The Heroes of the Young Republic

1. See Merrill Peterson, *The Jefferson Image in the American Mind* (New York, 1960).
2. For an account of the changing image of Franklin see Dixon Wecter, *The Hero in America,* Ch. IV.
3. See Walter Lippmann, *The Public Philosophy* (Boston, 1955).
4. *The Columbian Magazine,* II, 3.
5. *The Columbian Magazine,* I, 227.
6. *Monthly Anthology,* II, 345.
7. *Monthly Anthology,* V, 424.
8. *Monthly Anthology,* I, 526; II, 55.
9. *Analectic Magazine,* XIII, 9.
10. *Analectic Magazine,* XIII, 89.
11. *The Columbian Magazine,* II, 3.
12. *Analectic Magazine,* XIII, 9.
13. For an analysis of the theory and practice of moralism in English biographies see Donald A. Stauffer, *The Art of Biography in Eighteenth Century England* (Princeton, N.J., 1941), 309–52, 414–95 and Harold Nicolson, *The Development of English Biography* (London, 1928), 1–86, 109–31. For moralism in American biographies see Edward H. O'Neill, *A History of American Biography, 1800–1935* (Philadelphia, 1935).

14. *The Columbian Magazine,* V, 35.
15. *Monthly Anthology,* I, 462.
16. *Analectic Magazine,* XIII, 90–91.
17. Quoted in James P. Wood, *Magazines in the United States* (New York, 1956), 27.
18. *Monthly Anthology,* I, 378.
19. In a biography of the merchant William Powell. *Monthly Anthology,* II, 110.
20. *Monthly Anthology,* V, 641.
21. *Analectic Magazine,* I, 462.
22. *Monthly Anthology,* II, 121.
23. Philip Schuyler was praised by the *Monthly Anthology* for being "too intelligent to found his notions of political or civil government upon the perfectability of man." *Monthly Anthology,* I, 669.
24. *Monthly Anthology,* I, 669.
25. *Analectic Magazine,* XIII, 91.
26. *General Repository and Review,* IV (October, 1813), 357.
27. *Monthly Anthology,* I, 430, 472.
28. *Monthly Anthology,* I, 572.
29. *Analectic Magazine,* XIII, 274.
30. *Analectic Magazine,* I, 226–35. See also *Analectic,* I, 456–65 and XIII, 413–14.
31. *Analectic Magazine,* XIII, 413.
32. *Analectic Magazine,* XVI, 15. See also *Analectic,* I, 465 and *Monthly Anthology,* II, 344 for other examples.
33. *Analectic Magazine,* XIII, 9.
34. *Analectic Magazine,* XIII, 272. See also *Monthly Anthology,* I, 571, 669 and II, 54.
35. *Monthly Anthology,* I, 639; II, 121.
36. *Monthly Anthology,* I, Preface, iii; *Monthly Anthology,* II, 54; *The Columbian Magazine,* V, 36; *Monthly Anthology,* II, 110.
37. *Monthly Anthology,* I, 572; II, 53; II, 110; *Analectic Magazine,* XIII, 274; *Anthology,* II, 345.
38. *Monthly Anthology,* I, 430.
39. *Monthly Anthology,* II, 54; V, 134. See also *Anthology,* II, 124; II, 346; *Analectic Magazine,* XIII, 275.
40. *Monthly Anthology,* II, 110.
41. *Monthly Anthology,* I, 429; I, 640, 641.
42. *Monthly Anthology,* I, 571; II, 53.
43. *Monthly Anthology,* II, 110.
44. These articles appeared in an extensive random sample of *The Colum-*

bian, The Monthly Anthology, and *The Analectic* plus a much smaller test sample from Volume Four of *The General Repository and Review.*

45. *Monthly Anthology,* II, 110.
46. *Monthly Anthology,* I, 639.
47. *Analectic Magazine,* XIII, 269.
48. *Monthly Anthology,* I, 320. See also *General Repository and Review,* IV (October, 1813), 357–58.

Chapter 3
The Magazine Revolution of the Nineties

1. For a good analysis of this later phase see Theodore Peterson, *Magazines in the Twentieth Century* (Urbana, Ill., 1956), esp. 64–84.
2. Mott, *History of American Magazines,* III, 5; IV, 11.
3. Quoted in Mott, *History of American Magazines,* IV, 11.
4. Mott, *History of American Magazines,* IV, 364–68.
5. Flora Mai Holly, "Notes on Some American Magazine Editors," *Bookman,* XII (December, 1900), 357.
6. Mott, *History of American Magazines,* III, 468.
7. J. Henry Harper, *The House of Harper* (New York, 1912), 84.
8. Henry M. Alden, "Fifty Years of Harper's Magazine," *Harper's,* C (May, 1900), 950.
9. From a letter explaining the omission of a chapter in the publication of James's translation of Daudet's *Port Tarascon.* Quoted in *The House of Harper,* 620. See also the delightful comments on the gentility of the 1890's in Thomas Beer, *The Mauve Decade* (New York, 1926).
10. Donald Sheehan, *This Was Publishing* (Bloomington, 1952), 8, 9. This book gives an excellent sense of the atmosphere maintained by the chief publishing houses in this period.
11. Frank A. Munsey, *The Founding of the Munsey Publishing House* (New York, 1907), 9–10.
12. S. S. McClure, *My Autobiography* (New York, 1914), 150–61.
13. Mott, *History of American Magazines,* IV, 482–83; Mott, "John Brisben Walker," *Dictionary of American Biography* (New York, 1943), XIX, 348; D. M. Rein, "Howells and the *Cosmopolitan,*" *American Literature,* XVII (March, 1949), 49–55.
14. "The Publisher's Desk," *Munsey's,* X (October, 1893), 116.
15. McClure, *Autobiography,* 222.
16. McClure, *Autobiography,* 207–8.

17. All circulation figures are from *Ayer's American Newspaper Annual and Directory.*
18. Frank Luther Mott stresses the link between the self-improvement trend and popular magazines in "The Magazine Revolution and Popular Ideas in the Nineties," *Proceedings of the American Antiquarian Society,* LXIV (April, 1954), 198–204.
19. Robert Underwood Johnson, *Remembered Yesterdays* (Boston, 1929), 149.
20. *Ibid.,* 141.
21. Rosamond Gilder, ed., *Letters of Richard Watson Gilder* (Boston, 1926), 22–44, 99–102, 231, 294–99.
22. Johnson, *Remembered Yesterdays,* 87.
23. Editorial, *Century,* XXIX (March, 1896), 791.
24. Charles F. Thwing, "Young Men and the Preaching They Want," *Century,* XXVII (February, 1895), 638.
25. Editorial, *Century,* XXVII (March, 1895), 790.
26. Editorial, *Century,* LIII (December, 1896), 313.
27. Editorial, *Century,* XL (June, 1901), 317.
28. Editorial, "Bribery as a Foible," *Century,* XL (August, 1901), 632.
29. Editorial, *Century,* XLIII (January, 1903), 478–79.
30. Editorial, *Century,* XLIV (October, 1903), 949.
31. Andrew Carnegie, "Popular Illusions about Trusts," *Century,* XXXVIII (May, 1900), 143–49.
32. Henry Loomis Nelson, "The So-Called Steel Trust," *Century,* XLIII (December, 1902), 302–16; George Buckanan Fife, "The So-Called Beef Trust," *Century,* XLIII (November, 1902), 148–58; Franklin Clarkin, "The So-Called Sugar Trust," *Century,* XLIII (January, 1903), 470–80.
33. "The Real Danger in Trusts," *Century,* XXXVIII (May, 1900), 152–53.
34. McClure, *Autobiography,* 138, 139, 234.
35. *The Autobiography of Lincoln Steffens* (New York, 1931), 361–62. See also the accounts in: Ida M. Tarbell, *All in the Day's Work* (New York, 1939), 118–19, 154–55, 199; Ray Stannard Baker, *American Chronicle* (New York, 1945), 95–98; William Allen White, *Autobiography* (New York, 1946), 386–87. The only full biography of McClure is Peter Lyon, *Success Story: The Life and Times of S. S. McClure* (New York, 1963).
36. Tarbell, *All in the Day's Work,* 119.
37. McClure, *Autobiography,* 130–31.
38. *Ibid.,* 152–60.
39. See the advertisement in *McClure's* which denied the charge that the

cheaper magazines could not be of the same high caliber as the more expensive ones. *McClure's,* V (August, 1895), 287.

40. "The Edge of the Future," *McClure's,* II (January, 1894), 199–216.
41. *McClure's,* III (June, 1894), 545–61; (July, 1894), 163–68; (August, 1894), 195–206.
42. Tarbell, *All in the Day's Work,* 195–96.
43. "McClure's Magazine in War Times," *McClure's,* XI (June, 1898), 206.
44. *McClure's,* XIII (October, 1899), back cover.
45. Steffens, *Autobiography,* 358.
46. See for example: C. C. Regier, *The Era of the Muckrakers* (Chapel Hill, 1932); Louis Filler, *Crusaders for American Liberalism* (New York, 1939); Richard Hofstadter, *The Age of Reform* (New York, 1955), 185–96.
47. See McClure, *Autobiography,* 236–46; Tarbell, *All in the Day's Work,* 196–206; Steffens, *Autobiography,* 357–75.
48. Ray S. Baker, "The New Prosperity," *McClure's,* XV (May, 1900), 86–96.
49. McClure, *Autobiography,* 237.
50. Steffens, *Autobiography,* 375.
51. Editorial, *McClure's,* XX (January, 1903), 336.
52. The Editor, "Patriotism," *McClure's,* XXI (July, 1903), 336.
53. Ray S. Baker, "The Lone Fighter," *McClure's,* XXII (December, 1903), 194–97.
54. Quoted in Mott, *History of American Magazines,* IV, 484.
55. John Brisben Walker, "The 'Homestead' Object Lesson," *Cosmopolitan,* XIII (July, 1892), 572–75.
56. Sir Robert Harton, "The Discovery of Altruria," *Cosmopolitan,* XX (November, 1895–April, 1896), 85–93, 219–24, 321–25, 437–41, 544–47.
57. See for example: *Cosmopolitan,* XVII (April, 1894).
58. John Brisben Walker, "The Trusts and the End," *Cosmopolitan,* XXIX (July, 1900), 310–12.
59. Edward Everett Hale, "The Choice of an Occupation," *Cosmopolitan,* X (April, 1891), 761–63; "The Promotion of Laborers," *Cosmopolitan,* X (November, 1890), 121–23.
60. Walker's marginal comments on F. W. Morgan, "Recent Developments in Industrial Organization," *Cosmopolitan,* XXVI (April, 1899), 619–24.
61. Frederic C. Howe, "Men of Honor and Stamina Who Make the Real Successes in Life: I, Joseph W. Folk," *Cosmopolitan,* XXXV (September, 1903), 554.

62. Frank A. Munsey, *The Story of the Founding and Development of the Munsey Publishing House* (New York, 1907), 28.
63. See Munsey, *Story of the . . . Munsey Publishing House.*
64. George Britt, *Forty Years—Forty Millions, The Career of Frank A. Munsey* (New York, 1935), 4.
65. Munsey, *Story of the . . . Munsey Publishing House,* 8.
66. Mott, *History of American Magazines,* IV, 418.
67. Munsey, *Story of the . . . Munsey Publishing House,* 27.
68. *Ibid.,* 48.
69. *Ibid.,* 53–54.
70. Quoted in Britt, *Forty Years,* 16.
71. Quoted from the *Independent* in Mott, *History of American Magazines,* IV, 611.
72. "Publisher's Desk," "Fifteen Broad Minded Men," *Munsey's,* XVIII (April, 1898), 798.
73. "Publisher's Desk," "The Most Picturesque Yet," *Munsey's,* X (February, 1894), 561.
74. "Publisher's Desk," *Munsey's,* XVIII (March, 1898), 955.
75. Quoted in Mott, *History of American Magazines,* IV, 613.
76. William Kirkus, M.A., L.L.B., "The Episcopal Church in New York," *Munsey's,* XXII (February, 1900), 727.
77. Frank Lewis Ford, "The Vanderbilts and the Vanderbilt Millions," *Munsey's,* XXII (January, 1900), 468.
78. Frank A. Munsey, "Getting On in Journalism," *Munsey's,* XIX (May, 1898), 214.
79. Editorial, "The Government and the Individual," *Munsey's,* XI (May, 1894), 221.
80. Editorial, "The Reign of the Business Man," *Munsey's,* XV (June, 1896), 383; John A. Adams, "The Wealth of the Philippines," *Munsey's,* XIX (August, 1898), 664; Frank A. Munsey, "The Greatest Charity Scheme of the Century," *Munsey's,* XXIV (November, 1900), 234, 310.
81. Bird S. Coler, "The Political Wrecking of Business Enterprises," *Munsey's,* XXIII (May, 1900), 277.
82. James B. Dill, "The College Man and the Corporate Proposition," *Munsey's,* XXIV (October, 1900), 148.
83. Harvey Sutherland, "The Richest Americans," *Munsey's,* XXIX (April, 1903), 15.
84. Britt, *Forty Years,* 4.

Chapter 4
The Hero as Napoleon

In order to reduce the bulk of the repeated citations of the same articles within the chapters analyzing the magazine biographies in modern magazines, I have used the following procedure:

The first citation of any article is given in full. Subsequent citations of the same article give only the magazine, the date of issue, and the page.

1. S. S. McClure, *My Autobiography* (New York, 1914), 220.
2. Brooks Atkinson, ed., *The Complete Essays and Other Writings of Ralph Waldo Emerson* (New York, 1940), 503.
3. Frank Luther Mott estimates that by 1914 some 17,000,000 copies of the Alger series had been sold, but there is no authoritative estimate of the proportion sold by 1894. F. L. Mott, *Golden Multitudes* (New York, 1947), 158–59.
4. For accounts of the success cult in the period 1860–1900 see Griswold, "The American Cult of Success," Chs. 4–6, and Wyllie, *The Self-Made Man in America,* Chs. 1–7.
5. D. A. Saunders, "Social Ideas in *McGuffey Readers,*" *Public Opinion Quarterly,* V (Winter, 1941), 579–89. See also Richard D. Mosier, *Making the American Mind* (New York, 1947).
6. See the discussion of the mood of the nineties in Richard Hofstadter, "Manifest Destiny and the Philippines" in Daniel Aaron, ed., *America in Crisis* (New York, 1952), 173–200.
7. Muriel L. Zimet, "The Business Man in the American Novel," unpublished M.A. thesis, 1948, Columbia University.
8. A. W. Griswold, "New Thought: A Cult of Success," *American Journal of Sociology,* XL (November, 1934), 309–18. For a far more idealistic view of New Thought see Benjamin O. Flower, *Progressive Men, Women, and Movements of the Past Twenty-five Years* (Boston, 1914), 175–80 and H. W. Dresser, *A History of the New Thought Movement* (New York, 1919).
9. John B. McMaster, "Daniel Webster," *Century,* XXXVIII (November, 1900), 103–19; John Morley, "Oliver Cromwell," *Century,* XXXVII (February, 1900), 566–88; Rear Admiral William T. Sampson, "Admiral Dewey as a National Hero," *Century,* XXXVI (October, 1899), 927–30.
10. Eliot Gregory, "Unavailing Wealth," *Century,* XLIV (June, 1903), 242.
11. "We must study the age and the people of any great man if we sincerely desire the truth regarding his strength and weakness, his purposes

and inborn tendencies, his failures and successes." William M. Sloane, "Life of Napoleon Bonaparte," *Century,* XXVII (November, 1894), 3.

12. "In any attempt to measure a man and determine his size and force, it is essential that he be taken in his native surroundings, and compared, not with alien types and times but with his own fellows . . . in measuring the men themselves, each must be taken in his own home, and his greatness estimated by his ability to mould thought, purpose, and life there." Chester Holcome, "Li Hung Chang," *McClure's,* VII (October, 1896), 427–36. See also: Thomas C. Martin, "Nikola Tesla," *Century,* XXV (February, 1894), 582–85.
13. John C. Adams, "Lincoln's Place in History," *Century,* XXV (February, 1894), 590–96.
14. Arthur Warren, "Philip D. Armour," *McClure's,* II (February, 1894), 260–80.
15. See especially: Arthur Warren, *loc. cit.; Century* (October, 1899), 927–30; Julian Ralph, "John Davison Rockefeller," *Cosmopolitan,* XXXIII (June, 1902), 160–63; William A. White, "Hanna," *McClure's,* XVI (November, 1900), 57–64; *Century* (December, 1898), 202–19; William A. White, "Theodore Roosevelt," *McClure's,* XVIII (November, 1901), 40–47; John B. Walker, "The Story of Theodore Roosevelt's Life," *Cosmopolitan,* XXXII (November, 1901), 159–62.
16. Field-Marshal Viscount Wolseley, "The Young Napoleon," *Cosmopolitan,* XXXIV (January, 1903), 329–38.
17. R. H. Titherington, "Napoleon at St. Helena," *Munsey's,* XXVI (November, 1901), 215–18; "Literary Chat," *Munsey's,* XIII (May, 1895), 20.
18. Prince Fabian Colonna, "The Bonapartes of To-Day," *Cosmopolitan,* XXVII (October, 1899), 649–56.
19. McClure, *Autobiography,* 219.
20. *McClure's,* (February, 1894), 260–80; Samuel E. Moffett, "Levi Zeigler Leiter," *Cosmopolitan,* XXXV (July, 1903), 336–81. See also for example: Whitney Allen, "James Anthony Bailey," *Cosmopolitan,* XXXIV (December, 1902), 170–74; Horace Porter, "Campaigning with Grant," *Century,* XXXI (February, 1897), 485–500.
21. Britt, *Forty Years,* 28.
22. C. Vann Woodward, *Tom Watson, Agrarian Rebel* (New York: Macmillan, 1938), 340–42.
23. *Century,* (December, 1898), 202–19.
24. Clifton S. Smith, "Oliver Cromwell," *Munsey's,* XI (May, 1894), 136–40.
25. Samuel E. Moffett, "John Arbuckle," *Cosmopolitan,* XXXIII (Septem-

ber, 1902), 542–44. See also: Samuel E. Moffett, "Henry Huddleston Rogers," *Cosmopolitan*, XXXIII (September, 1902), 532–35; E. C. Machen, "A View of Pierpont Morgan and His Work," *Cosmopolitan*, XXXI (June, 1901), 177–81; John B. Walker, "Pierpont Morgan, His Advisers and His Organization," *Cosmopolitan*, XXXIV (January, 1903), 243–48; Richard H. Titherington, "George M. Pullman," *Munsey's*, XI (June, 1894), 253–55.

26. George A. Smith, D.D., "Henry Drummond as His Friends Knew Him," *McClure's*, XII (April, 1899), 954–55; Rev. John Watson, "The Life of the Master," *McClure's*, XIV (February, 1900), 295–310; C. T. Winchester, "Wesley's Days of Triumph," *Century*, XLIV (August, 1903), 492–510.
27. "Topics of the Time," "Wanted: Another Wesley," *Century*, XLIV (August, 1903), 633.
28. Lincoln Steffens, "Jacob Riis, Reporter, Reformer, American Citizen," *McClure's*, XXI (August, 1903), 419–25.
29. Hamilton W. Mabie, "Andrew Carnegie," *Century*, XLII (October, 1902, 956–58.
30. *Cosmopolitan*, (January, 1903), 243–48.
31. "Wealth and Its Blessings," *Success*, II (October, 1898), 18.
32. Edwin Lefevre, "Daniel Gray Reid," *Cosmopolitan*, XXXIV (January, 1903), 339–42.
33. *Cosmopolitan*, (June, 1901), 177–81.
34. *Cosmopolitan*, (January, 1903), 243–48.
35. *Cosmopolitan*, (January, 1903), 339–42.
36. *McClure's*, (February, 1894), 260–80.
37. Frank L. Ford, "The Vanderbilts and the Vanderbilt Millions," *Munsey's*, XXII (January, 1900), 467–77.
38. "As They See It: the Question Whether It Is More Desirable to be Born to Poverty or to Wealth," *Munsey's*, XIV (November, 1895), 151–54.
39. *Cosmopolitan*, (June, 1902), 160–63.
40. Richard H. Titherington, "The Good Gray Poet," *Munsey's*, XIV (November, 1895), 138–46.
41. *Century*, (October, 1902), 956–58.
42. *Century*, (June, 1903), 241–46.
43. *Cosmopolitan*, (December, 1902), 170–74. Joshua Reynolds's biographer claimed that the painter "so impressed himself upon his day that it is probable that had he choesn any other profession he would have become prominent." Anon., "Sir Joshua Reynolds," *Munsey's*, XVI (January, 1897), 448–56. An actress was said to be "not necessarily a stage genius. In almost any line of work she might have followed, Miss

Nethersole would have been heard from." Lavinia Hart, "Olga Nethersole," *Cosmopolitan,* XXXI (May, 1901), 14–24.

44. *McClure's,* (February, 1894), 260; Louis Siebold, "Richard Croker," *Munsey's,* XXV (August, 1901), 628; Henry F. Osborn, "A Great Naturalist: Edward Drinker Cope," *Century,* XXXIII (November, 1897), 10; *McClure's,* (November, 1900), 57; *Century,* (December, 1890), 202; T. C. Crawford, "Ernest Terah Hooley and His Guinea Pigs," *Cosmopolitan,* XXVI (November, 1898), 97; *Century,* (November, 1894), 3.
45. See for example: *Century,* (October, 1902), 956–58; Woodrow Wilson, "Edmund Burke and the French Revolution," *Century,* XL (September, 1901), 784–92; R. H. Titherington, "A Grand Old Man of New York," *Munsey's,* XXVII (December, 1902), 393–94; T. C. Martin, "A Family of Engineers," *Cosmopolitan,* XXV (May, 1898), 23–34.
46. John Swain, "John Alexander Dowie: The Prophet and His Profits," *Century,* XLII (October, 1902), 933–94.
47. See for example: *Cosmopolitan,* (September, 1902), 532–35; *Cosmopolitan,* (June, 1902), 160–63; *McClure's,* (August, 1903), 419–25.
48. See for example: *Century,* (October, 1902), 956–58; Anon., "The President of Columbia," *Century,* XLI (April, 1902), 910–12; Theodore Roosevelt, "Admiral Dewey," *McClure's,* XIII (October, 1899), 483–91.
49. See for example: *Century,* (April, 1902), 910–12; George W. Julian, "A Presidential Candidate of 1852," *Century,* XXX (October, 1896), 870–83; *Cosmopolitan,* (November, 1898), 97–104.
50. Murat Halsted, "The Defeat of Blaine for the Presidency," *McClure's,* VI (January, 1896), 159–72.
51. A. J. Gade, "Oliver Cromwell," *Cosmopolitan,* XXVI (March, 1899), 564–70; *Cosmopolitan,* (January, 1903), 339–42.
52. See for example: An Old Acquaintance, "The Personality of Theodore Roosevelt," *Century,* XLI (December, 1901), 277–79; *McClure's,* (February, 1894), 260–80; Harold Parker, "David Bennett Hill," *Munsey's,* XII (October, 1894), 16–18.
53. *McClure's,* (November, 1900), 57–64.
54. *Cosmopolitan,* (July, 1903), 336–38.
55. *Munsey's,* (October, 1894), 16–18.
56. *McClure's,* (November, 1900), 57–64.
57. *Century,* (October, 1902), 956.
58. George Holme, "Rosa Bonheur," *Munsey's,* (April, 1894), 58.
59. *Century,* (November, 1894), 3.
60. A. C. Post, "Judge Oliver Wendell Holmes," *McClure's,* XIX (October, 1902), 523.

61. *Century,* (November, 1897), 10–18; *McClure's,* (January, 1896), 159–72; *Cosmopolitan,* (September, 1902), 542–44; Fritz Morris, "The Czars Simple Life," *Cosmopolitan,* XXXIII (September, 1902), 483–90.
62. Frank A. Munsey, "Collis P. Huntington," *Munsey's,* IX (August, 1893), 421–23.
63. James M. Beck, "Stephen Girard and His College," *Cosmopolitan,* XXIV (January, 1898), 247–57.
64. *Cosmopolitan,* (June, 1902), 160–63.
65. R. H. Titherington, "A Brief Outline of McKinley's Career," *Munsey's,* XXVI (November, 1901), 161–73; *Cosmopolitan,* (June, 1902), 160–63. For other examples of this formalized attitude toward religion see: *McClure's,* (January, 1896), 159–72; Robert N. Burnett, "Jacob Henry Schiff," *Cosmopolitan,* (April, 1903), 698–700; *Cosmopolitan,* (September, 1902), 542–44; *Cosmopolitan,* (September, 1902), 483–90.
66. *Cosmopolitan,* (March, 1899), 564–70.
67. For leading examples of this total pattern see: *Cosmopolitan,* (December, 1902), 170; *McClure's* (November, 1900), 57; *McClure's,* (February, 1894), 260; *Cosmopolitan,* (March, 1899), 564.
68. Ida M. Tarbell, "Abraham Lincoln, Part II," *McClure's,* VI (December, 1895), 3; *Century,* (February, 1894), 590; *Cosmopolitan,* (May, 1901), 14; *Century,* (November, 1894), 3; *Century,* (October, 1896), 870; S. H. M. Byers, "Some Personal Recollections of General Sherman," *McClure's,* III (August, 1894), 214; G. T. Ferris, "Li Hung Chang," *Cosmopolitan,* XVII (October, 1894), 643.

    For other examples of the inner-directed disregard for popularity and companionship see: *Century,* (August, 1903), 492; *Munsey's,* (January, 1897), 448.

    For a good example of the hero placing principle above friendship see Woodrow Wilson's description of Edmund Burke: "His passion for the principles he served was deeper than his passion for his friend." *Century,* (September, 1901), 784. Where the *Century* biographies tended to stress the hero's principles, the other magazines stressed his ambition.
69. *Century,* (October, 1902), 933–44; Charles S. Gleed, "James Jerome Hill," *Cosmopolitan,* XXXIII (June, 1902), 169–72. For other outstanding examples of dominance see: *McClure's,* (November, 1900), 57–64; *Munsey's,* (August, 1901), 628–32; Franklin Chester, "The Man of Mafeking," *Munsey's,* XXIII (July, 1900), 563–64.
70. *Century,* (December, 1898), 202–19; *Cosmopolitan,* (December, 1902), 170–74; *Cosmopolitan,* (April, 1903), 698–700; *McClure's,* (February, 1894), 260–80.

71. *Cosmopolitan,* (March, 1899), 564–70; *Century,* (December, 1901), 277–79; *McClure's,* (February, 1894), 260–80; *McClure's,* (November, 1900), 57–64; *Century,* (October, 1902), 933–44; E. L. Snell, "Dr. Morton's Discovery of Anesthesia," *Century,* XXVI (August, 1894), 584–89.
72. See for example: *Cosmopolitan,* (March, 1899), 564–70; *Cosmopolitan,* (December, 1902), 170–74; *Cosmopolitan,* (June, 1902), 169–72.
73. *Century,* (August, 1903), 492–510.
74. *McClure's,* (November, 1900), 57–64.
75. *Century,* (February, 1894), 582–85. See also: Emma B. Kaufman, "Cora Urquhart Potter," *Cosmopolitan,* XXIV (December, 1902), 184–90; *Cosmopolitan,* (May, 1901), 14–24.
76. Anon., "A Parisian Etcher," *Munsey's,* XIX (May, 1898), 226–33; *Century,* (August, 1894), 584–89; *Cosmopolitan,* (May, 1898), 23–34; John D. Long, "Rear-Admiral William T. Sampson," *McClure's,* XIX (July, 1902), 214–16; *McClure's,* (November, 1900), 57–64.
77. *Cosmopolitan,* (September, 1902), 532–35.
78. *Cosmopolitan,* (January, 1903), 339.
79. John Ford, "Levi P. Morton," *Munsey's,* XII (December, 1894), 273; *Cosmopolitan,* (January, 1903), 329.
80. "As They See It: The Question Whether It Is More Desirable to Be Born to Poverty or to Wealth," *Munsey's,* XIV (November, 1895), 151; *Cosmopolitan,* (May, 1901), 14.
81. Compare the account of Rockefeller's youth in Julian Ralph, "John Davison Rockefeller," *Cosmopolitan,* XXXIII (June, 1902), 160 with the analysis in a mimeographed article by Kenneth Lynn, "Allan Nevins, An Algerine Captive," Explorations in Entrepreneurial History, 245–61.
82. C. Wright Mills, "The American Business Elite: A Collective Portrait," *Journal of Economic History,* Supplement V (1945), 20–44; William Miller, "American Historians and the Business Elite," *Journal of Economic History,* IX (1949), 184–208.
83. Ida M. Tarbell, "Bishop Vincent and His Work," *McClure's,* V (August, 1895), 242.
84. *Cosmopolitan,* (June, 1902), 160.
85. Bronislaw Malinowski, *Magic, Science, and Religion and Other Essays* (Garden City, N.Y., 1955), 126.
86. See for example: *Century,* (October, 1902), 956–58; *Century,* (August, 1894), 504–59; *McClure's,* (November, 1900), 57–64; *McClure's,* (December, 1895), 3–23; *Munsey's,* (November, 1901), 161–73; *Munsey's,* (October, 1894), 16–18; *Cosmopolitan,* (September, 1902), 532–35; *Cosmopolitan,* (May, 1901), 14–24.

87. *McClure's,* (November, 1900), 57.
88. See for example: *Century,* (December, 1901), 277–79; *Century,* (November, 1897), 10–18; *McClure's,* (October, 1902), 523–24; N. MacDonald, "A Genius of the Chisel," *Munsey's,* XIV (March, 1896), 671–74; *Cosmopolitan,* (March, 1899), 564–70.
89. Louis Seibold, "Theodore Roosevelt," *Munsey's,* XXVI (November, 1901), 182–94. See also: Margaret Field, "Juliet Ward Howe and Her Daughters," *Munsey's,* XII (February, 1895), 527–29.
90. *Century,* (November, 1900), 103–19; Ray S. Baker, "Theodore Roosevelt, a Character Sketch," *McClure's,* XII (November, 1898), 23–32; *McClure's,* (December, 1895), 3–23; *Century,* (November, 1894), 3–30. See also: *McClure's,* (November, 1900), 57–64; *Munsey's,* (August, 1901), 628–32; *Cosmopolitan,* (June, 1902), 160–63; *Century,* (February, 1894), 582–85.
91. *Century,* (December, 1898), 202–19; *Munsey's,* (May, 1898), 226–33; *Munsey's,* (April, 1894), 58–65; *Cosmopolitan,* (December, 1902), 170–74; *Cosmopolitan,* (September, 1902), 542–44. See also for example: *Century,* (November, 1897), 10–18; *Century,* (February, 1894), 582–85; Ida M. Tarbell, "A Great Photographer," *McClure's,* IX (May, 1897), 559–64; *Cosmopolitan,* (September, 1902), 532–35.
92. "Yes, it is quite necessary to have a genius for hard work. . . . Hard work has marked every milestone of this woman's career." *Cosmopolitan,* (May, 1901), 14–24. See also for example: Lincoln Steffens, "The Overworked President," *McClure's,* XVIII (April, 1902), 483–92; *McClure's,* (July, 1902), 214–16; *McClure's,* (August, 1894), 214–22; *Munsey's,* (November, 1901), 161–73; *Cosmopolitan,* (December, 1902), 184–80.
93. *Cosmopolitan,* XXXIII (June, 1902), 16–63; *Cosmopolitan,* (May, 1901), 14–24. See also for example: *Munsey's,* XII (October, 1894), 16–18; *McClure's,* (October, 1899), 483–91; *McClure's,* (February, 1894), 260–80; *Cosmopolitan,* (November, 1901), 28–29.
94. See for examples: *Cosmopolitan,* (March, 1899), 564; *Century,* (February, 1900), 566; *Century,* (November, 1897), 10; *Century,* (February, 1894), 582; *Munsey's,* (October, 1894), 16; *McClure's,* (February, 1894), 260.
95. See for examples: *Century,* (August, 1903), 492; *Munsey's,* (July, 1900), 563; *Cosmopolitan,* (April, 1903), 699.
96. See for examples: *Cosmopolitan,* (September, 1902), 542; *Century,* (October, 1896), 870.
97. For explicit examples see: *Munsey's,* (December, 1902), 393; *Munsey's,* (October, 1894), 16; Charles Hale Garrett, "The New American Sculp-

tor," *Munsey's,* XXXIX (July, 1903), 545; *McClure's,* (December, 1895), 3.

98. See for examples: *Century,* (October, 1902), 933; *Munsey's,* XXVI (November, 1901), 161. A far more social emphasis did appear, almost at the end of the decade in Lincoln Steffens, "Jacob A. Riis," *McClure's,* XXI (August, 1903), 419.
99. *McClure's,* (October, 1899), 483; *Cosmopolitan,* (March, 1899), 564.
100. *Century,* (October, 1902), 956.
101. R. H. Sherard, "Hall Caine," *McClure's,* VI (December, 1895), 80; Robert Bridges, "F. Marion Crawford: A Conversation," *McClure's,* IV (March, 1895), 316; Hamlin Garland, "Real Conversations: James Whitcomb Riley and Hamlin Garland," *McClure's,* II (January, 1894), 234; W. Morton Fullerton, "Monsieur de Blowitz," *McClure's,* I (July, 1893), 166. For further examples of artists strikingly protrayed in the terms of the general model see: *Cosmopolitan,* (May, 1901), 14; Isabel McDougall, "Verastchagin in the Philippines," *Cosmopolitan,* XXXIII (June, 1902), 148; *Cosmopolitan,* (December, 1902), 184; *Munsey's,* (April, 1894), 58.
102. Mrs. Lew Wallace, "William Wetmore Story," *Cosmopolitan,* XXI (September, 1896), 464.
103. Frank A. Munsey, "Stephen V. White," *Munsey's,* VII (April, 1892), 15.
104. *Cosmopolitan,* (January, 1903), 243–48.
105. W. Freeman Day, "The Diamond King," *Munsey's,* XI (July, 1894), 462.
106. *McClure's,* (February, 1894), 260–80.
107. Harold Parker, "Russell Sage," *Munsey's,* XII (March, 1895), 634.
108. *Munsey's,* (December, 1894), 274.
109. *Century,* (November, 1898), 13.
110. Editorial, "A New Alexander the Great," *Century,* XXXV (October, 1898), 955.
111. Joseph Benson Foraker, "The Young Man in Politics," *Munsey's,* XVIII (December, 1897), 398.
112. *Munsey's,* (December, 1897), 398; *Century,* (December, 1901), 277; John B. Walker, "The Story of Theodore Roosevelt's Life, Part III," *Cosmopolitan,* XXXII (January, 1902), 321 and "Part VI," (April, 1902), 624; *McClure's,* (November, 1898), 22; *McClure's,* (November, 1901), 40; *Munsey's,* (November, 1901), 182.
113. *Cosmopolitan,* (November, 1901), 28; John Brisben Walker, "A Working Man in the Presidency," *Cosmopolitan,* XXXII (November, 1901), 27; *McClure's,* (November, 1901), 40.

114. *McClure's,* (April, 1902), 483.
115. *McClure's,* (February, 1894), 260.
116. Harold D. Lasswell, *Psychopathology and Politics* (Chicago, 1930), 42.

Chapter 5
Progressive Publishers

1. Johnson, *Remembered Yesterdays,* 149.
2. See Hofstadter, *The Age of Reform,* Chs. 4, 5.
3. Mott, *History of American Magazines,* IV, 35; Mark Sullivan, *The Education of an American* (New York, 1938), 209, 193; Mott, *History of American Magazines,* 598–99.
4. See the tributes to P. F. Collier and Robert Collier in Norman Hapgood, *The Changing Years* (New York, 1930), 168–75; and the hands-off attitude of Cyrus Curtis, Mott, *History of American Magazines,* 687.
5. Steffens, *Autobiography,* 575–91.
6. See Eric Goldman, *Two Way Street, The Emergence of the Public Relations Counsel* (Boston, 1948).
7. For the view *Collier's* took of this battle see Hapgood, *Changing Years,* 180–90.
8. Steffens, *Autobiography,* 483, 502–15.
9. Sullivan, *Education of an American,* 275.
10. *Ibid.,* 238–40. See also Steffens's sense of the much higher status of journalists in America compared with Europe: Steffens, *Autobiography,* 702–3.
11. Filler, *Crusaders for American Liberalism,* 83.
12. Johnson, *Remembered Yesterdays,* 149.
13. Steffens, *Autobiography,* 448–49.
14. See Hofstadter, *Age of Reform,* 196–200.
15. "The Idea Back of *Collier's,*" *Collier's,* XLII (January 2, 1909), 15.
16. Oswald G. Villard, "Curtis, Cyrus Hermann Kotzschmar," *Dictionary of American Biography,* XXI (New York, 1944), 212–13.
17. Edward W. Bok, *A Man from Maine* (New York, 1923), 149–50.
18. *Ibid.*
19. See Mott's careful investigation of this claim: *History of American Magazines,* IV, 682–84.
20. *Ibid.,* 685–86.
21. Isaac F. Marcosson, *Adventures in Interviewing* (New York, 1920), 59.
22. Upton Sinclair, *The Brass Check* (*Pasadena,* 1919), 22; John Tebbel,

George Horace Lorimer and the Saturday Evening Post (Garden City, N.Y., 1948), 32.

23. Tebbel, *Lorimer*, 249–89.
24. *Ibid.*, 226.
25. David Graham Phillips, "Swollen Fortunes," *S.E.P.*, CLXXIX (January 12, 1907), 10.
26. Harrison Rhodes, "The Real Leisure Class," *S.E.P.*, CLXXXI (January 9, 1909), 10.
27. Maude R. Warren, "The Servant in the House," *S.E.P.*, CLXXXIII (July 22, 1911), 4.
28. Bok, *Man from Maine*, 149; Tebbel, *Lorimer*, 28.
29. Edward M. Woolley, "The Secrets of a Railroad Executive's Rise," *S.E.P.*, CLXXXIV (February 10, 1912), 34.
30. Bok, *Man from Maine*, 149.
31. The Editors, *The Saturday Evening Post* (Philadelphia, 1923), 11.
32. Cf. Richard and Beatrice Hofstadter, "Winston Churchill: A Study in the Popular Novel," *American Quarterly*, II (Spring, 1950), 12–28.
33. "Thrift—Incubating the Nest Egg," *S.E.P.*, CLXXXI (November 14, 1908), 22, 23.
34. Lorimer as quoted in Marcosson, *Adventures in Interviewing*, 59.
35. "The Editor's Column," *S.E.P.*, *CLXXVIII* (June 30, 1906), 1.
36. Rebecca H. Davis, "Religion in the Days of Our Fathers," *S.E.P.*, CLXXVIII (March 24, 1906), 6.
37. William A. White, *The Autobiography of William Allen White* (New York, 1946), 4, 51, 61, 77, *et passim.*
38. Walter Johnson, *William Allen White's America* (New York, 1947), 237.
39. "The Editor's Column," *S.E.P.*, CLXXVIII (May 26, 1906), 2.
40. Editorial, "The Business of Living," *S.E.P.*, CLXXVIII (July 15, 1905), 12.
41. Editorial, "Protecting Capital," *S.E.P.*, CLXXIX (October 6, 1906), 16.
42. Editorial, "What the People Want," *S.E.P.*, CLXXVII (January 7, 1905), 10.
43. Editorial, "Patching Up the Machine," *S.E.P.*, CLXXIX (August 11, 1906), 16.
44. Alfred H. Lewis, "Why Roosevelt Must Run Again," *S.E.P.*, CLXXIX (July 21, 1906), 3, 4.
45. Editorial, "Corruption by Intangible Means," *S.E.P.*, CLXXVII (January 7, 1905), 10.
46. Henry M. Hyde, "By Favor of the Boss," *S.E.P.*, CLXXVIII (May 26, 1906), 6.

47. Editorial, "The Professor in Politics," *S.E.P.*, *CLXXXIII* (October 15, 1910), 22.
48. Editorial, "Let Us Alone," *S.E.P.*, CLXXX (June 13, 1908), 16.
49. Editorial, "Combination and Regulation," *S.E.P.*, CLXXIV (January 6, 1912), 22.
50. Samuel G. Blythe, "The Complete Muckraker," *S.E.P.*, CLXXXI (November 14, 1908), 14, 15, and (November 21, 1908), 18.
51. Wallace Irwin, "The Shame of the College's," *S.E.P.*, CLXXIX (August 4, 1906), 8.
52. Editorial, "The Lesson of Exposure," *S.E.P.*, CLXXVIII (December 30, 1905), 12.
53. "The Editor's Column," *S.E.P.*, CLXXVIII (June 2, 1906), 1.
54. Alfred H. Lewis, "Shonts of the Isthmus," *S.E.P.*, CLXXIX (September 8, 1906), 15.
55. Alfred Henry Lewis, "Glasgow: Who Wants to Know," *S.E.P.*, CLXXIX (August 11, 1906), 24.
56. *The Autobiography of William Allen White*, 483–84.
57. *Ibid.*, 484.
58. Britt, *Forty Years*, 165–67.
59. "Is the Country More Moral than the City?" *Munsey's*, XLI (June, 1909), 476.
60. Morris Bacheller, "The Progress in the Millionaire Business in America," *Munsey's*, XLI (June, 1909), 405–16.
61. John F. Gregory, "Successful Sons of Rich Men," *Munsey's*, XLIII (August, 1910), 585–95; Isaac F. Marcosson, "Crown Princes of Capital," *Munsey's*, XLV (May, 1911), 151–66; J. Aubrey Tyson, "The Making of Railroad Officials," *Munsey's*, XXX (March, 1904), 61.
62. Editorial, "An Optimistic View of the Business Situation and Its Bearing on Investments," *Munsey's*, XXIX (April, 1908), 61.
63. Herbert N. Casson, "Quebec—A Land Without Trusts," *Munsey's*, XXXVII (July, 1907), 437–46.
64. For Munsey's views on muckraking see "The Shop," *Munsey's*, L (January, 1914), 649–52; and "The Business Situation and Something About Investments," *Munsey's*, XL (January, 1909), 483. Also see Herbert N. Casson, "The Wave of Reform," *Munsey's*, XXXIV (October, 1905), 17–28.
65. Herbert N. Casson, "The Wave of Reform," *Munsey's*, XXXIV (October, 1905), 26.
66. "Senator Robert M. La Follette," *Munsey's*, XXXVI (February, 1907), 655.

67. Judson C. Welliver, "If Bryan Is Elected to the Presidency," *Munsey's*, XL (October, 1908), 3.
68. Editorial, "The New Party's Prospect of Success," *Munsey's*, XLVII (September, 1912), 864.
69. Guy Warfield, "The Great Labor Unions and Their Leaders," *Munsey's*, XXXI (June, 1904), 358–65.
70. Erman J. Ridgway, *This for Rememberance, A Tribute* (Chula Vista, Calif., 1927), 17, 8.
71. Quoted in George E. Mowry, *Theodore Roosevelt and the Progressive Movement* (Madison, 1947), 212.
72. Editorial, "There Isn't Money Enough in the World To-day to Do the World's Work," *Munsey's*, XXXIX (May, 1908), 216.
73. *Ibid.*, 213.
74. "With *Everybody's* Publishers," *Everybody's*, X (February, 1904), 290; John Adams Thayer, *Astir: A Publisher's Life-Story* (Boston, 1910), 232.
75. Quoted in Thayer, *Astir*, 268.
76. See the analyses of Lawson in Filler, *Crusaders for American Liberalism*, 171–202 and in David Mark Chalmers, *The Social and Political Ideas of the Muckrakers* (New York, 1964), 57–65. David Graham Phillips wrote a novel based on Lawson: *The Deluge* (Indianapolis, 1905). Frank Fayant wrote a series of articles on "The Real Lawson" for *Success* in 1907–1908.
77. "A Brief History of *Everybody's*," *Everybody's*, XVI (June, 1907), 863.
78. Thayer, *Astir*, 251, 256, 289.
79. Thayer, *Astir;* Albert N. Marquis, ed., "Thayer, John Adams," *Who's Who in America, 1914–1915* (Chicago, 1914).
80. Albert N. Marquis, ed., "Ridgway, Erman Jesse," *Who's Who in America, 1914–1915* (Chicago, 1914).
81. "With *Everybody's* Publishers," *Everybody's*, XIII (July, 1905), 143–44.
82. O. Henry, "A Ruler of Men," *Everybody's*, XIV (August, 1906), 157; Charles E. Russell, "Where Did You Get It, Gentlemen?" *Everybody's*, XVII (August, 1907), 201; John Dennis, Jr., "Marshall Field—A Great Mercantile Genius," *Everybody's*, XIV (March, 1906), 291; "The Dollar Mark and the Hall-Mark of Fame," *Everybody's*, XV (September, 1906), 386.
83. "What Is a Good Man?" *Everybody's*, XVII (December, 1907), 850.
84. Editor's Note to Paul Latzke, "Romances of Success; James J. Hill: Builder of the Northwest Empire," *Everybody's*, XVI (April, 1907), 435.

85. Paul Latzke, "Romances of Success; George Westinghouse," *Everybody's*, XVI (May, 1907), 649.
86. For accounts of the origin of *Collier's* see: Mott, *History of American Magazines*, IV, 453–57; Sullivan, *Education of an American*, 204–9; "1879–1909," *Collier's*, XLII (January 2, 1909), 13–20.
87. Quoted in Mott, *History of American Magazines*, IV, 455.
88. "1879–1909," *Collier's*, XLII (January 2, 1909), 15.
89. Hapgood, *The Changing Years*, 167.
90. Hapgood, *The Changing Years*, 44.
91. See Mark Sullivan, *Education of an American*.
92. Hapgood, *The Changing Years*, 172.
93. "1879–1909," *Collier's*, XLII (January 2, 1909), 14.
94. "The Middle Ground," *Collier's*, XXXVII (September 8, 1906), 18, 19.
95. "1912," *Collier's*, XLIV (November 27, 1909), 22, 23.
96. Sullivan, *Education of an American*, 218.
97. Editorial, "Enforcement," *Collier's* XXIV (December 31, 1904), 6.
98. Editorial, "Opportunity," *Collier's* XLI (July 4, 1908), 8.
99. "1879–1909," *Collier's*, XLII (January 2, 1909), 16.

Chapter 6
The Hero as Politician

In order to reduce the bulk of the repeated citations of the same articles within the chapters analyzing the magazine biographies in modern magazines, I have used the following procedure:

The first citation of any article is given in full. Subsequent citations of the same article give only the magazine, the date of issue, and the page.

1. "1903—An Editorial Review of the Past Year," *Collier's*, XXXIII (January 2, 1904), 12.
2. Editorial, "Financial Idols Overthrown," *Collier's*, XXXVI (January 6, 1906), 13.
3. "In the House of the Interpreter. The Smashing of Idols," *American*, LXIII (November, 1906), 109–10.
4. Edward A. Ross, *Sin and Society* (Boston, 1907), 53.
5. Harry Thurston Peck, "Napoleon, the Greatest Man in the History of the World," *Munsey's*, XL (October, 1908), 82.
6. Lincoln Steffens, "U'Ren, the Law-Giver," *American*, LXV (March, 1908), 6.
7. William A. White, *Masks in a Pageant* (New York, 1928), 283–84.
8. Ross, *Sin and Society*, 86.

9. Editorial, "Contempt of Law," *McClure's*, XX (January, 1903), 336.
10. Lincoln Steffens quoted in George E. Mowry, "The California Progressive and His Rationale: A Study in Middle Class Politics," *Mississippi Valley Historical Review*, XXXVI (September, 1949), 239–50.
11. Introductory Letter by Theodore Roosevelt in Ross, *Sin and Society*, xi.
12. Ross, *Sin and Society*, vii.
13. Walter E. Weyl, *The New Democracy* (New York, 1913), 163.
14. Ross, *Sin and Society*, 151.
15. Ray Stannard Baker, "In the Land of Promise," *Collier's*, XXXVI (February 24, 1906), 20–22.
16. Editorial, "Opportunity," *Collier's*, XLI (July 4, 1908), 8.
17. "In the House of the Interpreter," *American*, LXIII (November, 1906), 109.
18. Alfred H. Lewis, "Shonts of the Isthmus," *S.E.P.*, CLXXIX (September 8, 1906), 15.
19. Peter C. Macfarlane, "James Whitcomb Brougher," *Collier's*, XLIX (March 30, 1912), 13.
20. Brand Whitlock, "The Mayor of Cleveland," *S.E.P.*, CLXXIX (February 23, 1907), 5.
21. William A. White, *The Old Order Changeth* (New York, 1910), 121 as quoted in Hofstadter, *Age of Reform*, 257.
22. Ross, *Sin and Society*, 6.
23. The following comments on Progressive villains are based upon these seven articles which fell within the one-ninth sample of biographies to be examined closely from the four best-selling magazines in the Progressive decade: Mark Sullivan, "Folk and Stone of Missouri," *Collier's*, XLI (July 25, 1908), 18; Gilson Gardner, "The Real Mr. Fairbanks," *Collier's*, XXXIX (June 1, 1907), 13; Will Payne, "A Plutocrat in Homespun," *S.E.P.*, CLXXIX (July 28, 1906), 10; Arthur E. McFarlane, "Where the Money Came From: Jay Gould," *S.E.P.*, CLXXVI (May 14, 1904), 3; Frederick Palmer, "Hearst and Hearstism," *Collier's*, XXXVII (September 22, 1906), 19; Samuel G. Blythe, "The New England Oligarchy, " *S.E.P.*, CLXXXII (April 30, 1910), 18; Peter C. MacFarlane, "Is Roger Sullivan a Boss?" *Collier's*, LII (August 8, 1913), 29.
24. Frederick Palmer, "One Kind Word for John D.," *Collier's*, XXXVII (June 30, 1906), 14, 24.
25. Albert Shaw, *The Outlook for the Average Man* (New York, 1907), 2.
26. "What Is a Good Man?" *Everybody's*, XVII (December, 1907), 850.
27. Peter C. Macfarlane, "Sunshine George of Boston," *Collier's*, LI (June 14, 1913), 7; William A. White, "Twelve Years of Mr. Bryan," *Collier's*, XLII (October 17, 1908), 12; Christian Brinton, "Maxim Gorky,"

Everybody's, XII (April, 1905), 464; Theodore Waters, "Plain Heroes of Science," *Everybody's,* X (March, 1904), 367; J. J. Dickinson, "The Trust Inquisitor—The Man Who Commands the Secrets of Every Business Concern in the Country," *S.E.P.*, CLXXVII (March 11, 1905), 13; Hrolf Wisby, "The New King of Norway," *Munsey's,* XXXIV (February, 1906), 555.

28. Albert Shaw, *The Outlook for the Average Man,* 45, 46.
29. Editorial, *S.E.P.*, CLXXVII (December 31, 1904), 14.
30. W. J. Ghent, *Socialism and Success, Some Uninvited Messages* (New York, 1910), quoted in A. Whitney Griswold, "The American Cult of Success," Ch. IX.
31. Weyl, *The New Democracy,* 154.
32. Ross, *Sin and Society,* 149–50.
33. *Everybody's,* (March, 1904), 367.
34. Carl Snyder, "Carrel-Mender of Men," *Collier's,* L (November 16, 1912), 12.
35. Peter C. Macfarlane, "The Unmuzzled Dr. Wise," *Collier's,* XLIX (June 1, 1912), 15; *Collier's,* (June 14, 1913), 7.
36. Samuel G. Blythe, "Great Men and Their Neighbors: William Jennings Bryan," *S.E.P.*, CLXXIX (June 29, 1907), 10.
37. Paul Latzke, "Romances of Success; George Westinghouse," *Everybody's,* XVI (May, 1907), 641.
38. Frank A. Munsey, "John D. Rockefeller," *Munsey's,* XXXIII (April, 1905), 99.
39. Theodore Roosevelt, *American Ideals* (New York, 1904), 62.
40. *Collier's,* (June 1, 1912), 15; John L. Mathews, "The Coming Ashore of Andrew Furuseth," *Everybody's,* XXV (July, 1911), 60; Herbert N. Casson, "Loeb, the Man at the Gate," *Munsey's,* XLIV (December, 1910), 309; Edward G. Lowry, "Keeping a President in Physical Trim," *Collier's,* XLVII (June 10, 1911), 19; Henry B. Needham, "Roosevelt Today," *Collier's,* XLV (May 7, 1910), 14.
41. Anon., "The Powers of a Strenuous President," *American,* LXV (April, 1908), 555.
42. Peter C. Macfarlane, "The President's Silent Partner," *Collier's,* LI (May 3, 1913), 31; *Everybody's,* (July, 1911), 60.
43. McCormick was quoted as saying: "I have one purpose in life and only one—the success and widespread use of my machines. All other matters are too insignificant to be considered." Herbert N. Casson, "The Romance of the Reaper," *Everybody's,* XVII (December, 1907), 755; *Collier's,* (June 10, 1911), 19.
44. Alfred H. Lewis, "David Rowland Francis," *Everybody's,* X (June, 1904), 753.

45. Arthur Train, "William Travers Jerome," *S.E.P.*, CLXXVII (December 9, 1905), 3; Alfred H. Lewis, "Moran of Massachusetts," *S.E.P.*, CLXXIX (October 20, 1906), 4; *Collier's*, (May 7, 1910), 14.
46. *Collier's*, (June 1, 1912), 15. See also: Peter C. Macfarlane, "The Black-Maned Lion of Seattle," *Collier's*, L (December 28, 1912), 21; John S. Gregory, "Oscar Straus, Progressive," *Munsey's*, XLVIII (November, 1912), 197. Elsewhere E. A. Ross explained that while charity was fine, it was not needed so much as were men who would uphold and improve "the rules of the game." Edward A. Ross, "What Is a Good Man?" *Everybody's*, XVII (December, 1907), 850.
47. Edward F. Harkins, "A Turning-Point in the Career of Governor Hughes," *Munsey's*, XXXVIII (December, 1907), 301; *Collier's*, (February 24, 1906), 20; *Munsey's*, (December, 1907), 755.
48. *Collier's*, (March 30, 1912), 13; *Collier's*, (December 28, 1912), 21.
49. *Collier's*, (June 14, 1913), 7.
50. *Ibid.*
51. Herbert N. Casson, "The Americans in America," *Munsey's*, XXXVI (January, 1906), 432.
52. *S.E.P.*, (February 23, 1907), 5. For other instances of a Progressive "awakening" see: *Collier's*, (June 1, 1912), 12; *Everybody's*, (July, 1911), 60.
53. *S.E.P.*, (December 9, 1905), 3.
54. *Everybody's*, (April, 1907), 435; *Everybody's*, (December, 1907), 755.
55. Day A. Wiley, "The Personality of Theodore Roosevelt," *Munsey's*, XXXI (May, 1904), 61; *Munsey's*, (November, 1912), 197; *S.E.P.*, (October 20, 1906), 4.
56. *Collier's*, (October 17, 1908), 12; *Collier's*, (May 3, 1913), 7; *Munsey's*, (December, 1910), 309; William A. White, "Taft, a Hewer of Wood," *American*, LXVI (May, 1908), 26; *Everybody's*, (July, 1911), 60.
57. John Brisben Walker's marginal comment on the article by F. W. Morgan, "Recent Developments in Industrial Organization," *Cosmopolitan*, XXVI (April, 1899), 619.
58. *Munsey's*, (December, 1910), 309.
59. Frederic C. Howe, "A Golden Rule Chief of Police," *Everybody's*, XXII (June, 1910), 814.
60. *Everybody's*, (June, 1904), 753.
61. *Munsey's*, (October, 1911), 3.
62. *Munsey's*, (September, 1904), 801.
63. Theodore Roosevelt, *An Autobiography*, 25, 26.
64. Ralph B. Perry, *Characteristically American* (New York, 1949), 82.
65. Quoted in C. Wright Mills, *White Collar* (New York, 1951), 56.

Chapter 7
Mass Magazines and the War

1. Walter Johnson, ed., *Selected Letters of William Allen White* (New York, 1947), 157.
2. Editorial, "Boxing the Compass," *S.E.P.*, CLXXXVII (May 1, 1915), 24. See also editorial, "The Best-Laid Plans," *Collier's*, LIII (August 29, 1914), 16.
3. For analysis of the end of muckraking see: Louis Filler, *Crusaders for American Liberalism*, Ch. 28; C. C. Regier, *The Era of the Muckrakers*, Ch. 12; and Richard Hofstadter, *The Age of Reform*, 194–96.
4. Editorial, "The New Republic," *Collier's*, LIV (October 31, 1914), 14.
5. For accounts of the advertising business after 1890 see: John Adams Thayer, *Astir: A Publisher's Life Story* (Boston, 1910); Ralph M. Hower, *The History of an Advertising Agency, N. W. Ayer and Son at Work, 1869–1949* (Cambridge, 1949); Frank Presbrey, *The History and Development of Advertising* (New York, 1929); G. P. Rowell, *Forty Years an Advertising Agent, 1865–1905* (New York, 1926); Neil H. Borden, *The Economic Effects of Advertising* (Chicago, 1942), Ch. II; Walter A. Gaw, *Some Important Trends in the Development of Magazines in the United States as an Advertising Medium*, unpublished dissertation, 1942, New York University. The figures for advertising expenditures in 1890 and 1914 are given in Borden, *Economic Effects of Advertising*, 48.
6. Presbrey, *History of Advertising*, 525, 544–52.
7. Peterson, *Magazines in the Twentieth Century*, 78.
8. Presbrey, *History of Advertising*, 483.
9. Quoted in Mott, *History of American Magazines*, IV, 497.
10. Hapgood's brief account of this break can be found in *The Changing Years*, 219–22. A fuller account appears in Mark Sullivan, *Education of an American*, 295–308.
11. For his own brief account of his editorship see Sullivan, *Education of an American*, 312–14.
12. Filler, *Crusaders for American Liberalism*, 368–70.
13. Quoted by Filler, *ibid.*
14. The essential facts about the transformation of *McClure's* are set forth in Mott, *History of American Magazines*, IV, 602–5. The dramatic personal story behind them is given in Peter Lyon, *Success Story: The Life and Times of S. S. McClure*, (New York, 1963), 330–37, 392–93.
15. *Collier's*, LVII (August 26, 1916).
16. *Collier's*, LVIII (January 13, 1917).

17. "Idealism and Commercialism," *Collier's,* LII (January 24, 1914), 25.
18. Editorial, "Reaction That Is Progress," *S.E.P.*, CLXXXVII (October 3, 1914), 26.
19. Editorial, "Shooting the Leaders," *S.E.P.*, CLXXXVII (October 24, 1914), 24. For similar sentiments see: Jonathan Bourne, Jr., "Menace of Bureaucracy," *Collier's,* LIV (December 26, 1914), 30; Isaac Marcosson, "How Is Business?" *Collier's,* LIII (August 15, 1914), 5; Editorial, "The New Freedom," *S.E.P.*, CLXXXVII (February 20, 1915), 24.
20. Editorial, "First to Fight," *S.E.P.*, CXC (July 7, 1917), 22. See also Samuel Blythe, "Dives and the Demagogues," *S.E.P.*, CXC (January 12, 1918), 8.
21. Editorial, "A New Discovery: Our Country," *Collier's,* LIX (May 12, 1917), 8. See also editorial, "Closing in on Wilhelm," *Collier's,* LXI (August 3, 1918), 15; David Lawrence, "The New Boss," *S.E.P.*, CXC (August 3, 1918), 19; Edward M. Woolley, "Packing for Pershing, First of a New and Important Series: Big Business in Arms," *McClure's*, LI (December, 1918), 24, 25, 45.
22. Editorial, "The Scale of Business," *Collier's,* LXI (July 6, 1918), 14.
23. Isaac Marcosson, "Business-Managing the Empire," *S.E.P.*, CXC (January 12, 1918), 18.
24. See *Collier's,* LVIII (January 6 and 13, 1917).
25. Charles M. Schwab, "Doing the Impossible," *Collier's,* LXI (September 7, 1918), 9.
26. Editorial, "The Meaning of the War," *Collier's,* LIII (August 22, 1914), 14.
27. Editorial, "Guilt Is Personal," *Collier's,* LIII (September 5, 1914), 14.
28. Editorial, "Are We Neutral?", *Collier's,* LIII (September 12, 1914), 16. See also in the same issue articles on "The German War Lust" and on "The Siege of Liege" from a Belgian viewpoint.
29. Editorial, "What Our Neutrality Means," *Collier's,* LIV (January 9, 1915), 12; Editorial, "The Problem of Foreign Exchange," *Collier's,* LV (October 2, 1915), 14; Editorial, "Lending to Ourselves," *Collier's,* LV (October 23, 1915), 14.
30. "The Last Message of Richard Harding Davis," *Collier's,* LVII (August 5, 1916), 19.
31. Franklin H. Giddings, "Our Challenge to Germany," *Collier's,* LVIII (March 3, 1917), 5; Editorial, "No Half Measures, Mr. President!" *Collier's,* LIX (March 17, 1917), 12.
32. Editorial, "A New Discovery: Our Country," *Collier's,* LIX (May 12, 1917), 8.

33. Editorial, "Managing the War," *Collier's*, LIX (May 5, 1917), 12.
34. Owen Johnson, "The New America," *Collier's*, LXI (May 11, 1918), 8, 9, 41–44.
35. Editorial, "Strange Alliances," *S.E.P.*, CLXXXVI (August 22, 1914), 22.
36. Corinne Lowe, "Taking the Cure," *S.E.P.*, CLVII (October 3, 1914), 14. See also the cartoon "Back From Europe" in the same issue, p. 27.
37. Sec the series of three articles by spokesmen for Britain, France, and Germany in *S.E.P.*, CLXXXVII (October 17, 24, and November 21, 1914); Irwin S. Cobb, "Being a Guest of the German Kaiser," *S.E.P.*, CLXXXVII (October 24, 1914), 14; Karl N. Llewellyn, "An American Private in the German Army," *S.E.P.*, CLXXXVII (May 8, 1915), 27.
38. Editorial, "The Barbarisms of Warfare," *S.E.P.*, CLXXXVII (June 5, 1915), 24; Editorial, "Why an Embargo?" *S.E.P.*, CLXXXVIII (August 28, 1915), 20; A. C. Laut, "When Half the World Goes Broke," *S.E.P.*, CLXXXVIII (September 4, 1915), 25; Editorial, "Entangling Alliances," *S.E.P.*, CLXXXVIII (February 19, 1916), 24; Editorial, "Scraps of Paper," *S.E.P.*, CLXXXVIII (July 3, 1915), 22; Editorial, "The Difference," *S.E.P.*, CLXXXIX (March 3, 1917), 24.
39. Editorial, "Our Needless Wars," *S.E.P.*, CLXXXVIII (July 10, 1915). See also Editorial, "Vox Populi," *S.E.P.*, CLXXXIX (November 18, 1916), 26; Editorial, "A Call to the Nation," *S.E.P.*, CLXXXIX (February 17, 1917), 24; Editorial, "In Safe Hands," *S.E.P.*, CLXXXIX (March 3, 1917), 24; Tebbel, *Lorimer*, 163, 179.
40. Gabriel Almond makes a perceptive analysis of some reasons for violent swings in American attitudes toward foreign policy in his book *The American People and Foreign Policy* (New York, 1950), 53–65.
41. "The Prussian Paranoia," *S.E.P.*, CLXXXIX (May 5, 1917), 5; Editorial, "The Prussian War Cult," *S.E.P.*, CXC (July 14, 1917), 24.
42. "Our Labor Plutocrats," *S.E.P.*, CXC (January 5, 1918), 10; Albert W. Atwood, "Big Money and What the Workers Are Doing with It," *S.E.P.*, CXC (September 7, 1918), 21. Business, of course, was pictured as sacrificing private interests or at least meriting special incentives in its leadership of the war effort.
43. Editorial, "Slackers and Pacifists," *S.E.P.*, CXC (May 25, 1918), 20.
44. Editorial, "Scum of the Melting Pot," *S.E.P.*, CXC (May 4, 1918), 22; Samuel G. Blythe, "Our Imported Troubles and Trouble-Makers," *S.E.P.*, CXC (May 11, 1918), 5.
45. Arthur Guy Empey, "Our Real Enemy," *McClure's*, LI (July, 1918), 21.
46. See especially David Lawrence, "Americans for America," *S.E.P.*, CXC (June 15, 1918), 23 and the cartoons of Herbert Johnson on September 21 and October 12.

47. Editorial, "Only the Stump of Dagon Was Left," *S.E.P.*, CXC (December 28, 1918), 20.

Chapter 8
The Heroes of World War I

In order to reduce the bulk of the repeated citations of the same articles within the chapters analyzing the magazine biographies in modern magazines, I have used the following procedure:

The first citation of any article is given in full. Subsequent citations of the same article give only the magazine, the date of issue, and the page.

1. Edwin Lefevre, "Unwritten Interviews," *S.E.P.*, CLXXXVI (March 7, 1914), 9.
2. Gerald S. Lee, "Suspicious People," *Cosmopolitan*, LXI (June, 1916), 41.
3. William Maxwell, "If I Were Twenty-One, A Business Man's Talks to Young Men," *Collier's*, LVIII (March 10, 1917), 10; LIX (March 17 and April 14, 1917), 10; "Salesmanship and Success," *Collier's*, LXI (July 20, 1918), 14.
4. William M. Sloane, "Life of Napoleon Bonaparte," *Century*, XXVII (November, 1894), 3–30.
5. See the editorial, "Opportunity," *Collier's*, XLI (July 4, 1908), 8.
6. C. J. Manning, "Romance and Radishes," *Collier's*, LIII (August 15, 1914), 28–30.
7. Will Irwin, "The Floating Laborer; The Case of John Smith," *S.E.P.*, CLXXXVI (May 9, 1914), 3–5, 41–50.
8. Herbert Kaufman, "Andrew Carnegie," *Cosmopolitan*, LXIII (July, 1917), 76.
9. Edward M. Woolley, "Money Sticking Out," *McClure's*, XLII (January, 1914), 109–16.
10. Mark Sullivan, "Lord Northcliffe," *Collier's*, LX (November 24, 1917), 20.
11. Herbert Kaufman, "Mr. Rockefeller," *Cosmopolitan*, LXII (April, 1917), 78–79; Herbert Kaufman, "Andrew Carnegie," *Cosmopolitan*, LXIII (July, 1917), 76.
12. Frederick Palmer, "England's Man of Common Sense," *Collier's*, LVII (September 9, 1916), 6; Ernest Poole, "Hoover of Belgium," *S.E.P.*, CLXXXIX (May 26, 1917), 14; James B. Connolly, "Sims of the Navy," *Collier's*, LX (November 3, 1917), 6; Poole, *loc. cit.;* Irvin S. Cobb, "An Interview with Lord Kitchener," *S.E.P.*, CLXXXVII (December

5, 1914), 3, 4; John T. Graves, "The Colossus of Panama," *Cosmopolitan,* LVI (January, 1914), 231–33; Isaac F. Marcosson, "Business-Managing the Empire," *S.E.P.,* CXC (January 12, 1918), 18.

13. *S.E.P.,* (January 12, 1918), 18–20; Edward M. Woolley, "Salary—$100,000 a Year," *McClure's,* XLII (April, 1914), 103–11; *Collier's,* (September 9, 1916), 5, 6; *Collier's,* (November 3, 1917), 5, 6; T. P. O'Connor, "Kitchener," *Collier's,* LIV (September 26, 1914), 7, 37; Harris Dickson, "Save and Serve with Hoover," *Collier's,* LIX (August 11, 1917), 5–7; *Collier's,* (September 9, 1916), 5, 6; Frederick Palmer, "Sir Douglas Haig," *Collier's,* LIX (April 7, 1917), 5, 6.
14. *Cosmopolitan,* (January, 1914), 231–33; Henry C. Emergy, "Our Prosperity and Peace, A Warning from Judge Gary," *Collier's,* LVIII (January 13, 1917), 5–7.
15. Washington Irving, "Biographical Notice of Captain Isaac Hull," *Analectic Magazine,* I, 226–35.
16. *S.E.P.,* (May 26, 1917), 14, 58–61.
17. *McClure's,* (April, 1914), 103–11; Edward M. Woolley, "Hunting Kilowatts for $100,000 a Year," *McClure's,* XLIII (October, 1914), 115–20.
18. *Collier's,* (November 3, 1917), 5; James Hopper, "The Man Joffre," *Collier's,* LIV (March 13, 1915), 13; Peter C. Macfarlane, "A Professional Peacemaker," *Collier's,* LIII (July 25, 1914), 11; Fred C. Kelly, "Newton D. Baker, Practical Scholar," *Collier's,* LVII (May 6, 1916), 21.
19. *Collier's,* (May 6, 1916), 21; *Collier's,* (September 26, 1914), 7; *Collier's,* (July 25, 1914), 11.
20. *Collier's,* (September 26, 1914), 7; *Collier's,* (May 6, 1916), 21.
21. *Collier's,* (September 9, 1916), 5; *Collier's,* (April 7, 1917), 5; *Collier's,* (May 6, 1916), 21; *Cosmopolitan,* (January, 1914), 231; Henry J. Forman, "Mr. McAdoo Speaks," *Collier's,* LX (March 9, 1918), 5; *Collier's,* (July 25, 1914), 11; *Collier's,* (April 7, 1917), 5; *Collier's,* (March 13, 1915), 13; *Collier's,* (November 3, 1917), 5; *Collier's,* (September 26, 1914), 7.
22. *McClure's,* (October, 1914), 115; *Collier's,* (March 13, 1915), 13; *S.E.P.,* (May 26, 1917), 14.
23. *Collier's,* (April 7, 1917), 5; *Collier's,* (November 3, 1917), 5.
24. *Collier's,* (July 25, 1914), 11; *Collier's,* (April 7, 1917), 5.
25. Grantland Rice, "The Grand Old Dope," *McClure's,* XLV (May, 1915), 36; *Collier's,* (April 7, 1917), 5; *McClure's,* (April, 1914), 103; *Collier's,* (September 26, 1914), 7.
26. *S.E.P.,* (May 26, 1917), 14; Richard Washburn Child, "How About Colonel House," *Collier's,* LVI (October 30, 1915), 11; *Collier's,* (March 13, 1915), 13.

27. Edwin Lefevre, "Daniel Gray Reid," *Cosmopolitan,* XXXIV (January, 1903), 339–42.
28. *S.E.P.*, (May 26, 1917), 14; *Collier's,* (August 11, 1917), 5; *McClure's,* (April, 1914), 103; *Collier's,* (March 13, 1915), 13; *S.E.P.*, (January 12, 1918), 18.
29. *Collier's,* (April 7, 1917), 5; *Collier's,* (September 9, 1916), 5; *Collier's,* (March 13, 1915), 13; *Collier's,* (April 7, 1917), 5; *Collier's,* (September 26, 1914), 7.
30. *Collier's,* (November 3, 1917), 5; *Collier's,* (September 26, 1914), 7; *McClure's,* (April, 1914), 103; *Collier's,* (March 9, 1918), 5; *Collier's,* (April 7, 1917), 5; *Collier's,* (May 6, 1916), 21; *Collier's,* (April 7, 1917), 5.
31. Winthrop Fox, "Halmi—Painter Laureate of Beauty," *Cosmopolitan,* LVI (April, 1914), 579; Fannie Hurst, "Samuel Merwin—Romantic Realist," *Cosmopolitan,* LXIV (November, 1918), 60.

Epilogue

1. Arthur Warren, "Philip D. Armour," *McClure's,* II (February, 1894), 260.
2. Henry J. Foreman, "Mr. McAdoo Speaks," *Collier's,* LX (March 9, 1918), 5.
3. Peter C. Macfarlane, "A Professional Peacemaker," *Collier's,* LIII (July 25, 1914), 11.
4. Owen Johnson, "The New America," *Collier's,* LXI (May 11, 1918), 8.

Index